LABOUR MARKET ISSUES
OF THE 1970s

Labour Market Issues of the 1970s

Edited by
D. J. ROBERTSON
and
L. C. HUNTER

Published for
The Scottish Economic Society
by
OLIVER & BOYD
Edinburgh

OLIVER AND BOYD

Tweeddale Court, 14 High St.
Edinburgh

A Division of Longman Group Ltd.

These papers were first printed in *Scottish Journal of
Political Economy,* Vol. XVII No. 2, June 1970, and were
available to subscribers to that journal in that form. They
are here reprinted for a wider audience under the title—
Labour Market Issues of the 1970s.

ISBN 0 05 002318 7

Printed by
THE CENTRAL PRESS (ABERDEEN) LTD.

THE CONTRIBUTORS

K. J. W. Alexander : Professor of Economics in the University of Strathclyde.

H. A. Clegg : Professor of Industrial Relations, and Director of the Centre for Industrial and Business Studies in the University of Warwick.

J. R. Crossley : Professor of Industrial Relations in the University of Leeds.

D. J. Flunder : Director, The Dunlop Rubber Co. Ltd.

J. W. Garbarino : Professor of Business Administration and Director of the Institute of Business and Economic Research in the University of California, Berkeley.

J. Gennard : Research Officer, Department of Industrial Relations, The London School of Economics and Political Science.

C. Grunfeld : Professor of Law in the London School of Economics and Political Science.

R. Hamilton : Research Fellow, Manchester Business School.

L. C. Hunter : Professor of Applied Economics in the University of Glasgow.

T. L. Johnston : Professor of Economics, Heriot Watt University.

T. Lupton : Professor of Organisational Behaviour in the Manchester Business School.

G. L. Reid : Senior Lecturer in Applied Economics in the Department of Social and Economic Research, University of Glasgow.

B. C. Roberts : Professor of Industrial Relations in the London School of Economics and Political Science.

D. J. Robertson   :   Professor of Industrial Relations in the University of Glasgow.

A. W. J. Thomson   :   Lecturer in Applied Economics in the Department of Social and Economic Research, University of Glasgow.

CONTENTS

THE EMERGING ISSUES

D. J. ROBERTSON and L. C. HUNTER

I

In the planning of a symposium volume such as this it is perhaps salutary to turn back and with the aid of hindsight consider how successful a similar venture, undertaken a decade ago with the 1960's in prospect, might have been as an exercise in prediction. Certainly, if one looks closely enough, the main elements that were to give shape to the development of the labour market and the industrial relations system during the 1960's were already present in 1960. This was the year when Selwyn Lloyd became Chancellor of the Exchequer and it was his name that was to become associated, shortly thereafter, with the imposition of a temporary 'pay pause' which was to launch the economy on a sustained policy of attempts to control the rate of increase of incomes—a policy which has persisted through to 1970. There can be no doubt that, whatever the success of the various versions of incomes policy introduced during this period in actually reducing the rate of increase of wages and salaries, the presence and the evolution of the incomes (and subsequent prices) policy have had far-reaching effects on the whole labour market and industrial relations environment.

In 1960, too, the first major comprehensive productivity agreement was concluded at the Esso refinery in Fawley, and while it took some time for the full implications of this to become known and evaluated, it would perhaps be no exaggeration to say that the major collective bargaining innovation of the 1960's has been the diffusion of some form of productivity bargaining throughout most sectors of industry. Probably the most critical note struck by this new approach has been the growing recognition of the desirability of restoring a closer relationship between increases in pay and increases in productivity. This established both new possibilities of mutual gain for management and labour through the collective bargaining process and provided a criterion for wage increases which, at least from the economy's point of view, was preferable to the prevalent grounds of comparability and cost of living adjustments. There were, however, other effects, for it

1

gave added point to the arguments of those who favoured a system of established wage negotiation based primarily on the plant or company concerned, rather than on the industry at large which was the dominant practice, at least in formal terms. Productivity bargaining also promised some prospect of being able to come to grips with those obstacles to the efficient utilisation of manpower which were held by many observers to be a primary root cause of Britain's lack of competitiveness in the world economy: features of the system such as restrictive practices adopted by unions and (more especially) work groups, and resort to overtime working on an habitual and systematic basis.

Thirdly, the year 1960 saw the emergence of the Trades Union Congress Report on disputes and workshop representation which brought clearly to the fore the growing dissatisfaction of the trade union movement with certain features of the industrial relations system and (perhaps more importantly still) with the internal organisation of the unions themselves. This of course was one of the issues that was to be picked up in subsequent discussions of industrial relations reform, which gathered momentum with the appointment in 1965 of a Royal Commission on Trade Unions and Employers' Associations. The Report of this Commission in 1968, the Conservative Party's detailed proposals for reform (*Fair Deal at Work*) and the Government's own proposals (*In Place of Strife*) that were to become the subject of a traumatic debate about the place of law in industrial relations, all added to the atmosphere of impending—if not yet accomplished—change that characterised the latter years of the decade.

Many more straws in the wind could be identified, but the real question is how far, in the circumstances of 1960, one would have been able to see in those small beginnings even a semblance of the full shape they were to take in the next decade. There is no certainty, either, that at any point of time such straws will be visible even to those most on the look-out for them. Would it have been possible in 1960 to predict the really drastic change in the role of government and its agencies in labour and industrial relations? It is not unreasonable to advance the view that in 1960 the industrial relations system, if not the labour market itself, was still regarded very much as a largely autonomous sub-system of society, one of the last outposts of laissez-faire. Ten years later it is widely recognised as occupying an integral position within the socio-economic framework, reflecting the growing recognition by government that many of its policy objectives, not just for labour but more generally also, can only be achieved through some measure of intervention in the system itself. One only has to mention the emergence of legislation on industrial training, conditions of employment, redundancy payments, the selective employment tax and its regional variant, together with the activities of the National Board for Prices and Incomes, of the new-look Department of Employment and Productivity, and of the new Commission for Industrial Relations, to get some conception of the scope of government-induced intervention in labour affairs; and the list by no means ends there. Could one have predicted this switch of policy in 1960?

In view of these difficuties, the theoretically simple task of the editors of a symposium such as this becomes much more problematical in practice. It was therefore with some hesitation that we embarked on the task of defining a set of issues on which we could pin our faith as certain runners during the whole course of the 1970's. Even then, the problems were by no means over, for once the subject is divided into its major topics, the next related task is to try to ensure that each topic will be covered adequately by someone really expert in that area. This is another hazardous stage of the enterprise because the best devised scheme for a symposium is useless without authors to match. We count ourselves extremely fortunate since we not only found ourselves with an embarrassingly large selection of possible topics within our subject area but were also able to obtain the ready co-operation of authors of real quality and distinction in dealing with those issues which we judged most important. It is the quality of our authors which we know will ensure that this symposium is an important contribution to the debate on the labour market issues of the 1970's. We are grateful to them for their contributions and their co-operation.

In the remainder of this introductory discussion we propose to try to isolate some of the central questions on which aspects of the recent debate have fastened and then will try to indicate the themes for future debate which we regard as already with us and likely to grow more urgent. The intention is to do a little modest scene setting before giving way to the authors on their various topics.

II

There was a time when British industrial relations were much admired by other countries. The British trade union movement has a long and honourable history. The development of collective bargaining in this country was followed at a respectful interval by other countries. We have from time to time enjoyed a special reputation for attempts to be fair and equitable in our settlement of terms and conditions of employment and to be forward-looking in our desire to protect the worker from abuses. We may then ask why it is that at this particular period of time we are witnessing such an outburst of controversy on our system, and what changes have induced this criticism of a well-established system.

The most obvious reply is to say that it has been too well established and has not been subject to enough change while all around it has changed. We can still regard the present system of collective bargaining and industrial relations in Britain as the culmination of a process of establishing the position of trade unionism and of providing for negotiation of terms and conditions of work between the worker in industry and his employer in a way that is free of legal or formal intervention. The historical image of the industrial relations system in Britain is certainly one of industrial and of manual workers and of struggle between weak unions and established employers. It is for this reason that trade unions were, for example, given their special privileges before the law, and the predominant system of collective bargaining at the industry level which has been so much a feature of British arrangements is one which effectively safeguards the weakest while not sufficiently considering the needs of the more sophisticated parts of the industry with which it concerns itself. It may well be that this type of arrangement is one which leads to conservatism and lack of response to changing circumstances at least until the point is reached at which pressure on the system builds up to a level at which something has to give. In the full employment and inflationary conditions of the postwar period the weakest link proved to be the control of labour costs and in the second half of the 1960's the need to restore a measure of control over these costs gave rise to a wholesale questioning of the system by which they got determined.

Unlike the collective bargaining arrangements of many other countries, British agreements have been largely concerned with wages and, at least formally, have neither encompassed the true complexity of the actual payment systems nor ventured far into the growing number of issues on the conditions of work which arise apart from the basic wage level. Instead, these issues tended to be dealt with informally and a greal deal depended on unwritten agreements, custom and practice. But the various pressures acting on the system gave rise to increasing difficulty in operating in this way, and much of the discussion and debate which preceded the establishment of the Royal Commission on Trade Unions and Employers' Associations was concerned with the need to replace this with a more formal and orderly system, possibly to be implemented by means of a more active role for the law in industrial relations. Despite the wide brief given to the Royal Commission, its Report focussed to a great extent on the manufacturing and manual sectors where these problems of disorderly structures and procedures seemed to be most prevalent.

It is indeed arguable that the Royal Commission saw itself essentially as dealing with changes required in the old familiar context of organised industrial relations in manufacturing industry and among manual workers, with the object of bringing this sector into line with the changing needs of the economy. But we ought to go on to observe that the context itself has now changed so much that this sector of interest in labour market issues, while continuing to be important, is no longer as central as it was and that we should look for the issues of the 1970's outside the area which has dominated our thinking—manual workers and industry. Such a formulation of the situation leads both to the feeling that the issues discussed by the Royal Commission and hotly debated since its publication will continue to require attention, and to the further feeling that most of the applications of the Royal Commission's thinking will require to be outside the area with which it seemed to be most concerned, so that the bulk of labour market issues will now develop outside the historic context of the debate. In other words, we may expect two sets of labour market issues in the 1970's: those arising out of the process of change in the traditional context and those arising out of new contexts.

In the traditional context of manual workers and of organised industrial relations involving trade unions in industry, we may perhaps diagnose four main categories of issues. First, it is apparent that questions on how to regulate the behaviour of trade unions and the organisation and conduct of collective bargaining have now become so dominant that they will continue with us for quite some time. It seems unlikely, however, that the choice will be simply one between the use of law and the freedom of informal organisation. It is already apparent that collective bargaining and the trade unions themselves will be the subject of more attention and more regulation by one means or another. The question is not one of the presence of regulation but the form it might take. One obvious possibility is that the T.U.C. might acquire and exercise substantial regulatory powers over the activities of its member unions, though this raises difficult issues on the nature of its authority and its power to impose effective sanctions. An alternative is to envisage a more extensive framework of law relating to the contractual nature of agreements and of procedures, and to the powers and status of the parties to the bargaining process, including a means of providing for and organising union recognition. There are again difficulties in devising effective sanctions and of integrating industrial relations into the normal fabric of the law. This latter point has caused some to advocate a somewhat different structure of law in this field with appropriate institutions to match. The debate has caused British industrial relations to look with active interest at other countries which have a more legalistic approach to these matters and especially to the U.S.A.

Secondly, the emphasis of the Royal Commission on the ' two systems ' of industrial relations and the need to take more cognizance of the situation in the factory is symptomatic of a wider realisation that negotiation on labour market issues will require to be conducted in more detail and with more resources on both sides, covering a wider range of issues. This change involves a number of aspects, among which the following have to be noted. It restores an emphasis on the industrial relations and collective bargaining problems of the firm in a way that was not always possible before. In so doing it raises questions about the resources and techniques available to the firm in coming to grips with the new situation and helps to pinpoint areas of actual or potential weakness which may in part have been responsible for symptoms of friction in the whole structure of industrial relations and the management of production and labour. It also restores emphasis on the relationship between payment and productivity and as a result brings into question the adequacy of existing systems of wage payment in fulfilling the functions required of them by all concerned parties—management, wage-earners and trade unions. It requires a renewed attention to the whole issue of productivity measurement and productivity improvement, as well as the analysis of causes of higher productivity. This may seem to be saying no more than that the ' two systems ' approach has paved the way for an extension of the productivity bargaining phenomenon, but it is surely more than this. Not only does it involve a new emphasis upon the need to consider many more aspects of the use and reward of labour than were previously thought necessary, but it also requires changes in attitudes to and acceptance of alterations in the organisational context of employment, and in technology. It also, and maybe still more importantly, allows one to look beyond the immediate but possibly short-term and ephemeral gains to be made from productivity bargaining *per se* to the more general development and acceptance of a system of company agreements in which a much wider spectrum of issues, both procedural and substantive, can be handled.

Thirdly, this type of negotiation is in turn going to require new actors upon the scene. Much of the criticism of shop stewards has been rather misdirected, because it has seemed to doubt the need for individuals acting in the interest of their fellows within the labour force. The real questions surely have been on the training and the function of the shop steward, and his role in a process of determination of conditions which has required the kind of detailed knowledge and detailed negotiation to which he aspires, but has not had a place for it firmly established. The fact that the shop steward has lived outside the context of formal contemporary bargaining has in many cases meant the wrong sort of shop steward. What is now needed, however, is a considerable increase of manpower engaged in discussing and determining the use of labour and the return to work at all manner of different levels, so that we may envisage both more ' shop stewards ' of a different type, and many more labour managers who, it is to be hoped, will turn out to be adequately trained, as well as more positive efforts in this direction from line management.

Finally, the effect of changes of this sort upon institutions in the industrial relations process can hardly be small and is likely to be most dramatic in relation to the trade unions themselves, so that there will be increasing issues of the type, organisation and number of trade unions required.

These issues of regulation of the form of bargaining, of the resources used for bargaining, and of trade union adjustment will be echoed, however, by increasing issues outside the traditional areas of organised industrial relations. The shadow of these other issues may be seen in the changing character of the labour force. The fastest growing sectors of employment are outside manufacturing industry and the professions are growing more rapidly than manual workers. Women have come to play an increasingly important part in employment. These changes imply an alteration in the balance of the labour market, a shift in the direction of traditional social and economic forces acting on wage determination and a questioning of the adequacy of normal labour market processes in bringing about the kind of changes in the structure of payment that an efficient market system is expected to exhibit. In particular it has to be recognised that in the growing sector of white collar workers the individual can no longer seek—or has no wish to seek—to determine his own conditions of work for himself. In an organised and complex labour force he too becomes party to the organised settlement of wages and conditions and is seeking new forms of association to help in the process. The adjustment of the new forms of organised relationship in white collar and professional groups to the present system of determining conditions of work will obviously create many difficulties, not least between old and new forms of workers' organisation. White collar workers are particularly important in the public sector and as a result its arrangements, and their relation to what happens elsewhere, are of growing interest.

This set of premises has been accompanied by another which has to do with the greater affluence of the labour force in general. This improvement in the well-being of the greater part of the labour force has served only to highlight the difficulties faced by those who for one reason or another have not been able to obtain a reasonable share in the growth of prosperity or who continue to suffer from major uncertainties about the flow of income from work or their security of employment. The main issue here has in the past been that of payment, but there are many more—such as the evolution of the fringe benefit type of reward, the emergence of payments in compensation for redundancy and, on the procedural side, the development of formal processes to cope with the problems of redundancy and dismissal in order to provide some safeguard to those with reason to doubt the security of their employment and incomes. While progress has been made there undoubtedly remains much to be done in these areas, and to them we have to add the renewal of interest in matters of equity and equality of opportunity, as reflected in the increasing attention now being placed on equal pay and minimum wages. The whole area is one which has received renewed scrutiny from government, and in some cases at least, the establishment of minimum standards.

More generally, however, as we observed at the outset the State has come to play a bigger role in the labour market and indeed this may well have been the greatest single change in the British labour market environment during the 1960's. The reasons for this expanded role are diverse, but they certainly include the growing awareness in public policy of the sensitivity of the economy as a whole, especially in its external relations, to the course of events in the labour market. As a result, there have been growing efforts to develop methods of influencing the labour market and, through that, the economy as a whole. These efforts range from the very general measures designed to control the level of unemployment within what have come to be regarded politically as the full employment limits, to a whole spectrum of policies aimed at more specific problem areas within the labour market: the latter include attempts to regulate the industrial distribution of the labour force, to improve the ease with which labour can adjust to the changed needs upon which much of our productivity growth depends and to provide a more efficient basis for the training of labour and its development through better planning for its utilisation. This of course is quite apart from and in addition to the growing concern of government for the consequences of unofficial strikes and other symptoms of unrest in the system of industrial relations, and the interest of government in encouraging and aiding in the evolution of improved procedures for the handling of grievances and the conduct of negotiations without undue friction.

Two questions then remain. First, it has to be asked what sort of effect these changes have been having on the total cost of labour to the employer, which has certainly been influenced by the new standards sought by the State to improve the relationships between the worker and his work, between the worker and his employer and even between the worker and society at large. Secondly, consideration needs to be given to the way in which government has developed, frequently in an *ad hoc* manner, a number of agencies designed to investigate—and to a variable extent, to guide or control—recognisable problem areas with the complex system of labour market and industrial relations activities. This includes the National Board for Prices and Incomes, the Commission on Industrial Relations, and the Department of Employment and Productivity which has taken over many of the responsibilities of the old Ministry of Labour, and has acquired some new orientations. But to this formidable list there has also to be added a number of other agencies which have, like the Monopolies Commission and a variety of specialist manpower Committees, been asked to play some part in planning for a more efficient use of labour for the benefit of society as a whole. It is arguable that the need now is for a rationalisation of these various agencies, so designed as to give the State adequate opportunity to cover the major problem areas already defined, as well as those that may be opened up as the 1970's unfold: one version of such rationalisation now being discussed is the proposed Commission for Industry and Manpower.

The main point that has been made here is that the traditional system of industrial relations and traditional thoughts in the labour market in Britain have been mainly concerned with only a part of the field, and with a declining part, and most of our debate up till now has been directed to improving the working of that sector with which industrial relations has been traditionally concerned. Wider issues are growing, and the 1970's like the 1960's will certainly turn out to be a decade of change.

A volume such as this can possibly help to identify the main issues and create some sense of perspective around them. At the beginning we observed some of the difficulties of identification and at the close of the 1970's there will no doubt be obvious omissions. We have, in selecting issues for discussion, left out a direct contribution on the future of incomes policy although of course this is a topic that recurs regularly throughout the contributions. In avoiding a direct approach we are not to be seen as denying the probable importance of incomes policy in the future, but rather as recognising that its longer-term influence has now fully permeated all discussions about, and the whole shape of, industrial relations and collective bargaining in Britain. While it is difficult to see the scope for any very new development in alternative methods of incomes policy as a short-term restrictive device, its presence in this capacity is a continuing background fact. We have no doubt that this particular tiger, though some believe, or pretend to believe, that it is made of paper, will emerge from time to time in the next decade and be given a shape and form specific to the needs of the day. We have left out of account as a separate issue the problems of union structure and amalgamation, though again this is a theme that recurs in the essays that follow. Mention could also have been made of the changing political role of the labour movement, the implications for the conduct of industrial relations in the emergence of the conglomerate enterprise and especially the multi-national company, while more attention could have been given to parallel developments in the industrial relations systems of other countries.

In the end, limits have had to be imposed. We can only hope that the final selection is one that highlights most, if not all, of the key issues for the 1970's, and that the collective whole will help to create that sense of perspective we believe to be an important factor in trying to understand a little more about our future.

THEORY AND METHODS OF NATIONAL MANPOWER POLICY*

J. R. CROSSLEY

I

THE BASIS OF MANPOWER POLICY

The development of labour market and manpower policy, no less than that of other major parts of national policy, needs to proceed from an adequate theoretical basis. This is not to say that its final objectives are not severely practical ones. On the contrary, the present needs for active, continuing and diversified measures of support are obvious to the most casual observer of the British labour market. The point is rather that a proper balance between these different measures, their most appropriate forms of administration, and a fruitful strategy for developing the research and information services upon which they depend, all require an agreed framework of ideas about what the policy is for, and how it is supposed to work.

In Britain this is lacking, and there has been a notable reluctance to borrow from Swedish and American authors[1] the notion that substantial public intervention is needed if the national labour market is to work like a market at all, and begin to live up to some of the claims made for its efficiency, from arguments founded more or less securely on theoretical welfare analysis, by the proponents of *laisser faire*. It is, indeed, bad form even to use the word ' market ' in association with labour, among British manpower administrators and legislators. But if this shows an admirable regard for the famous phrase in the founding charter of the ILO that labour is not a commodity, it also incurs the risk that individual members of the labour force will receive less than their economic dues. Freedom of job choice, to take but one example, is not a natural freedom which already exists in the labour market. It has to be created by meticulous and particularised attention to the needs of individuals and groups, and its achievement is both an enlargement of personal freedom, and a gain to the performance of the labour market. In the opening section of this chapter, we sketch some salient features of manpower and labour market policy, from the standpoint of economic theory, and for reasons of space we omit the many qualifications which flow from the fact that we are discussing human beings. Since there is no lack of emphasis on this point in the British literature, the reader should have no difficulty in supplying the qualifications himself.

* The author is grateful to Professor Mark Blaug for comments on an earlier draft of this article.
[1] Rehn (1962); Bakke (1963); Lester (1966).

It is true that human labour is not a commodity. Human beings are more accurately conceived as assets, from the economic point of view, and an adequate view of how the labour market works, for policy purposes, must start from this fact. Like other economic assets, people in the labour force have a present value which reflects the expectation that they will continue to earn real income in the future. How much income they are expected to earn, and hence their present values, can be thought of as depending on their locations, broadly conceived, within the labour force classified by occupation, industry, geographical locality and so on. Since a change of location usually involves an outlay on the one hand, and a change in the present value of discounted earnings on the other, it is essentially an investment decision. In an idealised model of the operation of the labour market, we imagine that these changes of location are made by individuals, whenever the prospective increase in present value exceeds the cost of change, as perceived by themselves.

We know, of course, that the costs of change are often large, and that there is much uncertainty about the permanence of the gain from movement. It is therefore not at all surprising that members of the labour force do not respond to wage changes in the same way as supplies upon a commodity market, and we can infer that the labour market is likely to develop other distinctive features as well. Prominent among these are institutional arrangements which minimise uncertainty about the gains from movements, which include the well known tendency towards rigidity in wage differentials, which preceded collective bargaining and has been reinforced by it. Wage differentials could scarcely have much allocative effect in a market where job changes are made with some expectation of continuing employment in the new job, if expectations about relative wages were being cheated through continual variation. What happens instead is that the return from the change of location is made to vary through changes in the investment outlay: the costs of job search shift between potential employer and employee for example, over the cycle, and they also differ greatly among individuals on each side of the labour market. It is a corollary of this institutional arrangement that more of the short period variation in demand will be taken out in the form of variations in employment rather than wage levels, and this explains the complementary institutional development of trade union unemployment insurance in the last century. A further peculiarity of the market, as Marshall stressed, is that property in human capital is vested in the individual himself. This has many implications, and in particular a large part of protective action by trade unions and the state can be seen as the defence of this property right against its expropriation, which in its extreme form is slavery. Where an employee contracts with an employer and there is on the job training, moreover, the human capital of the one, and the job arranged by employer on the other, come together in a jointly owned asset, and there will evidently be considerable scope for bargaining over the division of the total return.

If this is how the labour market works, we can see how the scope for labour market and manpower policy arises, by retracing the points made in the last paragraph. Neither the full *social* costs or benefits from what has been called a change of location will always be reflected fully in those perceived and incurred by the individual mover. In addition, his discount rate is likely to be higher than the social one, and the mover will typically be ignorant of all but a fraction of the investment opportunities available to him. His investment is moreover constrained in many cases by lack of funds, since the market for capital is far from perfect, especially when the borrower cannot offer himself as security. Secondly, the protective devices generated by uncertainty are by no means neutral in their overall social effects, and there is scope for replacing the more inhibiting ones by others which still maintain individual safeguards. Thirdly, although the individual has an inalienable property right in the human capital embodied in him, it is the case that much of the investment which created it was made by others: his parents, employers and the state, whose long term interests do not necessarily coincide with his own. This has provided a powerful argument for state subsidised education in the past, and continues to do so for many, who reject proposals to finance higher education by government loans to students, for example, on the ground that an equity participation in subsequent earnings would infringe the basic property right. Finally, since the scope for bargaining arises at least in part out of the existence of human capital, and its participation in what may be called the joint ownership of jobs, we should expect manpower policy to be bound up closely with industrial relations at the workplace, especially in respect of changes in job specification, and what these changes are worth to each side.

We can now define the aims of manpower and labour market policy in a rather more specific way than that of ' making the labour market work '. National manpower policy is concerned with making those public investments which will maximise the present social value of the human capital embodied in the labour force, subject to specific constraints. The constraints include those of the public expenditure budget itself, and various requirements with regard to the distribution of the economic costs and benefits, as well as purely social aims, such as a requirement that retraining facilities should be available to people of any age, whether or not they are likely to remain at work long enough to pay off the real costs of retraining. The policy can be implemented in many ways, but most of these are variants of the use of selective taxes and subsidies to alter the structure of incentives so as to bring optimising individual behaviour closer to that which is also optimal from the social point of view. In the rest of this paper we shall interpret national manpower policy as being concerned with public investments in human assets, and regard this as separating it from national labour market policy. The latter is a rather wider concept, under which the benefits may accrue in other forms, as for example through a downwards shift in the Phillips curve, which reduces the rate of inflation corresponding to a given overall rate of unemployment.

II

SOME THEORETICAL CONSIDERATIONS

Manpower policy as investment programming

Judged from the point of view of this definition, manpower policy at present lacks all but a few of the agencies, institutions, techniques and information flows which are needed to implement it, and for many years we shall continue to rely largely on personal judgments and *ad hoc* measures. This is no reason, however, for neglecting the basic principles, which apply irrespective of whether we ever reach the millennial state of knowledge which the more enthusiastic supporters of manpower forecasting envisage. At the risk of labouring the obvious, therefore, we now examine in a simplified and schematic way some of the main requirements which an adequate manpower policy should try to satisfy.

Suppose, for simplicity, that there are a finite number of well defined ' locations ' or categories of manpower, so that the present distribution of the labour force among the categories can be represented by a single vector. The simplest type of manpower policy would then proceed by forecasting the corresponding vector at some future date, and would rely upon its publication to validate the forecast. To the extent that governments already undertake manpower forecasting, it is frequently used in this way. It might be thought that the mere publication of a forecast would be unlikely to influence locational choices, but where there is much ignorance the publication of an authoritative forecast can in fact have marked effects. That is one reason for caution with this type of policy. There are others.

In the first place, nothing whatever is said about costs and present values. Suppose for a moment—as may be approximately true for marginal changes in a relatively static economy—that the vector of present values, which corresponds with the manpower distribution vector, is unchanged between the two dates. It will still be highly unlikely that the costs of changing location will be the same for individuals starting from different locations, and we shall therefore have a matrix of costs forming the entries in a two way table distinguishing destination by column, and origin by row. Given the manpower distributions at origin and destination, the investment problem is precisely that defined as the transportation problem of linear programming, for which straightforward methods of solution exist (Churchman et al., 1957). Leaving aside their technicalities, however, the important conclusions are that costs become relevant as soon as we move away from the simplest kind of policy, and it also follows that a programming method, i.e. a decision making technique, is needed *as well as* a manpower forecast. In this example, the manpower forecast is made quite independently of costs and present values, but if present values were indeed invariant, a better policy would be to *choose* that manpower distribution vector which maximised the increment of total present value, less costs.

As a next step in complexity, we note that the same linear programming technique can also handle the much more plausible case where the vector of present values corresponding to the forecast manpower vector differs from the present one. Each cell in the transportation matrix now has a gross change in present value, as well as a transportation cost. What is new is the forecasting of a set of present values, as well as a manpower vector, and this is the development which is needed to unify some of the different approaches to the analysis of manpower policy which exist in the research literature. These include, as the main competitor with purely quantitative manpower forecasting, the internal rate of return analysis, which has an obvious affinity with the present value technique proposed here. By itself, the internal rate of return approach also has some serious defects. In particular, by recommending that we should invest where present (or recent) rates of return are high, it neglects the forecasting of relative prices which is an indispensable part of any programme for efficient accumulation (Malinvaud, 1953; Masse, 1962). Even more seriously it assumes (in common with the forecasting model discussed in the previous paragraph) that the conditions of partial equilibrium analysis are satisfied, which rules out its relevance when changes of more than marginal size are envisaged.

To put this last point differently, there is a general functional relationship between the forecast manpower vector and the corresponding present value vector, and if we vary the first, the second will be altered too. There is an infinite set of these functionally related pairs of vectors, and in principle the task of manpower policy can be expressed as that of scanning the future by examining all feasible pairs, and picking out the *optimum optimorum* by repeated application of the transportation programming model.

Since we are at this stage concerned only with conceptionalisation and pure theory, the precise form of the functional relationship between the vectors of manpower quantities and present values can be left unspecified. Evidently a general equilibrium approach is needed, which allows for future technological changes and changes in tastes and other factor supplies, as well as product and factor substitution. The problem is essentially that of programming investment projects which have interdependent effects (sometimes called dynamic external economies), and some literature exists on the development of practical techniques (Chenery, 1959).

Any decision-making technique which attempts to follow the scheme outlined so far will have to reckon with a further complication, which is the existence of uncertainty. Instead of a single vector of present values, for a given manpower vector, there is in theory a set of present value vectors, only one of which will be realised, being chosen, in the language of game theory, as nature's strategy. If the vectors corresponding to the different strategies which may be chosen by nature have probabilities attached to them, the decision-making techniques now include a game-theoretic element, and it is the excess of *expected* present values over costs which is maximised. There is a far-reaching implication of this extension of the model to include uncertainty, which is best seen if we return to the simpler specification in which there is no interdependence between the manpower and present value vectors. There is then a single matrix of present values, arranged by column according to nature's strategies and distinguished by category of manpower, in each row. Under these conditions, it will not matter how many people move into any particular manpower category, since present values are independent of manpower distribution. Now it is well-known proposition in game theory that the optimal strategy in a game played against nature will often be a mixed one. In a long series of plays, that is to say, the decision-maker will vary his choice among different rows, in proportions determined by the numerical data of the game. This strategy is not available to the individual manpower investor, whose opportunities for repeated plays are very limited, and if left to himself he will normally choose conservatively. By contracting with others, however, in a national manpower policy, he can raise his expected pay-off since the mixed strategy can be played by the group as a whole. If we do not know how technology is going to change, we can agree that some of us should be trained to cover one possible outcome, some for another and so on. But while the expected pay-off to the group can be raised by the use of a mixed strategy, it will involve some people in losses which they would have avoided if they had not contracted to play as members of the group. Consequently there must be an arrangement for redistributing the income streams actually realised, in order to compensate individuals for the unforeseen effects of technological change, if society is to meet uncertainty by training the labour force in this flexible way. The precise form of the redistributive arrangements will in principle need to take account of differences between individuals in risk aversion, and of the disincentive effects of redistribution (Friedman, 1953).

Manpower policy for optimal economic growth

Although we have tried to show the relevance of some existing decision-making techniques to the improvement of national manpower policy, it will never be possible to do more than get somewhat closer than we are at present to the goal of maximising the expected net present value of human capital. A further theoretical development is helpful as a background to the evaluation of practical techniques. Among the factors determining the gains from investment in human capital, we can distinguish between static and dynamic ones, and attempt to form a view as to their relative importance. The case for manpower forecasting rests largely on the belief that it is dynamic elements such as technological change which provide the opportunities for high returns from properly chosen manpower investments. On the other hand one may ask whether a scanning of the present value vectors corresponding to alternative manpower distributions under *present* technology would not also yield substantial gains. It is implicit in much of our present concern with productivity bargaining and the efficient use of manpower in Britain that most observers would answer this question with a strong affirmative. In one sense this is encouraging, since it means that solutions to the technically most difficult parts of the policy scheme, which are those involving the forecasting of technological change, are not immediately needed, for substantial benefits to be attainable from manpower investment. But by the same token, if we are not at present somewhere in the neighbourhood of the optimal manpower distribution for our present technology, it is quite invalid to attempt to produce manpower forecasts based on an optimal growth model of some kind, until the first problem has been solved, in the interpretation of the available data. It is a necessary condition for staying on the optimal growth path that we should first get onto it. This consideration invalidates most, if not all, of the manpower forecasts which have been produced in the United Kingdom up to the present time. It does not necessarily invalidate them as stages in the development of methods, however, and as a final theoretical exploration we consider briefly some implications of optimal growth theory for the possible future development of forecasting methods.

As a first step, it is necessary to give some theoretical meaning to what has just been distinguished as the objective of the static element in manpower policy, which is the optimal manpower distribution for the *present* technology. Suppose, following Von Neumann (1945), that technology is specified as a spectrum of techniques of the discrete, linear programming, kind, except that the production process takes time, between the input of factors at the beginning of the period (a year, say), and the output of commodities at its end. These latter become the factors used in the next production period, and so on. Suppose further, in order to simplify the exposition, that there are only two ' commodities ' which are both inputs and outputs, and that these are an economic good which satisfies both production and consumption requirements, and ' training ' which is embodied in members of the labour force who would otherwise remain unskilled. Training is assumed to be durable, so that the total stock of skilled men is carried forward from one period to the next, with an increment depending on the amount of new training given to unskilled workers during the period. It is assumed that each activity uses both inputs and produces both outputs, though in varying ratios. Unskilled labour is also an input, but it is for simplicity ' netted out ' by deducting from the output of the economic good of each activity a fixed wage, at which unskilled labour is assumed to be in perfectly elastic supply. Similarly, the wage of the skilled labour used in each activity is deducted from its output of the economic good. Skilled labour, however, is not available in whatever quantity is needed during the period. It is available only in a fixed quantity, inherited from the previous period, and the same is true of the stock of the economic good which is left over for use as a productive input, after the payment of wages. The respective levels of these inherited stocks will evidently depend upon the choice of activities and the levels at which they are operated. If it is the object of economic policy to maximise the rate of growth, it is not difficult to show that under these assumptions only two activities will be selected from the technology set. They will also be combined in a fixed proportion, held constant over time, which maximises the rate of growth at which stocks are passed on from one period to the

2

next, in the proportions required as inputs by the two activities taken together. This will also be the maximum rate at which the whole economy can grow. Given that this is the objective of economic policy; the particular choice of techiques which it implies, and the rate of investment in training, determine a particular fixed distribution of total manpower input between skilled and unskilled, and this can be interpreted as the optimum distribution for the given technology, which it is the target of static manpower policy to attain.

Since the model described is a linear programming one, we expect it to have a dual in terms of prices and the rate and interest, and this can easily be shown to have the same solution as the original problem, in the sense that the same two activities will be chosen on the optimal growth path, because they are the only ones which make non-negative profits. It follows that under the special assumptions of the Von Neumann model, a cost-benefit approach to the choice of manpower investments, which works in terms of trial calculations of accounting profitability, will lead to the same solution as the quantitative balance approach which is so popular among manpower forecasters. This conclusion is a reminder, however, of the very limited scope for the purely quantitative approach to manpower forecasting, rather than a sound theoretical basis for it, because the decomposition into separate quantity and price problems occurs only if the linear programming formulation is an appropriate specification of the efficient allocation problem. For other kinds of linear model, which probably come closer to a realistic description of the growing economy, such as the dynamic Leontief model, with different kinds of trained manpower each having its own supply function, there is no escape from the need to solve the full set of general equilibrium equations corresponding to the present technology.[2]

The Von Neumann model can also be used to throw some light on another interesting question, from the theoretical point of view, which is how to incorporate forecast changes in technology into the model, in order to make it truly dynamic. Suppose, for example, that the technology set changes every five years, in a way which can be foreseen, and that economic policy now includes the objective of preparing, during the present five years, to begin the next five years with an assortment of stocks which will be optimal, both in scale and composition, under the new technology. There are two things which can be said about this situation which have implications for manpower forecasting. One is that the forecaster has to foresee not only the spectrum of new techniques available in five years time, but also the optimal choice which will be made from it. It is against this theoretical requirement that actual forecasting techniques have been assessed. A second feature of the situation is more comforting. The preparation of the appro-

---

[2] The linearity assumption is made in the dynamic Leontief model because it brings the general equilibrium problem within range of approximate solution by empirical methods. In the context of manpower forecasting, its use does not imply, as Blaug (1967) has recently contended, a belief on the part of the forecaster that input coefficients are ' really ' fixed, under a given technology.

priate mixture of stocks for the epoch of the new technology will obviously take us off the optimum growth path for part of the current five year epoch. We can, however, draw from the turnpike theorems of linear growth theory the conclusion that we shall remain on the optimal growth path of the current technology for most of the time (Morishima, 1964, Chap. VI). More generally and realistically, if technology changes every year, or if we revise our five year forecasts every year, we may conjecture that a policy of maximising growth, while providing a changing assortment of manpower stocks for technological change, will normally require a choice of activities in any one year which is in the neighbourhood of the choice which would be made if that year's technology were to continue indefinitely. We turn now to consider some implications of the foregoing discussion, for the future development of manpower policy in the United Kingdom.

III

THE DEVELOPMENT OF POLICY TECHNIQUES

If manpower policy is conceived as the use of public funds to improve the process of human capital formation, its first and main concern is with the potentialities and needs of individuals. In a free society, individual choice is the primary decision mechanism, and the belief that what is best for the individual will often be best for society as well is not invalidated when the operation of an efficient labour market is seen in human capital terms, but merely given a more complicated form. Almost everybody prefers not to be unemployed, to take an obvious example, and an identity of individual and social interests is seen in the traditional macroeconomic policies for full employment. These latter are certainly a part of manpower policy as defined here, since the real net benefits of a move from unemployment into productive work are immediate and large. But manpower policy needs to go much further than that. The traditional macroeconomic policies can at best provide no more than some kind of employment for most people, and the extra jobs created—for example by public works—may offer neither much choice nor much permanence of employment. Optimal investment in human capital, by contrast, involves a time horizon covering the whole working life, and this point must be continually reasserted against the policies which emphasise the immediate or short period perspective. Even the attempts to move away from complete reliance on the traditional macroeconomic measure and make national economic plans on a five year basis, for example, run considerable risks of discounting the future too heavily. And the long time horizon should also make us question the wisdom of relating the intake into Government Training Centres, as at present, to data which include occupational vacancy rates which have a substantial cyclical component.

Individuals also differ greatly, in job satisfaction needs as well as capabilities, and a manpower policy which starts from the need to improve individual investment decisions must eventually develop diversified and particularised services, with a detailed regard for the requirements of different groups. For a well-informed choice, the individual requires good information, both about the market and about himself. In this respect, the success of the Adult Occupational Guidance Scheme of the Department of Employment and Productivity has been a revelation, both of the large unsatisfied needs for individual help, and of an unsuspected willingness to use the public employment service as it develops new roles. This particular service is available only in some of the large exchanges, and it points the way to more specialised staffing in what should in any case probably be a concentration of resources in fewer but larger exchanges.

While the provision of information and counselling services to improve individual decision making is one line of development from the investment concept of manpower policy, another follows from the fact that there is quite frequently a divergence between private and social net benefits from investment in human capital. It is no accident that Pigou (1932) drew his examples largely down this field of application, when illustrating and developing the distinction between private and social costs and returns. A distinction has to be made between two kinds of social gain. First are those which arise from the possibility of collective insurance, where investments are too risky to be undertaken by the individual. In theory this may appear in a lower social rate of discount than the individual one, but the tendency of government policy, if anything, has been to discount the future too heavily, as has just been noted. The Redundancy Payments Act, on the other hand, does approximate fairly well to the alternative approach to risk-bearing implied by the games theory treatment of uncertainty which was outlined earlier. It should be added that some educational policy makers now recognise that individual human capital can be diversified as an insurance against unforeseen technological changes by extending the period of general education; but there has been little discussion yet of the relative costs of these social provisions against uncertainty.

Secondly, a divergence between social and private net product may arise even in a world of perfect foresight. The private costs of the geographical mobility of a few key workers may easily be offset by the gain in national product where they relieve a bottleneck for example, and hence have complementary effects in promoting further employment on the supply side, as well as multiplier effects on that of demand. The existence of such a gain is already apparent in the willingness of some employers at the receiving end to pay some of the major costs like those of housing. But here again there are great differences between individuals, and the need is not so much to increase the total volume of geographical mobility as to change the structure of incentives so as to make it more productive. The present subsidies available from the Department of Employment and Productivity have been criticised for being too low, but a more serious fault is that they allow little scope for discrimination. In terms of the matrix of transportation costs and gross value changes proposed earlier, there may be differences between the social and private matrices, and discriminatory subsidies will usually be needed if private decisions about changes of location are to conform with a human investment programme chosen on the basis of the social matrix. It is no answer to say that discrimination always provokes some complaints and political lobbying by special groups (which it does) because the principles of discrimination are now widely applied in other areas of manpower policy, as for example in the Selective Employment Tax, the Regional Employment Premium, and the grant and levy systems used by the Industrial Training Boards. Taken as a whole, these are measures which seek to bring individual optimising behaviour into line with what is needed in the national interest by using differential net subsidies to alter the structure of incentives. Their further development involves several distinct problems.

First is the need for a much wider and more critical use of cost-benefit modes of thinking on the part of manpower administrators. What is needed in the next few years is not a set of detailed, comprehensive and fully quantified studies (though there is indeed much scope for academic research in this field) so much as a general awareness of the existence of the various kinds of external effects and the habit of mind which seeks to list both costs and benefits comprehensively, and enquires as to their incidence. As one example we may take the basic assumption of the Industrial Training Act of 1964 that training is ' general ' in the sense that while it may be acquired in one firm, it is no less productive in its application in others. It is this assumption which lies behind the use of grants and levies to spread the costs of training ' more equitably ' and to reduce the ' poaching ' of recently trained men. But the argument for redistribution of costs does not apply if training is specific to the particular technology and other circumstances of the firm, having no value elsewhere. There is empirical evidence that a considerable proportion of training costs are in fact incurred in specific training (Thomas, et al. 1969) so that it is quite possible that the present net grants cause a misallocation of resources. This risk is particularly large where an attempt is made to redistribute the whole of the cost which falls upon enterprises, as under the grant and levy system of the Engineering Industry Training Board. There is, of course, no general presumption that the appropriate restructuring of incentives need involve the redistribution of all costs and returns, in any case. One must also ask why the levies and grants are restricted to enterprises, and do not apply to trainees as well, since they surely incur some of the costs and benefits of training also? This last point is taken for granted, for example, in proposals for financing higher education through a system of loans as well as grants to university students. Among the various subsidies now in operation, the Regional Employment Premium was exceptional in respect of the publication of a fairly full official analysis of its possible economic effects. As another example of the greater willingness to cross intellectual boundaries in policy making which an investment orientation should promote, there is a need for declining *and* improving investment opportunities to be sought out and presented to the policy maker *together,* as part of the same information scheme. At present the balance of political pressures is such that the policy maker tends to see the declining industry or region as a social phenomenon in its own right, and not as the counterpart of potential new growth and development. The consequence is that emergency programmes for job creation are improvised, or measures taken to prop up the declining industry, in the absence of a previously worked out list of alternative new investments in the manpower displaced. Manpower policy needs active portfolio management, as well as an occasional overdraft.

The ability to see the full range of costs and benefits, and the interrelations between different manpower measures, should also be one of the decisive factors underlying the *organisation* of manpower policy. It is one which has not been given sufficient weight in the United Kingdom, where different parts of the policy, having been developed on an *ad hoc* basis to meet different needs at various times in the past, remain scattered among several Government Departments and other organisations. This is not a complaint against *ad hoc* development itself, which on the contrary typifies in the United Kingdom experience precisely the adaptive learning capability which a good manpower policy should cultivate. Nor is it simply a plea for administrative tidiness, for a detailed analysis of the ramifications of manpower policy soon takes one into spheres which are, and must inevitably remain, those influenced by other Government Departments. An illustration is the need for local authority housing policies to take account of the requirements of geographical mobility, not only by a greater willingness to waive the usual residence requirements, in favour of high priority immigrants to the locality, but perhaps more radically by promoting greater uniformity among local authorities in their rates of subsidy to council tenants. Such a change would be a major matter of national policy to be argued out, presumably, at Cabinet level. It raises the question, to which one returns repeatedly on taking up particular issues, whether manpower policy has a sufficiently high status, in the present machinery of government, for its advocacy to be assured at the highest levels. It is not a satisfactory answer to say that there are already several senior Ministers who have some responsibility for manpower, at the Departments of Education and Science, Employment and Productivity, Housing and Regional Planning, Technology and Defence. The dividing lines of responsibility are frequently the same as those where policy is weakest, and it is hardly surprising that this is so. Which Department is responsible for the training and deployment of managers, for example, or of technicians, or for the introduction of school children to the world of work? It would probably be wrong to follow the Canadians, in setting up a separate Ministry of Manpower, since in the United Kingdom, at least, manpower policy is not separable from that which cover wages and industrial relations. But the strengthening of the Department of Employment and Productivity, during the last few years, has not moved uniformly on the two fronts.

The problems of organisation do not end there. In retrospect it now seems to have been a mistake to place the main administrative responsibility for industrial training at industry level, in the Industrial Training Act. Something can be done, under the Act, to strengthen the Central Training Council, but it is doubtful whether this would go far enough to meet two needs. One is the ability to steer industrial interests on a course consistent with national interests, if a divergence appears between the two. Another need is for the administration of industrial training to be reconciled with that of educational policy. There are many sensitive issues here, but we may note, as one example, and ask where it should be leading us, that the U.G.C. and the Research Councils have already begun to alter the structure of the output of the higher educational system through the allocation of funds for development and scholarships etc. in a way not altogether dissimilar from the intervention of the Training Boards in industry. For policy making and administration below the national level, a reorganisation of industrial training along regional lines would bring it into line with the general trend in other policy areas, and could also give some flexibility where it is needed most, which is at the local level.

Information Needs

We consider next the development of information systems for manpower policy and distinguish first between statistics relating to the present position, and manpower forecasts. From the point of view of the theoretical scheme proposed earlier, analysis of data relating to the present should not stop short at a mere description of where we are now in terms of human capital and its utilisation. It has to go on and indicate where we ought to be, given present technology, tastes and resources. This analysis is conceptually distinct from and preliminary to manpower forecasting, which introduces future changes in technology etc., although the policy recommendations based on the two may of course be brought together. It is one of the most surprising features of manpower policy discussions in the United Kingdom in recent years that while many of the most active participants (including some trade union leaders as well as employers) have repeatedly stressed the gains which can be made from it, the critical evaluation of present manpower utilisation has been almost entirely neglected by the professional analysts. No serious attempts have been made to verify the numerous guesses about the overall rate of manpower underutilisation, for example, which have varied between 5 per cent. and 50 per cent. of the labour force. And there has been little acknowledgement among those who have projected recent employment trends, that the present may be a disequilibrium position from which we wish to escape rather than perpetuate, being supply-determined where there are shortages at current relative wages, and demand-determined in the converse case. It may be that this reflects a belief in the capacity of the labour market to adjust quickly to a position in the neighbourhood of long run equilibrium (nowithstanding the durability of human capital, of which the belief itself is an excellent example), but in that case why bother to analyse the data and make projections?

In the United Kingdom there is therefore as much scope for the development of knowledge about the present, and a particular urgency about the need to make some radical changes, since developments in the statistical system have a very long gestation period. This is not to say that the fault lies mainly on the side of the data; on the contrary and as with manpower forecasts, the blame lies more on their neglect and misuse.

An overriding practical constraint on the development of manpower statistics is that the total number of official enquiries regularly addressed to establishments has now reached a saturation level. Since the need for economic and social data continues to grow, alternative channels of information must be developed. As the author has argued elsewhere (Crossley, 1966), household surveys provide a potential source of information on manpower, and one which is superior to establishment surveys on the personal correlates of employment data, such as earnings, age, education and household characteristics, which are so important in the analysis of labour supply. There has recently been an expansion of the Household Expenditure Survey in this direction, but no attempt has yet been made to substitute this channel for some of the topics covered by the establishment surveys of the Department of Employment and Productivity. Such a development, together with the bringing together into a multipurpose survey of at least some of the several different enquiries, addressed to similar samples by the Department, would create scope for the collection of new data from establishments to meet new needs. Another contribution to the same end would be a review of the continuing usefulness of some of the present statistical series, which exhibit, like most British labour market institutions, a remarkable tendency to survive in the form appropriate for meeting all the contingencies which have arisen in the past, should they ever recur again. One may seriously ask, for example, whether much of the present occupational data ought not to be scrapped, since the use of a different occupational classification for each major topic covered makes comparisons and the search for relationships virtually impossible. Perhaps they should at least be suspended, until the Department of Employment and Productivity produces the meaningful occupational classification which so many manpower research studies in the United Kingdom have shown to be our greatest statistical need. Among the new topics to be covered by establishment surveys, priority should be given to the collection of comprehensive job vacancy statistics, with supporting data on starting rates of pay and other conditions. These are needed for the development of policies for improving current utilisation, and while current vacancies are *not* necessarily a reliable guide to future ones, there is something to be said, from the technical point of view, for learning to measure current shortages before we make serious attempts to forecast future ones. In the United States and Canada, there has been extensive research on establishment surveys of vacancies during the last few years (N.B.E.R., 1966; U.S. Congress, 1966). This has been prompted, especially in the United States, by the recognition that the well known shortcomings of the employment exchange job order data make them an unreliable source of operating data for the exchange service itself, to say nothing of the needs of policy analysis. The difficulties encountered in these studies suggest that it may have been over-ambitious to attempt to meet both these needs at once. Personnel executives do not commonly use the concept of a vacancy, nor are vacancy records always kept centrally, or for long, when they are kept at all. Moreover, although good statistical practice requires that a vacancy should only be said to exist when some concrete action has been taken by an enterprise to fill it through one or more sources, the long evolution of the corresponding concept of unemployment, used in the United States Current Population Survey, suggests that considerable experimentation will be needed to establish a suitable definition. If operating as well as analytical uses of the data are to influence this process of experimentation, priority should be given to the operating needs of enterprises and job seekers themselves.

Manpower forecasting

It was emphasised earlier that manpower forecasting is ancillary to decision making, and some of the disappointingly slow progress with the development of manpower forecasting methods, both in this country and elsewhere, can be attributed to a failure to acknowledge this fact. Since there are many decision-makers in the labour market, with widely differing needs, it is unlikely that a single multipurpose forecast can meet all needs. It may indeed succeed in meeting none of them, yet this is the type of forecast which is typically generated by the whole economy econometric models, on which a substantial amount of research has concentrated. It has been encouraged by potential users who have in effect asked their researchers to go away and produce some factual forecasts on which their decisions will then be based. Since the decisions are to be made by those whose actions will affect events in the labour market, i.e. the 'facts' to be forecast, this procedure involves a major logical contradiction which can only be avoided if the policy action is recognised as something to be chosen, rather than forecast.

A more diversified approach would recognise that there are some continuing trends in the structure of employment which are already clear to professional students of the labour market, without the need for very sophisticated methods of analysis, but which could, nevertheless, be more widely publicised, for example among new entrants to the labour force. At the other extreme are questions put by policy makers to which the forecaster must have the courage to say that no answer can be given. If he fails to do so, the policy itself may fail to come to terms with uncertainty, and it is for the policy maker, not the forecaster, to decide whether the risks of a particular course of action should be incurred. It is indispensable, for this purpose, that the assumptions on which the forecast is based should be communicated fully to the policy maker, but the forecaster cannot evade his own responsibility for choosing assumptions which have a high likelihood of being realised, among all possible sets of assumptions. Such an evasion of responsibility seems to be implied in the distinction which is sometimes made between forecasts and projections; the latter being said explicitly to be conditional upon assumptions which may turn out to be wrong. But forecasts cannot avoid being conditional upon some assumptions, and by definition an assumption may be wrong. Provided the assumptions are explicit, as they should always be, the relevant distinction is between those cases where the forecaster is instructed to make certain assumptions, and those where he is not and must therefore use his judgment. Communicating the implications of his judgment will often involve the forecaster at least as much in an analysis of the decision process itself, as in actual forecasting. It may be an uncomfortable experience for the policy maker to have to write down lists of his objectives and the means at his disposal, but it is an indispensible preliminary task, since ideally what should be forecast is the future *relationships* between the items in these lists. The choice of a particular set of numbers, as a target, is then the outcome of a policy decision, rather than the forecasting process. The Industrial Training Boards, six years after the Act, have not in general considered very carefully what they can expect from manpower forecasting, and when they can realistically expect it, and in the absence of very clear guidance from the Department of Employment and Productivity on the present technical capabilities of manpower forecasting, there is a risk that the whole edifice of the new industrial training arrangements will turn out to lack a foundation, when the scaffolding is removed.

For the present technical capabilities are very limited, if one wants detailed and accurate forecasts of the occupational employment structure five or ten years ahead, given certain general objectives with respect to economic growth say, regional policy and the accommodation of faster technological change. This judgment on the progress of manpower forecasting may seem pessimistic to those who have studied its development in the United States.[3] It is true that the technical standards set by the Department of Labor are very high, but the projections have been published with less regard for optimality criteria, of the kind discussed earlier in this article, than seems to have been demanded in the European countries. The latter have been much more cautious in believing that the publication of a forecast, even a fairly good one, will do little harm and perhaps some good.

There are at present two competing approaches to manpower forecasting, in which the forecasts are prepared centrally by specialist economists and statisticians in the one case, and by the enterprises themselves in response to a sample survey in the other. In support of the second method, as used for example in the biennial surveys of highly qualified scientific manpower requirements, it is said that whereas one may be able to make a fair estimate of the age of a ship's captain by fitting a multiple regression model to the displacement, maximum speed and other measurements of the ship, the estimate will be much improved if the question is put directly to the captain.

[3] See, for example, the Symposium on Manpower Projections in *Industrial Relations*, May, 1966.

This is valid only insofar as the future is already determined by decisions which enterprises have taken, or where they can be shown on other grounds to have more knowledge of uncertain events than the centralised forecasting team. These are matters of fact, on which the present evidence does not favour the enterprise method. The provision of additive forecasts, on a common set of assumptions, requires not only that enterprises should already have a forecasting capability—which is true only of a minority—but that the capability should be sophisticated and flexible enough to meet the special requirements of the questionnaire. There are in addition biases towards optimism, since declining firms are reluctant to report their condition, and also towards conservatism, which appears in a tendency for the dispersion of anticipated changes to be consistently less than realised ones.

Where enterprises lack a manpower forecasting capability, we might expect them to report the closest substitute information in response to a questionnaire, which is their knowledge of current vacancies, the latter being more accessible to special enquiry within the enterprise. The author has examined this conjecture in the data from an area skill survey for North Carolina, which was chosen as representative of the many such skill surveys which have been undertaken in the United States. (*Employment Outlook*, 1966; U.S. Dept. of Labor, 1965.) The study asked for forecast employment increases over the period 1966 to 1970, for 107 occupations, from more than 2,800 employers in a selection of 35 industries, and also for current vacancy data for the same occupations. Among the 36 occupations which had at least 1,000 employees each, in the sample at the base date, the correlation coefficient between forecast employment increases and current vacancies (both expressed as a percentage of the number employed in the base period) was $+0.87$, which is highly significant in a sample of 36. It means that approximately three-quarters of the information contained in the forecasts was already contained in the vacancy data. It does not follow, of course, that good forecasts can be made from vacancy data, even if the vacancy data are good. The point is simply that in the present state of manpower forecasting, little seems to be gained by asking for anything more than current vacancies. (Crossley, 1968.)

Up to the present there is sufficient experience of both methods only for relatively short periods of a year or less, and for fairly large employment aggregates. For this type of problem, the centralised agency using statistical methods (often of a simple kind) seems to perform best. Where longer term forecasts are required, as in the French and British national plans, there has usually been a combination of the two methods. This seems to be the most promising approach. There are some components, notably the development of new techniques and products, which are more accurately foreseen by the sector specialist, while he on the other hand has little knowledge of what may be happening in other product and factor markets. If we recall the earlier discussion of linear growth models, it seems that manpower forecasting can in principle be divided into two main elements. One is the forecasting of a set of production techniques for each industry, which is a matter of technological forecasting, and best done at the decentralised level. The other is the solution of the general equilibrium system at the whole economy level, which gives factor and product prices and hence the efficient choice of techniques (Kornai, 1967; Holt et al., 1960). The first attempt to forecast the efficient choice of techniques, on the basis of general equilibrium considerations, however crude, is an appropriate function for a central agency. But sector experts would no doubt wish to suggest revisions, perhaps very substantial ones, to their technology forecasts, when a first approximation to the equilibrium sets of factor and product prices becomes available. The rate of take-up of the new technology will moreover depend upon constraints which may exist upon investment funds, and the average technology will depend upon current scrapping rates and past investment outlays, as described in growth models of the 'vintage' technology type. It appears to be in the occupational composition of each industry's labour force that most of the mutual adjustment occurs between new technological possibilities, and manpower supplies. Since the *average* technology at one point of time was typically the best practice technology some five to ten years previously, and hence observable several years in advance, it should be possible, in theory at least, to foresee most of the manpower implications of new technology over a period of at least five years. The use of vintage models is complicated however by the consideration that the best-practice lag has both a technology and an economic variability of its own, being governed apparently by a logistic rather than a steady diffusion process, and providing a form of capital-for-labour substitution, since it varies inversely with changes in the wage-rental ratio. Some of this will no doubt be set out before long in econometric models at industry level, but in building up from that to an operational forecast through the process of mutual consultation with sector experts, and adjustments of forecasts, it would be surprising indeed if only one or two iterations, as in the British National Plan of 1965, converged on a solution which was acceptable from both points of view.

If we are still a very long way from having this procedure, there are some components in it where an immediate opportunity for progress exists.

Technological forecasting is a rapidly developing field of study, but it has proceeded independently of manpower forecasting, and indeed of general economic forecasting, in many cases. Labour economists can no more expect to be professionally competent in applied science and technology than in the other disciplines with which they have traditionally been associated in multi-disciplinary research, but a new dimension now has to be added to such research. Another development indicated by the theoretical analysis which is surely overdue is some extension of forecasting techniques, including those which use input-output methods, from purely quantitative data to the forecasting of price and income structures. In a market economy it is scarcely conceivable that quantitative planning can be effective unless there is an assurance that the structure of incentives will guide decisions in the right direction, and few would deny that the recent prices and income policies have lacked an overall strategy for the relative prices of products and factors.

The fact that large gaps exist in an overall manpower forecasting system need not deter the forecaster from pushing ahead with specific forecasts for well-defined occupations of particular importance. The margins of error arising from ignorance about what is happening to imperfect substitutes in the rest of the labour force may lie within the confidence intervals of the forecasts; and if they do not, that may indicate that the elasticities of supply and substitution are large enough in any case for the forecasts to be unnecessary.

There is one further line of development suggested by the earlier analysis of manpower forecasting in a general equilibrium setting. We have pointed out that enterprises are only now beginning to forecast their own demands. They can scarcely be blamed, however, for not being able to make forecasts of market supply, and it is in respect of manpower supply, for which the Department of Employment and Productivity has special responsibility, that the biggest gap exists in the forecasting system. There was probably no single forecast of more importance in the 1965 National Plan than that concerning the reduction in the rate of growth of the total labour supply, but the implication seems to have been overlooked that the Government should now go on to present this forecast analysed by region and by type of training (no doubt very crudely defined, to begin with) and eventually in terms of gross flows into and out of the labour force. Such a gross flow analysis would link up with a statistical model of the industrial training system, which seems to be needed in its own right as a device for describing in a comprehensive way and monitoring the progress of the Industrial Training Boards. It has been an unfortunate and unwarranted assumption of much of the public discussion of manpower policy in the United Kingdom in recent years that the structure of demand is sovereign and that manpower supply must be made to adapt to it. It would be a useful first step towards improving the efficiency of the labour market to recognise that it requires a mutual adjustment, in which employers will have a stronger incentive to find new ways of meeting labour shortages, if they are confronted with better information about the supplies which are likely to be available to them.

University of Leeds

References

BAKKE, E. Wight (1963). *A Positive Labor Market Policy.* Merrill.

BLAUG, Mark (1967). 'Approaches to Educational Planning.' *The Economic Journal,* June 1967.

CHENERY, Hollis B. (1959) 'The Interdependence of Investment Decisions' *in* Abramovitz, Moses and others, *The Allocation of Economic Resources.* Stanford.

CHURCHMAN, C. West, ACKOFF, Russell L. and ARNOFF, E. Leonard (1957). *Introduction to Operations Research,* Part V. Wiley.

CROSSLEY, J. R. (1966). 'Essential Statistics for Manpower Forecasting' *in* Roberts B. C. and Smith, J. H. (eds.) *Manpower Policy and Employment Trends.* L.S.E.: Bell.

CROSSLEY, J. R. (1968). 'Labour Market Data and Procedures for Estimating Current and Prospective (Medium and Long Term) Scarcities of Manpower.' *O.E.C.D. Expert Group Meeting on Reporting Enterprise Labour Requirements and Defining Scarcities in the Labour Market.* O.E.C.D., May 1968.

Employment Outlook (1966). *Employment Outlook for Selected Occupations in North Carolina, 1966-70.* Employment Security Commission of North Carolina, December 1966. B.E.S. No. E—252.

FRIEDMAN, Milton (1953). 'Choice, Chance and the Personal Distribution of Income.' *The Journal of Political Economy,* August, 1953.

HOLT, C. C., MODIGLIANI, F., MUTH, J. F. and SIMON, H. A. (1960). *Planning Production, Inventories and Work Force.* Prentice-Hall.

KORNAI, J. (1967). *Mathematical Planning of Structural Decisions.* North-Holland.

LESTER, Richard A. (1966). *Manpower Planning in a Free Society.* Princeton.

MALINVAUD, Edmond (1953). 'Capital Accumulation and Efficient Allocation of Resources.' *Econometrica,* April 1953.

MASSE, Pierre (1962). *Optimal Investment Decisions.* Wiley.

MORISHIMA, Michio (1964). *Equilibrium, Stability and Growth; a Multisectoral Analysis.* Oxford.

N.B.E.R. (1966). *The Measurement of Job Vacancies.* National Bureau of Economic Research, 1966.

PIGOU, A. C. (1932). *The Economics of Welfare.* Fourth Edition. Macmillan.

REHN, Gosta (1962). 'Manpower Adaptability and Economic Growth.' *The O.E.C.D. Observer,* No. 1, November 1962.

THOMAS, Brinley, MOXHAM, John and JONES, J. A. G. (1969). 'A Cost-Benefit Analysis of Industrial Training.' *British Journal of Industrial Relations.* July 1969.

VON NEUMANN, J., (1945). 'A Model of General Economic Equilibrium'. *Review of Economic Studies,* 1945-6.

U.S. CONGRESS (1966). *Job Vacancy Statistics.* Hearings before the Subcommittee on Economic Statistics of the Joint Economic Committee, Congress of the United States, 89th Congress, Second Session, May 17 and 18, 1966. U.S. Government Printing Office, 1966.

U.S. DEPARTMENT OF LABOR (1965). *Area Skill Survey Handbook on Employment Security Job Market Research Methods.* November, 1965.

TRENDS IN PLANT AND COMPANY BARGAINING

B. C. ROBERTS AND JOHN GENNARD

I

THE GROWTH OF PLANT AND COMPANY BARGAINING

It was the view of the Donovan Commission (1968) that the growth in collective bargaining at the plant and company level had fundamentally changed the pattern of industrial relations in Britain. This conclusion was apparently thought by the Commission to be self-evident since no attempt was made to investigate in full detail the extent to which local bargaining was in fact taking place. The purpose of this article is not to seek to fill the whole of this gap left by the Commission, since this could only be done by a comparative survey carried out by or through the Department of Employment and Productivity, but to examine the factors making for the development of plant and company bargaining, and on the basis of more limited evidence, the scope and coverage of the agreements that have been reached.

The Department of Employment and Productivity has for many years collected details of agreements made between trade unions and employers' associations covering an entire industry or section of an industry, but it has not attempted to collect systematically agreements made at the plant and company level. However, under prices and incomes legislation the D.E.P. has obtained details of a large number of agreements which have had to be checked against the norms and criteria laid down. Following the recommendations of the Donovan Commission the Department is now seeking to develop and maintain a register of plant and company agreements mainly concerned with procedure.

The task of comprehensively surveying plant and company agreements is not an easy one, since the range of these agreements is wide and their pattern is highly complex. Agreements at the plant and company level may be made between the employer and a single trade union or a number of unions; they may cover all or specific groups of employees in a company, whether they be employed in one or more locations. There may, however, be separate agreements in each plant or location, for different groups of employees and with different unions. Where the firm produces a single range of products in a multiplicity of plants, it is likely, though by no means certain, that an agreement in one will have a counterpart in another. Where, however, the firm is a 'conglomerate', it could quite easily happen that one subsidiary had enterprise and plant agreements and another subsidiary had not.

Since trade unions in Britain organise horizontally there are few companies which recognise and negotiate with only one union. It is, therefore, not uncommon for a union representing particular groups of employees such as draughtsmen, clerks, transport workers, or electricians and maintenance mechanics, either to negotiate separate agreements, or to have their particular interest distinguished in a company agreement which covers all groups.

Companies belonging to an employers' association which have negotiated separate wages agreements will nevertheless generally follow the procedural agreement covering the industry. However, some firms have adopted their own procedures which may supplement or even be a substitute for the arrangements made for the industry. The role of procedure has become of increasing importance with the development of plant and company agreements which are negotiated for a specific term. It is not always possible to distinguish agreements covering procedural matters from those that deal with issues of substance, since both elements may be included in the same agreement.

The greatest difficulty in analysing the growth and development of plant and company agreements arises from the fact that a large proportion of the agreements made at these levels are not negotiated as entirely new and clearly distinguishable contracts. They are supplements and additions that are added to previous agreements in an almost continuous process of bargaining that has no finite boundaries or term. Many agreements are merely verbal undertakings made by management and they become a part of the normal conditions of employment without ever being written down or incorporated in a formal signed agreement. It was this kind of fragmented ambiguous type of collective bargaining which led the Donovan Commission to emphasise the need for a clearly defined plant and company bargaining procedure at the conclusion of negotiations and the signing of a written agreement.

Unfortunately it is impossible to give any precise indication of the extent to which the various types of plant and company agreements have increased during the past decade. At the time when the first Fawley Productivity Agreement was signed in 1960, which might reasonably be taken as marking a most important stage in the development of enterprise bargaining, no figures of the number of workers who might have been working under plant or company agreements exists. The only information that is available is an estimate of the number of workers thought to have been covered by collective bargaining machinery at that time made by the Ministry of Labour. This figure referred primarily to workers covered by industry-wide collective bargaining, not to those working under plant and company agreements.

In its evidence to the Donovan Commission the Ministry of Labour (1965, para. 48) listed 500 separate industry-wide negotiating arrangements, including statutory wage-fixing bodies, for manual workers alone. It estimated that some 14 million workers were covered by this machinery in

1964, out of a total of 16 million. Collective bargaining machinery of a similar kind covering non-manual workers existed mainly in the public sector. Out of a total of 7 million non-manual workers it was estimated that less than 4 million were covered by collective bargaining arrangements. Though it was known that many companies had their own bargaining arrangements comprehensive information as to the number involved was lacking.

Since the report of the Donovan Commission the Department has been collecting, with the voluntary assistance of the companies, the procedural agreements in existence in all those firms with more than 5,000 employees on their pay-roll.[1] The size of the firms asked to report will be gradually reduced and the notification made compulsory under the projected industrial relations act. At a later stage agreements covering matters of substance such as pay and conditions of employment made at the plant and company level may also have to be reported.

Under the Prices and Incomes legislation agreements covering pay, hours of work and productivity that might have been in breach of the norm, have had to be registered with the Department of Employment and Productivity. However, there can be no certainty that all agreements have been notified. Moreover, agreements made at the company level covering such matters as sickness schemes, pensions and redundancy provisions would not be covered by the necessity to notify the Department since they would be unlikely to be in conflict with the norm.

Nevertheless, in spite of the limitations in coverage mentioned the Register of productivity agreements compiled by the D.E.P., though it also includes national agreements, provides the most important source of information on the growth of plant and company agreements. The Register was started on 1 January 1967 following the period of standstill on increases in incomes. On 24 October 1969, 3,788 agreements covering 7 million workers had been reported. These agreements were entirely in the private sector of the economy, since agreements made in the public sector are not registered with the D.E.P., but with the Department directly involved which consults with the D.E.P. on the policy implications of the agreements concerned.

Some indication of the growth since 1 January 1967 in the number of these agreements during the various phases of the incomes policy as marked by the successive White Papers listed below can be gained from the following figures:

1. Prices and Incomes Policy Standstill: Period
    of Severe Restraint, (Cmnd. 3150)   1.1.67 - 30. 6.67   330 cases
2. Prices and Incomes Policy after 30 June
    1967, (Cmnd. 3235)   1.7.67 - 20. 3.68   619 cases

[1] The Employment and Productivity Gazette for December 1969 reported that more than 300 companies, nationalised corporations and large local authorities, employing in all more than 6 million people, had been invited to register their agreements. The response had been good.

3. Productivity Prices and Incomes Policy
  1968-69, (Cmnd. 3590)   21.3.68 - 31.12.69   3,236 cases

The number of cases reported to the D.E.P. averaged about 60 per month during 1967; for the first five months of 1968 it was 75 a month, but in June 1968 the figures went up to 200 per month. The rate of reporting remained at this high level throughout the remainder of 1968, but fell slightly in 1969 to about 160 a month.

Since August 1968 the D.E.P. has made a broad industrial breakdown of the cases reported for permission to exceed the standard norm of $3\frac{1}{2}$ per cent. on grounds of productivity improvement. Table I below indicates the distribution of these cases under the main S.I.C. orders:

Table I

INDUSTRIAL DISTRIBUTION OF CASES REPORTED TO D.E.P.

Order No.	Heading	No. of Cases
I	Agriculture, Forestry and Fishing	4[1]
II	Mining and Quarrying	7
III	Food, Drink and Tobacco	243
IV	Chemical and Allied Industries	103
V	Metal Industries	0
VI	Engineering and Electrical Goods	477
VII	Shipbuilding and Marine Engineering	58
VIII	Vehicles	98
IX	Metal Goods	97
X	Textiles	35
XI	Leather, Leather Goods, etc.	3
XII	Clothing and Footwear	1
XIII	Bricks, Pottery, Glass, etc.	36
XIV	Timber, Furniture, etc.	11
XV	Paper, Printing and Publishing	126[2]
XVI	Other Manufacturing	45
XVII	Construction	12
XVIII	Gas, Electricity and Water	0
XIX	Transport and Communications	161[3]
XX	Distributive Trades[4]	80[5]
XXI	Insurance, Banking, etc.	32
XXII	Professional and Scientific Services	0
XXIII	Miscellaneous Services	16
XXIV	Public Administration and Defence	3[6]

Source: Department of Employment and Productivity.

Notes: 1. None in agriculture.
    2. Over 50 per cent. of which are in newspaper printing.
    3. 69 in road passenger transport.
    4. Includes oil distribution.
    5. Mostly Wage Councils accepted on low pay criteria.
    6. All in civilian sector.

Of particular interest is the relatively large number of productivity agreements made in Food, Drink and Tobacco, Transport and Communications, Paper, Printing and Publishing and Engineering and Electrical Goods.

It is now quite clear that in these industries a substantial number of employees are working under plant and company agreements. In many other industries and areas of employment only a small minority would appear to be specifically covered, but nevertheless, many employers would be paying wages substantially above the levels laid down by industry-wide agreements.

It is common practice in smaller firms for employers to follow general trends in local labour markets by allowing earnings to drift up under competitive pressures. Increases will often be given and improvements made in conditions of employment following submissions from shop stewards, but the process of negotiation and agreement will be quite informal. In many cases only if a dispute arises will a full-time official be called in to take part in negotiations. In other cases he may attend a meeting to give formal approval to an offer an employer is prepared to make in the knowledge that others in his area have made similar increases. This kind of agreement may be included in the figures of agreements collected by the D.E.P., which cannot be taken as indicating the true extent of systematic plant and company bargaining.

A distinction must also be made between a once and for all productivity agreement which involves the buying out of a particular practice and the entering into a plant or company agreement which is the first of a series, thus establishing bargaining at this level as a normal pattern. It cannot, therefore, be assumed that the 7 million workers covered by productivity agreements reported to the D.E.P. are covered as a matter of course by comprehensive and systematically negotiated plant or company agreements. Some element of collective bargaining exists in every organised plant, but the number of workers who are covered by formally negotiated and signed collective agreements would seem to be only a minority. Since most of the 7 million workers were employed in large-scale enterprises, it is clear that the number of medium-sized smaller scale firms which have formerly negotiated plant and company agreements is small. The number is, however, growing. Although the shift to plant and company bargaining has not yet become the normal pattern replacing industry-wide agreements in all sectors it has taken firm root for the reasons we shall now examine.

II

Factors in the Growth of Plant and Company Bargaining

The factors responsible for the growth of plant and company bargaining may be listed under three headings, (a) economic, (b) institutional and (c) the role of the government.

a) *Economic*

In the period 1920-1940 the average unemployment figure was 13·1 per cent.[2]; this high level of unemployment and the lack of competitive demand

---

[2] Calculated from the London and Cambridge Key Economic Statistics.

for labour prevented a strong upward pressure on money wage rates. In fact, for much of the period, the pressure was tending to push wages down; in these circumstances industry-wide agreements not only set the minimum wage rate, they were also effectively setting the ceiling, too. In this situation power in the unions lay with the national officials and the job of the shop stewards was to try to ensure at plant level that the national rates were observed. For the past 25 years the British economy has experienced a period of high demand for labour. Taking unemployment figures as a crude measure of the state of the labour market in the period 1945-1966 the average level was 1·8 per cent.[3] The lowest annual average, 1·26 per cent., was recorded in 1951 and the highest, 2·6 per cent., in 1963.

The maintenance of virtually absolute full employment has fundamentally altered the significance of industry-wide bargaining. It is easier under conditions of economic prosperity and a strong competitive demand for labour to push money wages up by negotiations at the level of the plant or enterprise. The industry-wide agreement has now become both a basic minimum from which workers in highly profitable firms can step up pay to higher levels, and a way of pushing up the entire structure of earnings. This has given rise to the phenomena of earnings drift. The difference between increases in average hourly wage rates and average hourly earnings in the post-war period has been considerable. The Royal Commission on Trade Unions and Employers' Associations estimated that in 1938 ' there was only a modest gap between the rates laid down for a normal working week in industry-wide agreements and the average earnings which men actually received. By 1967 the two sets of figures had moved far apart ' (Donovan, 1968, para 57).

In the post-1945 era full employment greatly increased the bargaining power of the shop stewards. Rising prices and rising expectations created a strong pressure from union members for higher levels of pay than those the unions were securing at the industry level. The shortage of labour undermined the resistance of employers to demands from their own employees and they have been prepared to concede higher levels of pay in order to attract and retain the labour they required.

Along with full employment and wage drift the British economy has experienced relatively slower rates of increases in output per man than in the U.S.A. and the main continental economies. In the period 1957-1966 the average annual increases in output per head in the U.K. was 2·2 per cent. (National Board for Prices and Incomes, 1969). This low labour productivity and a growing awareness of the need to adjust to technological change encouraged employers to seek to raise productivity by capital expenditure and negotiating changes in the utilisation of labour.

It was the need to produce a better rate of return on capital employed that led to the development of productivity bargaining in the highly capital intensive chemical and oil refining industries. Changes in the utilisation of labour and capital had to be worked out at the plant level since industry-

[3] Ibid.

wide agreements were inappropriate for this purpose, although it might have been possible to lay down a framework at this level.

The Redundancy Payments Act, the Selective Employment Tax and the increased charges for social insurance have contributed to making employers much more conscious of labour costs during the past five years. Entry into export markets and growing competition from overseas have also made a growing number of British firms more conscious of the need to improve manpower efficiency. In the face of these problems management had to find ways of coming to terms with the power of militant shop stewards, who were strongly supported by their members and not inhibited by the industry-wide agreements signed by the unions when they called unofficial strikes to push up wages.

b) *Institutional change*

The growth in the independent power of the shop stewards has been due to the readiness of employers to bargain with them and to the failure on the part of the unions to adjust their organisation to the shift in the economic situation which was bringing about the increase in local bargaining. In the absence of any positive union response to the new circumstances during the past twenty-five years, shop stewards have extended their organisation through joint committees at both plant and enterprise level. These developments were at first quite outside of the control of the unions and even at the present time most stewards enjoy a considerable degree of independence from the formal processes of union control. The full-time union officials were at first opposed to the development of bargaining of the Fawley type on the grounds that it would lead to an increase in the power of the shop stewards, and thus make it more difficult to regain control over them. This fear gradually gave way to a recognition of the advantages a union could gain from participating in productivity bargaining.

Experience of the negotiation and operation of productivity agreements has led to the national union officers changing their attitudes. Opposition is now mainly encountered at the level of district committees in the A.E.F. which is mainly inspired by a fear that the privileges and power conferred by craft status may be undermined.

The changes in the attitudes of firms to collective bargaining have been accompanied by changes in the function of personnel management. The traditional role of the personnel manager as largely responsible for recruitment and the administration of wage and welfare policies has changed in many companies to responsibility also for relations with the unions. The industrial relations role has grown in significance with the rise in the importance of plant and company bargaining. In many large companies the Personnel Director is chief negotiator and his status has risen accordingly. A recent salary survey has shown that personnel managers enjoyed a faster rate of salary increase in 1968 than any other managerial specialist[4] (Times Business News, 1969).

The development of a specialised industrial relations function means that the larger companies are no longer dependent upon employers' organisations for expert service in this field. They are capable of carrying out their own negotiations without assistance. In this connection the influence of foreign investment in British industry should be mentioned. United States firms have tended to bring with them the U.S.A. labour practice of plant or company bargaining. In the past many of the companies that have bargained unilaterally have had U.S.A. parentage, for example, the Ford Motor Company, Vauxhall Motors and Woolworths. Recently a number of formerly British firms that have been taken over by American corporations have moved towards plant or company bargaining. A good example of this is Rootes Motors, which was reorganised when Chrysler, an American company, secured a majority share-holding. As a result in 1968 and 1969 a series of company pay and productivity deals were concluded and the firm has since announced its intention of leaving the E.E.F. when its present subscription lapses and conducting its own labour relations.

Foreign investment has helped the trend away from industry-wide bargaining in another way. U.S. companies have tended to compare their British operations with their American ones. It was a comparison by Standard Oil of its performance at Baton Rouge with its Esso plant at Fawley that led to the major innovation in British industrial relations in 1960— namely, the Fawley Productivity Agreements.

The employers' organisation on their part have, with some reluctance, come to recognise that plant and company bargaining are likely to continue to be of major importance. At the outset the employers' associations opposed plant and company bargaining on the grounds of generating excessive wage demands, which the marginal firms might not be able to meet. This meant the low cost firms had to leave their employers' associations or conform with less efficient firms, e.g. Esso over its distribution productivity agreement. However, most employers' associations no longer seek to prevent plant and company negotiations and are adjusting their functions accordingly. The chemical, rubber and electrical contracting associations have taken significant steps to assist member firms in the negotiation of productivity agreements. The chemical employers' association has set up a special advisory committee and made arrangements for special training courses to be provided by Strathclyde University for managers who are involved in the negotiation and administration of plant and company productivity agreements. Perhaps the most significant change is that made by the largest and most influential employers' organisation, the Engineering Employers' Federa-

---

[4] This Survey was undertaken by A.I.C. and was an examination of the trend of median salaries since 1965 of 15 job categories. Personnel managers' median salary had increased by 52 per cent. and was greater than that of any of the other categories, e.g. chief accountant (39 per cent.), cost accountant (43 per cent.) and production controllers (39 per cent.).

tion. The E.E.F. has recently established an employers' advisory service and a research department in response to the needs of member firms. Although agreement has not yet been reached with the unions the E.E.F. has recognised after a long period of hesitation, that the industry's long established procedural agreement should be revised to permit a more flexible and speedy settlement of disputes at the level of the enterprise.

c) *The Role of Government*

The Government's incomes policy has been a major factor in encouraging the growth of plant and company bargaining. Since the policy took the form of laying down a ' norm ' for wage increases but with a number of exceptions allowing the norm to be breached, it provided an opportunity to evade its restrictions. Apart from the Standstill phase of the policy (July-December 1966) one of these exceptions had been . . . ' where the employees concerned, for example, by accepting more exacting work on a major change in working practices, make a direct contribution towards increasing productivity in the particular firm or industry '.[5] This allowed, with the approval of the Ministry of Labour, a wage increase of any magnitude so long as it was associated with a commensurate increase in productivity. The vetting procedure carried out by the Ministry was inevitably influenced by practical expediency. It is a relatively simple matter for a government to regulate national agreements, but it is much more difficult to control increases in pay at the plants since these can be disguised in so many ways. Since pay increases could be made legitimate by a productivity link it is not surprising that unions and employers quickly took advantage of the opportunity created. The results of the productivity policy have been by no means merely inflationary, and it would be wrong to suggest that all productivity agreements have been ' phoney ', but it is widely agreed in industry that the productivity factor has not always been as tightly controlled as it was hoped the policy would achieve.

Nevertheless, the emphasis given by the Government to the need to improve productivity and the work in this connection of the National Economic Development Council and the little Neddies, and the pressure to improve training facilities and manpower utilisation have all had an effect in creating a link between productivity and pay at the level of the plant and company. There has been a considerable increase in output per man achieved during the last two years[6] and this probably owes a good deal to the considerable growth in productivity consciousness on both sides of industry which the policy has engendered.

[5] Prices and Incomes Policy Cmnd. 2639 para. 15; Prices and Incomes Policy Standstill; Period of Severe Restraint Cmnd. 3150 para. 27; Prices and Incomes Policy after 30 June 1967 Cmnd. 3235 para. 22; Productivity, Prices and Incomes Policy 1968 and 1969 Cmnd. 3590 para. 34.

[6] Output per head increased by 4·0 per cent. in 1968 and 2·9 per cent. in 1967 as opposed to an average of 2·2 per cent. 1957-1966 (National Board for Prices and Incomes, 1969).

III

SCOPE AND CONTENT

The groups of workers covered by plant and company agreements

While it is impossible to say how many workers are concerned or what proportion of enterprises in each industrial classification have negotiated agreements it is possible to give some information about the occupational groups covered in two collections of agreements we have been able to analyse.[7]

The first of these two samples is a group of agreements made by firms who are members of the Engineering Employers' Federation. The number of agreements involved is 67 and they were negotiated over the three years 1967, 1968 and 1969.

As Table II shows the group of workers covered by these agreements were mainly manual workers. However, when the miscellaneous and larger group of 92 agreements collected by Incomes Data Services was examined (see Table III) it was found that they covered a rather wider spread of occupations and included a much higher proportion of clerical workers.

Table II

TYPE OF WORKERS INVOLVED IN SAMPLE OF ENGINEERING AGREEMENTS

Type of Worker	1967	1968	1969	Total
Supervisory staffs	0	1	1	2
Clerical workers	0	2	0	2
Draughtsmen	3	2	0	5
Other technical staff	0	0	0	0
Skilled manual workers	6	20	19	45
Semi-skilled manual workers	6	20	20	46
Unskilled manual workers	6	19	18	43

Source: Engineering Employers' Federation.

The contents of agreements

Tables IV and V, classifying the contents of the agreements, show a very high correlation in rank order of subject matter. As might be expected from the emphasis given to productivity bargaining under the influence of incomes policy the major subjects of plant and company negotiation appear to be the reform of wage structures and incentive schemes, changes in

[7] Unfortunately owing to the attitude of employers who are only prepared to make returns if the information they give is kept completely confidential, the D.E.P. is unable to permit non-governmental research workers to examine any agreements which have been collected by the Department. We are extremely grateful to the Engineering Employers' Federation and to the Incomes Data Services for allowing us to carry out an examination of the agreements which they have been able to obtain during the past four years.

(July 1966 - October 1969)

Type of Worker	Number of Workers covered	1966	1967	1968	1969	Total	Industries
Supervisory staffs	5,300	0	0	0	1	1	Transport
Clerical workers	41,230	0	6	6	13	25	Vehicles; Transport; Insurance; Banking and Finance; Paper, Printing and Publishing; Food, Drink and Tobacco; Engineering; Shipbuilding
Draughtsmen	1,860	1	2	2	0	5	Vehicles; Shipbuilding; Engineering
Other technical staff	5,500	0	1	1	0	2	Vehicles; Food, Drink and Tobacco
Skilled manual workers		6	10	11	14	41	Food, Drink and Tobacco; Engineering; Transport; Paper, Printing and Publishing; Metal Man.; Chemicals; Shipbuilding; Vehicles
Semi-skilled manual workers	583,460	6	9	11	18	45	Food, Drink and Tobacco; Shipbuilding; Engineering; Chemicals; Transport; Metal Man.; Vehicles
Unskilled manual workers		7	9	11	18	45	Food, Drink and Tobacco; Shipbuilding; Engineering; Vehicles; Chemicals; Transport; Metal Man.
Sales staff	16,000	0	3	1	2	6	Distributive trades
Catering staff	35	0	0	0	1	1	Vehicles
Transport drivers	2,350	2	3	1	0	6	Chemicals; Food, Drink and Tobacco; Paper, Printing and Publishing
Miscellaneous	10,000	1	3	1	2	7	Chemicals
Total	665,735	23	46	45	69	184	

Note: 1. Total number of agreements studied was 92.

Source: Incomes Data Service Records.

working practices and the more flexible use of labour. Coming next in importance seems to be the development of fixed term agreements, then overtime rather far behind the reform of procedures and fringe benefits of various kinds. The reform of wage structure through the introduction of job grading on the basis of job evaluation had started on a minor scale with the increasing use by industry of consultants. However, the biggest impetus came with the phase of Incomes policy March 1968 to December 1969, when the White Paper for this period allowed exceptions to the norm. It stated, ' Reorganisation of wage and salary structures which can be justified on grounds of economic efficiency and increased productivity may be justified under this criterion '.[8] The amendment of existing incentive schemes also developed strongly in this post-devaluation phase of the policy. The most important changes were the introduction of measured day work and the setting of performance levels through work measurement techniques and replaced existing conventional incentive schemes. These new incentive systems were much tighter and helped to give the employer a much greater degree of control over wage costs and the employee stability of earnings. In 1969 there also appears to have been a sharp increase in the number of agreements having fixed termination dates.

Table IV

CONTENTS OF ENGINEERING AGREEMENTS[1]

Subject	1967	1968	1969	Total	Rank
Overtime	1	4	4	9	5
Labour flexibility	3	11	8	22	2
Manning levels	2	1	1	4	7
Restrictions on output	0	0	0	0	9
Changes in working methods, e.g. shift work, tea breaks	3	9	8	20	3
Wage structure reform	1	6	7	14	4
Amendment to existing Incentive scheme	2	12	14	28	1
Procedures	0	2	3	5	6
Annual salaries	0	0	0	0	9
Holidays	0	0	0	0	9
Fixed term agreements	0	2	7	9	5
Hours of work	0	0	0	0	9
Staged increases	0	2	3	5	6
Sickness benefits	0	0	1	1	8
Employment Security	0	0	1	1	8
Good intentions	2	3	0	5	6

Source: Engineering Employers' Federation Records.
Note: 1. Engineering here refers to the engineering collective bargaining unit and not the S.I.C. Order.

[8] Productivity, Prices & Incomes Policy in 1968 and 1969, Cmnd 3590, paragraph 36, April 1968.

Table V

CONTENTS OF AGREEMENTS

Subject	1966	1967	1968	1969	Total	Rank
Overtime	1	2	1	5	9	7
Labour flexibility	2	9	5	13	29	3
Manning levels	2	2	1	2	7	9
Restrictions on output	0	0	0	0	0	14
Changes in working methods, e.g. shift work and tea breaks	0	5	2	9	16	5
Wage structure reform[1]	2	4	9	15	30	2
Amendment to existing Incentive schemes[2]	4	8	12	10	34	1
Procedures	2	1	1	6	10	6
Annual salaries	0	0	0	3	3	11
Holidays	2	5	3	4	9	7
Fixed term agreements	0	1	2	9	17	4
Hours of work	1	1	0	0	2	12
Staged increases	1	1	0	3	5	10
Lower paid	0	2	0	0	2	12
Past productivity	0	1	0	0	1	13
Profit sharing	0	0	1	0	1	13
Sickness benefits	0	0	1	2	3	11
Employment Security	0	0	1	1[3]	2	12
Pension rights	0	0	1	0	1	13
Redundancy payments	0	0	0	1	1	13
Trade union membership	0	1	0	1	2	12
Good intentions	0	0	5	3	8	8

Source: Incomes Data Service Records.
Notes: 1. Refers to the rationalisation of job grading through job evaluation.
      2. Refers to changes like—the introduction of measured day work;
                          the setting of performance levels through work
                          measurement techniques (Premium Pay Plan).
      3. In this particular agreement (Ford 1969) the security was by off pay in the event of a work stoppage at another plant bringing work to a standstill.

Technological advance has compelled many companies to examine their methods of wage payment. The incentive systems which were adopted wholesale during and immediately after the second world war, as an easy and cheap means of securing higher output at a low cost, in terms of supervision and management, have often degenerated to the point where they have become a costly penalty on investment in modern technology. The inadequacies of out-of-date wage structures and methods of wage payment has been brought to the attention of management by rapid increases in the role of industrial consultants in the bringing about of change since the much publicised Fawley Refinery agreements. As existing patterns of wages were often highly inequitable and limited as well as offering opportunities for high but unstable earnings, workers have been prepared to consider changes. Since cost savings could be large the possibility of securing very substantial increases in pay, once grasped, has stimulated the cooperation of unions with management in negotiating company agreements and revising wage systems.

Changes in wage systems are inevitably linked to changes in working practices. The more efficient utilisation of labour has necessitated the negotiation of agreements to achieve the abandonment of restrictive definitions of jobs, the imposition of rigid boundary lines between the work done by different grades of skill and limitations on the volume of output. Negotiations which involved changes in long-established and apparently highly profitable restrictive practices could not be carried out through the industry-wide bargaining system, they could only be carried out in the enterprise. Bargaining of this kind is hard and if it is to be successfully carried through negotiations must be carefully prepared by both sides and based on detailed cost information about the firm's activities. The process is delicate, time-consuming and results may be less than expected when both sides have to face the harsh necessities of change.

Although both unions and management will often arrive at an agreement exhausted and ready to welcome a period of standstill, they both know that under modern technological and economic conditions they will have to continue the process again. This means that both sides are ready to enter into fixed term agreements. The growth of this type of agreement is becoming, as the figures show, increasingly important. Fixed term agreements have far-reaching implications for the future development of plant and company bargaining.

Fixed term agreements alter the approach to bargaining since they carry within them the concept of exchanging peace and cooperation on specific terms for a definite time period. In the traditional British system of industry-wide agreements the peace obligation in terms of time was never clear. Since the agreement was open-ended[9] the parties were free to bring the agreement to an end at any time they might choose. The *reductio ad absurdum* was reached when, as has happened on numerous occasions, notice was given of a new claim within a week or two of signing an agreement. The excuse for an immediate new claim has been the length of time taken to negotiate the agreement just signed. However, the effect was to give notice of repudiation of the new agreement and to invite workers to take any steps they felt capable of taking to demonstrate their dissatisfaction with it and to achieve improvements on the agreement to which their union had just put its signature. When an agreement covered the whole industry this policy was not only made feasible but likely to succeed.

The negotiation of fixed term agreements at the plant and company levels are likely to be much more specifically related to conditions applying to the workers concerned. Moreover, the workers themselves are more directly and immediately involved through their elected shop stewards. Plant and company agreements negotiated for a fixed term, therefore, carry a more direct obligation to observe their terms for the time period concerned. However, two kinds of problem inevitably arise during the period of a fixed

---

[9] Some industries have had fixed term agreements for some time. For example, the printing industry has had three year agreements since 1950 and one was in fact five years (1950-1955).

term agreement. The first is if there is any major change which alters the basic assumptions on which the agreement has been made; the second is the interpretation of provisions which give rise to dispute.

Many fixed term agreements seek to reduce the problem of changes in background circumstances by including automatic increases in general wage levels at the end of each year covered. Some, until frowned upon by the N.B.P.I., included a cost-of-living escalator clause which inflated or deflated the wage rates in accordance with agreed changes in the consumer price index. An alternative to an automatic adjustment is to provide for the possibility of reopening negotiations by either side on particular items, normally wages, at the end of a specific time period. In some of the agreements studied there were clearly defined methods of dealing with changes in circumstances during the term of the agreement. One company (Storey Bros. & Co. Ltd. in chemicals) which had negotiated a term agreement had conceded wage increases at intervals during the contract but these were only to be paid if the productivity savings calculated to pay for the claim had in fact been achieved. An agreed formula (a Target Index) had been devised to decide this fact.

The settlement of disputed issues of interpretation suggests the need for an effective disputes procedure. There are signs in a number of plant and company agreements that both sides are beginning to see an advantage in an arbitration procedure that can bring a speedy settlement in place of such long drawn out methods of resolving shop floor issues as, for example, in the case of the existing Engineering Industry Procedure.

IV

FUTURE TRENDS

So long as high levels of employment, rapid technological advance and high rates of economic growth continue, the conditions will be favourable for the further development of plant and company bargaining. Should there be a drastic change in economic circumstances and a return to the kind of unemployment levels that prevailed before the second world war, it is probable that the unions would be compelled to retreat behind the defences of national agreements. Since such a dramatic shift in economic circumstances appears to be unlikely, it can be assumed that the basic economic conditions will foster the trend towards plant and company bargaining.

The establishment of the Commission on Industrial Relations and the enactment of the further measures to give effect to the proposals of the Donovan Commission will give additional support to the trend. The encouragement of systematic bargaining through the registration of agreements, the assistance of the C.I.R. and the work of the Industrial Relations Officers of the D.E.P. will have a positive effect in the consolidation of plant and company bargaining.

The Manpower and Productivity Service of the D.E.P., established to help firms with procedure agreements, reported in the *Employment and Productivity Gazette,* December 1969, that between 1.1.69 and 30.11.69 the service had visited 192 firms to give advice on redundancy, grievance and dismissal procedures.

More important, however, than the help and encouragement that is available from the new governmental institutions, will be the developments within industry and the unions themselves. The trend towards large scale and often multi-national corporations will continue. With this trend will come an ever-increasing growth of the capital-labour ratio. In these technological and economic circumstances the role of labour will become increasingly crucial. Of particular importance in this respect will be the position of highly skilled, manual, technical and clerical staffs. All of these occupational groups are likely to be highly organised and will seek compensation for their contribution to the enterprise through collective bargaining. Industry-wide agreements will not meet the special needs of these groups which are bound to be closely related to the particular situation of the firms for whom they work.

Although the incomes policy was a powerful stimulus to plant and company bargaining it is almost certain that, had there been no incomes policy, there would have been a shift from industry-wide to plant and company bargaining for economic and technological reasons. At the present time the Labour Government has all but abandoned incomes policy as a major means of combating inflation. The Conservatives have stated that they will not seek to regulate collective bargaining through a Prices and Incomes Board or by other administrative devices. This means that both parties will be faced with the problem of preventing inflation by budgetary and monetary means—in short by allowing the unemployment figure to rise when necessary. We have already stated that there does not seem to be any objective reason in the immediate future why there should be a massive slump. On the other hand, it is likely both for reasons of economic stability and for structural reasons that the average level of unemployment will be higher during the next decade than it was in the last. It does not follow, however, that if unemployment averages out at around 3 per cent., instead of 2 per cent., this will have an adverse influence on the trend towards plant and company bargaining.

The absence of a Government administered incomes policy may put pressure on the unions and the employers through the T.U.C. and the C.B.I. to arrive at a Swedish type central framework agreement as an alternative to Government imposed cuts in spending, higher taxes and 'dear' money. Within such a framework there will be pressure on firms and unions to conform, but as we have seen in Scandinavia this is not likely to prevent a considerable amount of wage drift. In the event of there being no national incomes policy of any kind the situation will be one in which plant and company bargaining will be free to develop as employers and unions wish.

It is unlikely that the shift in the structure of bargaining will bring about any major change in the pattern of wage differentials. There has been some narrowing of differentials in advanced industrial societies but in all those in which there has been a substantial degree of free collective bargaining, changes have come about very slowly. The development of plant and company bargaining with its emphasis on efficiency and productivity may well lead to a widening of differentials again. Only if collective bargaining were eliminated altogether, as in Communist countries, could the wages of the lower paid workers be quickly brought substantially closer to the higher paid wage and salary earners.

There is, in these circumstances, likely to be considerable public emphasis on the need to protect the interests of the lower paid workers, since those workers who are in weak bargaining positions are not likely to be helped by the development of plant and company bargaining.

There is the question of what will be the role of the industry-wide national agreement in the future. The Donovan Commission saw such agreements as being confined to matters that could be controlled at the national level, for example, the length of the standard working week and the amount of annual paid holiday. The Commission's analysis of two systems of industrial relations and the ineffectiveness of the national agreement is possibly true of the engineering collective bargaining unit and the manufacturing sector of British industry. However, there is a large part of industry where the national agreement has been effective, for example, the nationalised industries, public services and parts of the private area of employment, and there is little at present to suggest that this sector of employment will depart from the national agreement. The public sector employs nearly 6 million workers and contains some of the quickest growing occupations. *The Pattern of the Future* (1964) predicted increases in employment in the electricity supply industry, the national and local government service and the educational services (which increased employment by 44 per cent. between 1953 and 1963). It is also possible that the size of the public sector will be further increased by nationalisation.

The content of the agreement in these industries generally covers the whole range of substantive and procedural matters. The evidence from the recent past does not suggest that the industry-wide national agreement is likely to be discontinued in the public sector. The British Steel Corporation devised a national job evaluated wage structure but in one of the few industries with a tradition of company bargaining met trouble at the former Steel Company of Wales from blastfurnacemen. These workers had previously received a higher rate than similar employees in other steel plants and the Corporation refused to advance them the full amount of a wage increase granted to steel workers in order to achieve a national rate. The Welsh blastfurnacemen reacted by striking. Although the Corporation paid the claim in full after a Court of Inquiry, it is still their aim to have an agreed national rate for all workers of a similar grade.

It is, however, interesting to note that as soon as a union has managed to push out a salient, such as in the case of the higher paid groups of workers at the Rootes Midland factory, it then resorts to arguments in favour of bringing everybody up to this level. Parity can, of course, work both ways. It can stimulate demands to restore differentials. It can also open the way to the return to the situation where there is only an industry-wide collective agreement.

The Prices and Incomes Board was asked in April 1969 to examine the general question of pay and conditions of airport ground staff. Pay structure differed widely between the three authorities owning 35 civil publicly owned aerodromes. The Board condemned the existing separate negotiating arrangements and suggested the establishment of unified negotiating arrangements to cover all airport ground staff and supported by an expert advisory unit on efficiency. If this is accepted, then agreements will become national, covering the whole range of substantive and procedural agreements.

It is more likely, therefore, that the old type of national agreement will continue in the nationalised industries and the public service (e.g. local government and the civil service). In the private sector the national agreement may continue with the negotiation by employers' associations and trade unions of minimum terms and conditions of employment. If these are to be a genuine minimum and not, as previously, a means of increasing general levels of pay those above the minimum will receive nothing. Only in this way could national minimum terms and conditions of employment for each industry be effectively evolved. A development of this kind would at the same time as helping the lowest paid worker encourage the development of plant and company agreements, since these would be the only way in which an increase of earnings above the minimum levels could be achieved apart from overtime.

The development of plant and company bargaining on a systematic basis makes considerable demands on the bargainers. The employers have begun to recognise the need for more expertise and are greatly strengthening their resources. However, the unions seem to be lagging behind in making radical improvements to their organisation. Some unions, e.g. the T. & G.W.U. and U.S.D.A.W., are providing productivity advisory services for their officials and shop stewards. The need to service local negotiators has been recognised by a number of unions who are making efforts to supply their local officials and shop stewards with an appropriate flow of information. Most unions are, however, grossly understaffed to meet the commitments of decentralised systems of sophisticated collective bargaining. To remedy this deficiency would require a considerable increase in expenditure on salaries of staff and officials which could only be financed out of a substantial increase in contributions. Most unions are extremely reluctant to raise their contributions to the levels needed to finance the improvements in their organisation which the situation requires. They fear that there would be a revolt of the rank and file which prefers to have its interests looked after by shop stewards who receive merely an honorarium for the work that they do.

It is this problem that has led the Government to propose the establishment of a system of public subsidies to help the unions modernise their organisations. In introducing their proposal, the Government believes that it is doing no more than extend to the unions the principle of assisting in industrial rationalisation and the raising of efficiency, that is carried out by the Industrial Reorganisation Corporation. Unions are, however, likely to be reluctant to take money from the Government for fear that they might be exposing themselves to certain pressures, as an enterprise does when it accepts I.R.C. support.

The fundamental problem that has still to be solved is the bringing to an end of unofficial strikes and other breaches of agreements. Industry-wide agreements have often broken down because they clearly seemed no longer relevant to both sides. The assertion of militant authority by the shop steward and the unofficial strike were an inevitable feature of a transition from industry-wide to plant and company bargaining in circumstances of institutional rigidity. If plant and company agreements constantly break down, employers with the support of public opinion are bound to press for legal sanctions and the Government will be under pressure to support the case for establishing greater stability. It may be recalled that the Donovan Commission recommended that procedural agreements should be reformed first of all and if this does not lead to a decrease in unofficial and unconstitutional strikes then ' it may be necessary to reconsider the desirability and practicability of giving some legal support to procedure agreements '. (Donovan, 1968, paragraph 476.)

The changes in the pattern of collective bargaining that are taking place are bringing the British system of industrial relations much closer to the American pattern. It is unlikely that this emerging new British system of industrial relations will adopt every aspect of the American system, but it would be surprising if we did not develop a legal framework that is similar in some important respects to theirs.

If the Conservative Party is returned to power at the next election and it carries out its expressed intention in its policy statement on industrial relations (*Fair Deal at Work*, 1968), collective agreements will be made legal contracts, except where the parties decide they do not wish to be legally bound. The present Government has said it intends to include in its proposed Industrial Relations Bill a clause to modify section 4(4) of the Trade Union Act 1871 to facilitate the direct legal enforcement, where the parties wish, of agreements between trade unions and employers' associations, and to provide that agreements should be legally binding if they include an express provision to that effect (*In Place of Strife*, 1969). The present legal position is that an individual employer and a trade union can, if they so decide, make a collective agreement legally binding, but the Act of 1871 makes agreements between trade unions and employers' associations unenforceable. The development of fixed term agreements is a step in the direction the Donovan Commission thought to be essential. Although unions are strongly against any extension of the law and many employers are not too anxious to be restricted by legal regulations, there are some indications that some employers believe it might be an encouragement to better industrial relations procedures if their agreements were under-pinned by a legal framework. At

4

least one company, Henry Wiggin Ltd, has thought it worthwhile to negotiate a fixed term contract which it was the intention of the company to make legally binding.[10] Attempts to develop this concept of contractual bargaining further at another plant have run into considerable opposition from some, but not all, of the unions concerned.

In the last few years public opinion towards the law in industrial relations does appear to have been changing. In the last few years there has been growing evidence from gallup polls of a shift in public opinion towards a greater degree of legal regulation in industrial relations. The shift away from pure power bargaining has happened everywhere but in Britain. What is perhaps most significant is that in none of the former dominions and colonial territories which inherited the British system of industrial relations has it survived. Experience has shown that the naked power struggle between employers and unions can be civilised by an appropriate legal framework and guided into a more constructive role by more efficient collective bargaining institutions. This does not mean of course that *all* strikes can be prevented, or should even be deterred by legal restrictions and institutional intervention.

It is impossible to predict exactly where the British system of industrial relations will settle down in the future, but it is clear that the bargaining structure will contain important elements at plant, company and national levels. To the extent that plant and company bargaining are established as important permanent features the system will be different from what it was like at any previous period in the history of industrial relations in Britain.

London School of Economics
and Political Science

---

[10] This agreement was made in reasonably favourable circumstances since the area in which the company's establishment is relatively lowly unionised and unmilitant.

REFERENCES

DONOVAN (1968). *Report* of the Royal Commission on Trade Unions and Employers' Associations. Cmnd. 3623. London, H.M.S.O.

Fair Deal at Work (1968). Conservative Political Centre, No. 400. London.

In Place of Strife (1969). Cmnd. 3888. London, H.M.S.O.

MINISTRY OF LABOUR (1965). *Written Evidence* to the Royal Commission on Trade Unions and Employers' Associations. London, H.M.S.O.

NATIONAL BOARD FOR PRICES AND INCOMES (1969). *Fourth General Report.* Cmnd. 4130. London, H.M.S.O.

The Pattern of the Future (1964). Manpower Studies No. 1. Ministry of Labour. London, H.M.S.O.

THE TIMES BUSINESS NEWS (1969). *Survey of Executive Salaries and Fringe Benefits in the U.K., 1969.* T.B.N., 28 November, 1969.

PUBLIC SECTOR AND WHITE COLLAR BARGAINING

T. L. JOHNSTON

White-collar workers have come to occupy a strategic place in both the economic and the institutional working of the labour market. '. . . if the trade union movement is to continue to play an effective role in the British industrial relations system, it must reverse the present downward trend of the density of unionisation by expanding its membership among the poorly-organised areas of the labour force, particularly among the rapidly increasing numbers of white-collar employees in private industry' (Bain, p. 99).

The occupational shift from blue to white collar employment has been well documented in recent years, and need not be repeated in detail here. There has been a decline from 81 per cent. in 1911 to 66 per cent. in 1961 in the proportion of the labour force employed in manual occupations in Britain, with a corresponding rise in managerial, administrative, professional and technical occupations, and in particular a fast growth in the clerical group between 1911 and 1951. During these forty years the clerical group more than trebled in numbers and doubled its proportion of the labour force from 4·8 per cent. to 10·7 per cent. From 1951 to 1961 the clerical group did, however, lose place as the fastest growing group to scientists, engineers and technologists, and industrial technicians, groups whose rapid recent growth has been strongly associated with technological innovation.[1]

The Donovan Report (1968) pointed out that white-collar trade union membership is at its highest in national and local government (over 80 per cent.), relatively low in insurance, banking and finance (31 per cent.), and very low in distribution (13 per cent.) and manufacturing industry (12 per cent.). In manufacturing the rapid growth in the absolute number of organised white-collar workers since 1948 has led to only a slight increase in density of unionisation, because of the matching increase in white-collar employment. According to Bain (1967, p. 29), 'In real terms this membership boom is non-existent.' Of course it is not only in the United Kingdom that shifts in the composition of the labour force, away from blue collar to white collar employment, have posed problems for trade unionism seeking to maintain its blue collar hold and increase its penetration rate among white collar workers. In the U.S.A. and Canada the degree or density of unionisation has also fallen, in part because white collar unionism has not been buoyant enough (Kassalow, 1968).

The purpose of this paper is to examine the characteristics and trends in the economic and institutional aspects of white collar unionism in Britain.

[1] The figures given here are taken from Barnes (1967). They are somewhat higher than the figures calculated by Bain, who does, however, state that his calculations are probably on the low side for white collar workers. Op. cit. p. 5.

We begin by looking at the public sector, where unionism has taken a much firmer hold than in the private sector; then we look at the private sector and examine its features; in the final part the implications will be examined for the future developments of white collar unionism. This is an extremely important question, not least in the terms in which Bain chose to present it in his research paper for the Donovan Commission. The vitality of trade unionism may depend in future on an adequate inflow of white-collar blood, if such a metaphor may be permitted.

I

WHITE-COLLAR UNIONISM IN THE PUBLIC SECTOR

The high density of unionism in the public sector undoubtedly gained most of its thrust from the introduction of Whitleyism into the Civil Service in 1919. Although it was introduced rather reluctantly for non-industrial civil servants by the government of the day, under great pressure from the staff associations, it has come to constitute a *de facto* collective bargaining model for determining pay and conditions in the Civil Service. Local authorities and the nationalised industries have followed the Whitley pattern, both organisationally and in the comprehensive national agreements which set standard pay and conditions in their appropriate segments of the public domain. It is true that national pay rates were not achieved overnight, but only after a long struggle, for example in local government, the railways, and the Post Office; but no contemporary assessment of public sector collective bargaining could possibly conclude that there is the cleavage which Donovan sought to demonstrate between a formal, and largely empty, national (or industrial) tier for settling terms and a grass roots or local tier ' where the action is '.

What are the distinctive characteristics of the public sector model which has on the one hand been applied to white-collar groups and, on the other, has generated a highly saturated membership position?

Whitleyism is undoubtedly a clear and orderly system of bipartite decision-making which found ready application in a governmental system with a single employer, readily identified, and a clear and integrated administrative apparatus. The orderly procedure for the conduct of government's business could readily be applied to the relations between the employer and employees in the system. The bureaucratic form of organisation, which Lockwood (1958, pp. 141 et seq.) has identified as important, was almost a definition of the way in which public activity is organised. The large work groups with homogeneous job groupings, and the clear vertical hierarchy of jobs, make for orderliness. In turn, the class structure of the Civil Service produced clear organisational lines for the trade unions (staff associations) which sought to organise the various groups in the hierarchy. Indeed, in this setting trade unions, in Prandy's formulation (1965, p. 73), are less protest bodies than administrative unions, and their function is not so much to challenge the system as to make it work more efficiently by providing for the representation of staff opinions and reactions.

The Whitley model in the public sector has not been without its problems. The first has related to the deceptively simple notion of the ' single employer '. In reality the constitutional source of power for the decisions which the employer has been willing to make has often been fudged, indeed deliberately obscured. The Treasury (1965) has found a nice form of words for handling the problem in the central civil service; but the locus of employer authority has frequently proved irksome to unions such as the National and Local Government Officers' Association (NALGO) in the Health Service Whitley Councils; here the Treasury has been able to exercise its influence behind the scene. As far as the unions are concerned they have never confidently known who is the ultimate source of employer authority, the Management Side. More accurately, they have known very well that it is the Treasury, but they cannot make it an explicit part of the Health Service bargaining system. Local government itself does not seem to have suffered from this inability on the part of the Management Side to identify a ' last offer ' situation which was known by both sides to be so. This depth in the defences of management has not of course always worked to the disadvantage of the unions when they were encouraged to keep searching for the ultimate managerial power. It has on occasion led them to 10 Downing Street, whereas in the private sector the last stop would usually prove to be 8 St. James's Square (the Department of Employment and Productivity).

The other problem in the public sector has concerned the search for a proxy for a productivity basis for bargaining. Where not only the aura of the public purse and public accountability pervade, but also the difficulty of measuring output in many types of public activity, a substitute has had to be found for a productivity base. Since the Priestley Commission (1955), this has become explicit in the comparability principle. In the case of the Civil Service this principle has been applied diligently through detailed pay research which has provided the ammunition for bargaining; in local government pay research has been less detailed, but the general doctrine that public servants follow pay trends in outside employment rather than setting a lead has become well established. Even in those sectors of public employment in which an output or throughput has been identifiable, such as the railways, fair comparison was given authoritative endorsement by a Court of Inquiry (1955, para. 10).

The twin pillars of public sector pay settlement have thus been standard rates and (some kind of) grading for settling the substance of terms and conditions; the Whitley machinery has settled procedural matters through systematic channels for grievance handling.

This type of collective bargaining system is, however, under challenge of change, as a result of the activities of the Prices and Incomes Board and the proposals for reorganising the structure of the Civil Service produced by the Fulton Committee (1968). Fulton has proposed that fair comparison should continue to be the governing principle for civil service pay; this is to be distinguished from the subversive work which the P.I.B. has carried on against the use of fair comparison as a pay argument, if not a principle, throughout the private sector. In the matter of the standard rate Fulton has however suggested a change which could have far-reaching implications.

> In all except the top grade, we think it important that there should be more flexible progression through the pay-scale of the grade. Fixed annual increments, in our view, do not give enough incentive to effort, and make possible too easy a progress for those who do not pull their full weight. We believe that it should be possible to reward merit by extra pay as well as by promotion (op. cit. para. 229).

The fundamental point which has come out of various P.I.B. studies of public sector white-collar pay is that, outside the civil service proper, there has in recent years been considerable salary drift, and what in the American jargon is termed 'grade creep'. Despite the evident adherence to standard pay systems, there has been much greater flexibility in pay and grading than had been generally realised. While accepting that in the gas industry, for example, regrading of staff workers had probably been due in the main to changing levels of skill required of staff, the P.I.B. (1968d, para. 24-27) exposed regradings which had occurred because a rise in salary was necessary to recruit and retain the staff required. In local government it is clear that the practice of 'excess rates' has been meant to permit flexibility and allow local additions to standard pay in order to meet the pressures of the local labour markets.[2]

Fulton also proposed a drastic simplification of the grading system in the civil service, envisaging a cut from 47 general and 1,400 departmental classes to some 20, an approach roughly comparable to the General Classification of the U.S. Federal Civil Service. It explicitly foresaw that this restructuring will 'surely lead to structural changes among the (staff) associations themselves ',[3] since the rigid class structure of the Service which is reflected in the occupational classification of unionism will disappear. Secondly, the new grading structure is to be based explicitly on job evaluation, and the P.I.B. (1968c, para. 136) has pointed out that the introduction of such job evaluation would impose certain limitations on the Civil Service Unions' freedom to bargain in respect of particular grades.

One of the most intriguing features of British Whitleyism and its carry-over into other public sector activity is that this process has not then readily moved further into private white-collar mechanisms and procedures. Balkanisation of institutional arrangements is reflected in the differences between the two sectors in white-collar union activity. Other countries have had similar experiences.

---

[2] Donovan Commission, Evidence (1967) p. 2644. See also PIB (1967c, para. 16) for salary drift among senior local authority officials.
[3] Fulton Committee (1968) para. 273.

In the U.S.A. the passage of the Wagner Act in 1935 helped manual workers in major industries, the C.I.O. sector, but stimulated neither private nor public white-collar unionism or bargaining. White-collar unionism in the private sector has remained modest in scope. In the public sector, however, an Executive Order (No. 10988) of 1962 has encouraged unionism in the Federal civil service, and there has been a spin-off into State and local government organisation (reflected too in the barrage of academic research and publications on the subject among American academics). Yet there is no full-blooded right of collective bargaining under the arrangements which the Executive Order initiated, and explicitly no right to strike. With such a weak model in the central or Federal government sector there is little likelihood of a carryover to white-collar unionism in the private sector. This fits with British experience, though the British public sector model is, of course, much more bipartite in scope.

In Canada the most recent Dominion legislation, The Industrial Relations and Disputes Investigation Act, 1948, included in the term ' employee ' persons doing clerical or technical work, but did not include managerial functions or professionals. There is, said the recent Task Force (1968, p. 26), considerable scope for the growth of trade unionism in general in a number of industries, ' particularly in white-collar occupations, in banking and finance and in much of retailing.' Yet, as in Britain, staff associations in the Canadian Federal civil service have generated enough momentum, particularly since they obtained consultative rights in 1944, to bring about a new Public Service Staff Relations Act of 1967. This provides a dual bargaining structure. Under one type of bargaining Canadian civil servant unions can now adopt a system which includes the right to strike; alternatively, they can opt for a system which incorporates arbitration as the final step in the negotiating process. The question then is whether this development will spill over into white-collar organisation in industry.

Sweden provides a quite explicit causal sequence which shows a distinct interdependence between public and private. Blue-collar workers had had the right to organise and bargain *de facto* for many years when the Right of Association and Negotiation Act was passed in 1936. This was intended to promote organisation among white-collar workers in private industry, and it has succeeded to a point where the white-collar trade union movement in Swedish industry and commerce is extremely well developed and a high degree of organisation among white-collar workers has been attained. It was not the intention of the 1936 legislation that organisation of public servants for collective bargaining should be promoted; the special problems of public servants were meant instead to be settled by provisions of 1937 and 1940 which provided limited rights of consultation to civil servants and local authority employees respectively (Johnston, 1962, Ch. V). Yet one of the most fascinating developments of Swedish industrial relations since then has been the growth of white-collar unionism in the public sector to the point where the government recognised in 1965, after many enquiries and much heart-searching, that public servants should be given essentially the same rights to bargain, including the right to strike, as workers and white-collar employees in the private sector. There are two points to note here. First, legislation promoted private white-collar unionism. Second, as in Canada, Swedish public sector unions showed that they could bring enough pressure to bear to modify a consultative position and install a complete collective bargaining system which includes the right to resort to direct action in support of claims. Indeed, the bargaining power is, in constitutional and legal foundation, if not in practice, a stronger one than that covering the British civil servant, for whom the right to strike is still somewhat obscure.

The important point seems to be that if machinery is set up in the public sector there is not necessarily a spin-off into the private; Britain exemplifies this. The U.S.A. provides too weak a form of staff consultation in the Federal civil service to be certain of its thrust and power of transfer; in Canada it is too early to judge. If, however, machinery is set up by law for the private sector, as in Sweden, it is difficult to stop it penetrating the public sector as well. Of course the Swedish case, in this as in other matters, is unique, but at least it is suggestive for the use of legislation to promote the right to organise and bargain. We return to this point in Section III.

As to the public sector itself the system—unified employer, administrative coherence and clear channels of communication—can evidently accommodate the institutions of collective bargaining without significant signs of indigestion.

Another contrast can be drawn between the Swedish treatment of public servants on the one hand and the civil servant in Canada, the U.S.A. and Britain on the other. In the last three countries there is an explicit use of the principle of pay comparability with outside employment. The British and Canadian systems have used two-stage pay research and bargaining (or consultation in the pre-1967 Canadian Model). The Salary Reform Act of 1962 introduced into Federal pay in the U.S.A. the principle of comparability based on annual nation-wide surveys of white-collar pay in private industry conducted by the Bureau of Labor Statistics. In Sweden no such explicit comparability machinery has been devised, and the parties can deploy their own fact-finding trawls in support of their bargaining postures. However it is achieved, fair comparison in the public sector may well be a device which obviates the need for private white-collar workers to organise. Is there in essence a feed-back effect—public sector pay is based on systematic comparisons with private white-collar pay; and there is nothing to prevent white-collar workers in the private sector in turn from using the public sector as their bench-mark? It will be argued in the next section that in Britain mechanisms are being introduced into the private sector which will promote this kind of transmission, and may weaken the transfer of the *institutions* of public sector bargaining to the private sector.

II

WHITE-COLLAR UNIONISM IN THE PRIVATE SECTOR

While plausible arguments can be advanced in support of the successful introduction of white-collar unionism into the public sector, there is a dearth of systematic explanations of the sluggish growth of private white-collar unionism. Lombardi and Grimes (1967) have suggested that the socioeconomic situation as perceived by the white-collar worker will be an important variable affecting their organisation:

> ' any factor signalling the employee that his position is becoming insecure, that his status within the firm is declining, or that his wage level relative to other groups is diminishing.'

Social and economic factors include the pattern of economic change, structure of relevant industry, and the proximity influence; they resemble closely what Mills (1956, p. 304 et seq.) called ' the objective circumstances of the work situation ' which influence the psychology of the white-collar worker, including his strategic position in the technological or marketing processes of an industry, which condition bargaining power.

In addition to the socioeconomic factors, Lombardi and Grimes identify three other variables, the threshold level of unionisation of the group, leadership, and public policy. Their main thesis, however, in examining these variables, is that advancing technology may mean for some white-collar workers a positive improvement in their position and security through increased personal specialisation; specialists in the medical and legal profession come to mind. For others, specialisation of task may lower skill requirements, increase routine and reduce responsibility and security. It does not follow from this, however, that increased personal specialisation militates against unionisation, or that the depressing of skills will in itself promote unionism. Public policy and the utilisation of a ' ripe ' situation by leaders affect the response. Lombardi and Grimes are pragmatic in their conclusion, that it is necessary to review each group of white-collar workers separately —a case study approach—in evaluating the socioeconomic conditions and their effects on unionisation.

Two of the most buoyant British white-collar unions exemplify the wisdom of a case study approach. The Draughtsmen's and Allied Technicians' Association (DATA) is a white-collar union whose members are office workers employed on ' staff conditions '. It has many of the characteristics of an occupational craft union. Yet it is essentially open-ended, nearly all of its incoming members being drawn from the manual worker ranks and, at the other end, the drawing office providing a traditional stepping stone for promotion. A fair number of DATA members leave the Association when they are promoted out of the drawing office into other jobs. It has two other noteworthy features. First, it has succeeded in having the status quo concept incorporated in its disputes machinery in engineering, something that other unions in the industry are still wrangling over. Second, it is very heavily involved in promoting the technical proficiency of its members (Donovan Commission, Evidence, 1967b). The Association of Scientific Technical and Managerial Staffs (ASTMS) is by contrast neither a craft nor an industrial union, but an inter-industry union which is willing to recruit members from among very senior executives.

A pragmatic approach has the merit of avoiding any assumption of a ' special relationship' between the employer and salaried employee, an assumption which has often led to the dismissal of white-collar organisation as a non-starter. Donovan (1968, para. 221) made this point by viewing the special relationship notion as ' increasingly unrealistic and out of date.'

Despite this, there is evidence of a persisting difference in the treatment by employers of their blue and white-collar workers. The recent survey of earnings conducted by the Department of Employment and Productivity showed that basic pay forms a much higher proportion of pay for white-collar than blue-collar workers, and, conversely, overtime pay is lowest for professional and clerical staff and highest for manual, particularly unskilled workers. (Against that, it should be noted, just to confuse the issue, that the London Clearing Banks have been forced into a very explicit overtime scheme for their staff below managerial status.[4]) Again, non-manual groups are less likely to lose pay than manual workers when they are absent voluntarily, are sick, arrive late or finish early.[5] Evidently, there is still a tendency to regard white-collar workers as ' part of the overhead ', a fixed rather than a variable cost. This is a powerful point in the setting of the various devices, discussed below, by which white-collar workers can latch on to pay increases generated for manual workers in the setting of productivity bargains. At least one British team of managers and trade unionists has shown concern about this status difference :

> The terms and conditions of employment in the American chemical industry do not erect a barrier between the staff and the hourly-paid. The hours of work and the principles upon which fringe benefits are based are usually the same for each group. Such differences are fast disappearing.
>
> *Recommendation:* In the development of collective bargaining, particularly when related to productivity improvements, British managements and trade unions should examine how and how quickly fringe benefits and terms of employment for salaried and hourly-paid workers may be brought into alignment (Chemical EDC, 1967, p. 56).

Do white-collar workers in fact need to organise in industry? Traditionally, white-collar workers have longer pay scales than blue-collar counterparts, and do not reach earnings maxima so quickly; nor are they so exposed to incentive pay systems (payment by results) which result in a

---

[4] PIB (1970).

[5] *Employment and Productivity Gazette,* August 1969, p. 727, Table 43 (for make-up of occupational pay), and September 1969, p. 825, Table 53 (for employees paid for less than their normal basic hours).

decline of earnings for older workers. (Dentists, who are in essence paid by results, are the exception that illustrates the rule.) Again, white-collar workers often exist in a system with *overlapping* pay scales, and can, as in banking, continue, even in the non-managerial jobs, to obtain intermittent pay increases once they have gone beyond the age-related scale. Few have as explicit a grind as the General Accident Life Assurance Company with one of its pay scales concluding at age 46—a structure which the P.I.B. (1967b, para. 29) deplored.

As in the public sector, the P.I.B. has exposed a great deal of salary drift in the private sector. There is a strong implication in I.C.I.'s salary system that it does not need a collective agreement for salaried staff. Indeed it claims that the individual contracts of employment of its staff employees are ' agreements which genuinely raise productivity and increase efficiency ' (PIB, 1969a, para. 22). The system is a two-tier one, covering general and individual aspects, with considerable scope for rewarding individuals within the system; this is in fact an essential feature of it.

The P.I.B. has also done much to promote an awareness of comprehensiveness of pay systems, and the interdependence of blue-collar and white-collar pay, in the reports which it has published on a) efficiency (productivity) bargaining (P.I.B., 1966; 1967a; 1969b), b) payment by results (P.I.B., 1968a), c) job evaluation (P.I.B., 1968c) and d) salary systems (P.I.B., 1969c). Let us look at these in turn.

a) The third report on productivity clearly envisages an extension of productivity bargaining beyond blue-collar jobs and workers to comprehend the total labour force of a company. Techniques of Organisation and Method Study and job analysis can be applied to non-manual work and improvements in productivity can be quantified. Clerical work can be measured, and this is desirable as a way of moving away from remuneration on the basis of comparable employment.[6]

b) Payment by results systems. Fragmented bargaining and consequent pay anomalies were found to characterise many of the conventional PBR systems which the Board examined for the purposes of its study. Examples of various plant-wide incentive schemes of the Rucker or Scanlon type were studied.

c) Job evaluation. In the study which it made for its report on Job Evaluation the Board found that the highest coverage by broad occupational groups in its sample was managerial (30 per cent.), staff (27 per cent.), followed by manual (26 per cent.), and craftsmen (11 per cent.). In a number of its other reports it has also seen job evaluation as a means of moving away from fragmented bargaining and pay anomalies, and as a method which can be used for determining pay levels for dissimilar managerial, professional and technical jobs, and fitting them into a comprehensive wage and salary hierarchy.

[6] PIB (1968b). Chapter 2 examines the measurement of clerical productivity.

d) In its report on salary structures the P.I.B. brought together in a systematic way its earlier analysis of anomalies and its commendation of techniques such as job evaluation and work measurement. Its examination of general salary reviews led it to the conclusion that excessive reliance was placed on comparisons with supposed market rates, instead of settling salaries in relation to contributions to productivity.

On the basis of these studies, it can be argued that the development of systematic managerial techniques for analysing jobs and setting pay will provide an adequate substitute for white-collar unionism. Why organise if management can be seen to be developing systematic systems which are equitable and efficient inside the firm and take account of market developments outside the company? Two points work against such a rash conclusion. First, the process of job evaluation must be distinguished from the process of pay setting or the establishment of pay curves; the latter can be (as in the Civil Service) the subject of bargaining. Secondly, a point the P.I.B. has stressed, job evaluation schemes may be more readily accepted if unions play a part in their establishment. Nevertheless, it is one of the facts of life that many managerial, executive, professional and technical staff do negotiate their remuneration outside the usual process of collective bargaining, and if more systematic techniques for pay setting are introduced this is likely to make the process of unionisation no less easy. In the terminology of Lombardi and Grimes (1967), the threshold level of unionisation of groups may be raised; it is unlikely to be lowered if these techniques are seen, or felt, to be efficient and just.

There is another dimension to salary setting in the private sector, namely its increasing interdependence. It was suggested earlier that the principle of comparability increased interdependence between the public and private sectors. There is a widespread use by companies of salary surveys as a way of obtaining information about market rates. While seeing the case in principle for this, the P.I.B. has criticised the standard of information generated in such surveys and their uncritical use by employers. More profoundly,

> the danger of overmuch reliance on comparing salaries revealed by surveys is that it tends to perpetuate a circular process whereby each group strives to retain a particular position in relation to the rest and so contributes its share to keeping the general level constantly moving up; the consequence is that a further increase soon becomes inevitable if the desired relationship is once more to be restored. We have found a number of examples of firms which try to keep ahead of the field in this way. The dangers are much worse when, as sometimes happens, firms rely not on a real survey at all but on hearsay, advertisements or the evidence of isolated cases which may prove to be exceptional (P.I.B., 1969c, para. 93).

The following sequence of the Carousel theme can then be identified—blue-collar workers obtain increases, perhaps under a productivity agreement, and staff workers feel they should benefit. This happened in the gas industry, and it was the introduction of a systematic manpower utilisation and payment scheme for blue-collar workers in I.C.I. which sparked off the salary adjustments which led to a reference to the P.I.B. (1969a). Increases transmitted within a company on the ground of internal comparability can then be transmitted by external comparability to other companies, and rationalised by the device of the salary survey.

Dr. Routh (1965) has told a fascinating story about the stability of occupational pay structure over the years, even though pay structure is in an almost constant state of change. Apart from the narrowing of differentials in periods of inflation, the Just Wage has carried over from its medieval origins into industrial society. His verdict is that trade unions cannot do much more than institutionalise and direct drives and aspirations that are already present in the individual workers (op. cit. esp. p. 147 et seq.). This of course resurrects the hoary controversy about ' the impact of the union '. The point to be raised here, however, is that if research suggests this conclusion about past changes in the twentieth century, future analysis will have to take account of the devices discussed above which are tending to improve the transmission lines for carrying pay changes across from blue to white-collar groups.

This is of course very speculative, and cries out for a carry forward of the type of analysis which Routh conducted up to the year 1960 to comprehend the years covered by the activities of the P.I.B. Even the crudest measure of comparability between average earnings of manual workers and average salary earnings is, however, suggestive; the respective indices (1955 = 100) rose to 208·1 (manual workers' earnings) and 206·9 (salary earnings) in 1968. The regular series on salaries published by the D.E.P. do not allow analysis by occupation, since the data are arranged by administrative, technical, and clerical and analogous categories; and while the new earnings survey conducted by D.E.P. does tackle the distribution of earnings by occupations for a number of salaried (and other) occupations it is of course only cross-section data for September 1968, and no time series is yet available on this basis. It is to be hoped that future toilers in the field of salaried occupations will have better data to till.

Apart from the salary drift identified in the public sector, private arrangements for settling salaries have shown that it is perfectly possible without the presence of a trade union to develop pay systems for white-collar workers that are collectivised up to a point, but which do give scope for individual supplementation to reward responsibility, experience and special expertise. One of the reasons for the success of the Swedish Union of Clerical and Technical Employees in Industry has been its recognition of this distinction; it has not tried to push the rate for the job down the throats of white-collar employees.

It has been the purpose of the P.I.B. in many of its reports to widen pay-determining horizons from an intra-plant to at least a plant and even a company level; and the Donovan Commission provided the *raison d'être* for company bargaining in its proposals for the reform of collective bargaining in Britain. A similar company-wide vista arises very naturally in the context of manpower planning, where there is increasing awareness of the internal manpower market as well as the mobility of labour in occupational, industrial and geographical terms. The Industrial Training Boards, after their early preoccupation with blue-collar skills, are now also turning their attention to the more heterogeneous ranges of salaried jobs and manpower. Job security, one of unionism's traditional concerns, is a secondary issue if manpower policy is not only active but comprehensive. All this promotes an awareness of, and interest in, interdependence in manpower utilisation.

The conclusion of this section is that there is a large array of pressures at work in private industry, few of which seem to point in the direction of greater insulation of white-collar workers from the fruits of collective bargaining in the traditional sectors. It does not follow at all that white-collar workers need to organise in order to stay in the economic networks of the labour market. Institutional changes other than unionisation are seeing to that in addition to the forces of the market itself.

It is not without significance that the Prices and Incomes Board has dealt explicitly with 33 white-collar pay cases in the 74 reports on incomes it has issued to date (February 1970), and several other reports, such as those on productivity bargaining, are now comprehending white-collar segments of the labour force. Even when the P.I.B. does not endorse a salary determination in a case referred to it, and adopts a disapproving stance, white-collar workers may not be moved to organise; in such a situation they may see the employer as a willing accomplice to pay improvements who is being frustrated by a public agency. Where then is the presure to be found which may generate a greater density of white-collar unionism in private industry?

IV

PROMOTING WHITE-COLLAR UNIONISM

An endogenous view of white-collar union growth suggests that the threshold level of unionisation may be rather high, given the tentative conclusions of the previous section. There may not be enough internal surge from within the white-collar ranks to spawn sturdy growth. But the approach to white-collar union growth in Britain in recent discussion is really quite different. It is not too much of an exaggeration to see in Bain's analysis and conclusions, quoted at the beginning of this paper, the case for exogenous pressure in order to make white-collar unions grow. If the survival of British trade unionism is held to depend on organising white-collar workers in private industry the question is what pressure to bring to bear on it from outside.

The Donovan Commission (1968, para. 737) was firmly of the view that collective bargaining is the best method of conducting industrial relations, not only for manual but also for white-collar employment. After reviewing the degree of white-collar unionism the Commission summarised the position as follows:

> Consequently, there is now a dilemma for public policy. Collective bargaining is recognised as the best way of conducting industrial relations and as depending on strong trade union organisation. The proportion of employees who are organised has however been declining. Employment is increasing in areas which have proved difficult to organise, so that the effect of obstacles to the development and recognition of unions in these areas is assuming greater importance for the future of collective bargaining. The evidence is that if these obstacles are to be surmounted more effective means of dealing with problems of trade union recognition are needed. (*Op. cit.* para. 224.)

How in particular is organisation among white-collar workers to be advanced? One approach, that of relying on the tolerance, if not the active encouragement, of employers is clearly ruled out of court. Despite its embarrassment at the bitterness which its predecessor's (in)famous circular of June 1964 had aroused among unions, the Confederation of British Industry (C.B.I.) was anything but positive at the time it submitted evidence to Donovan. 'At the moment our policy is waiting and seeing.' (Donovan Commission, Evidence, 1967a, p. 822.) The initiative must then come from outside.

Various forms of outside pressure to force employers to recognise white-collar unions can be distinguished. As is well known, Donovan's own preference was for a legal/administrative solution rather than a direct legal enactment along (say) the Swedish lines declaring the right in law to organise and bargain. Unilateral arbitration was envisaged for a situation where an employer refused to grant recognition to a union after a recommendation had been made by the proposed Industrial Relations Commission that recognition should be granted. (Donovan Report, 1968, para. 273.)

A Commission on Industrial Relations has been established, and its first efforts in this field have now become known. Indeed the Commission's first three reports (C.I.R.,1969a, b, c) dealt with the matter of trade union recognition for (a) supervisory and technical staff, (b) employees of a large insurance company, and (c) fish handlers and lorry drivers. Apart from the question of multi-unionism and the need for the unions to determine spheres of influence (in the case of The Associated Octel Company Ltd.), something which the unions seem willing to resolve, the main thread running through the recognition issues has been the whole matter of representativeness. Which comes first—recognition in order to assist unions to organise; or evidence of adequate representativeness by the unions in order to convince employers that they should grant recognition? The difficulty is well focused in the reference involving the General Accident Fire and Life Assurance Corporation Ltd.

The C.I.R. discovered that the Corporation was not opposed to trade union membership, and was willing to recognise the union (The Union of Insurance

Staffs) provided it was satisfied as to its representative capacity. It obviously was not, and the C.I.R. had a similar difficulty as to degree of representativeness. What is proposed is a two-stage solution. As a first stage there would *not* be joint regulation of pay and conditions, but the company would accord consultative rights to the Union of Insurance Staffs on matters of joint concern, including pay and conditions, with the right to initiate representations to management, and establish a grievance procedure. Whether or not these limited consultative rights would be extended to embrace full recognition, stage two, was however, in the view of the C.I.R.,

> best left for determination in the light of developments which would provide empirical answers to the questions about the Union's actual and potential representative capacity. Varying opinions have been expressed about the attitudes and wishes of the members of the staff who are at present unorganised but there is not yet sufficient information on the subject. We considered the possibility of holding a ballot or attitudes survey to remedy this deficiency. However, we came to the conclusion that the lack of information could best be met by assessing the position when the staff are fully aware of the possibilities open to them. (C.I.R., 1969b, para. 50.)

There has always been reluctance in Britain, e.g. in the Civil Service, to specify representativeness in numerical terms, and it is evidently the intention of the C.I.R. to continue this tradition of a qualitative rather than a precise quantitative approach to what is meant by ' a substantial proportion '.

The main comment on, if not criticism of, this approach must surely be that it is Fabian-like, and may be a slow process. It is of course consistent with the Donovan Commission's gradual approach to the reform of collective bargaining in general. Put another way, the Donovan Commission received a considerable amount of testimony, not least from unions, which favoured legal recognition arrangements; but its dilemma was that it had turned its face against a legal basis for collective agreements. If it had then provided for the legal enactment of the right to organise and bargain the difficulty might have arisen that employers would seek to insist that bargaining which was forced on them by law ought to culminate in agreements which were enforceable by law.

The Conservative Party's approach is to envisage a legal duty on employers to recognise, and negotiate with, registered trade unions subject to the conditions that the employer may call for a secret ballot among his employees and be compelled to recognise the union or unions ' only where the results show that a majority of his employees—or of those in a particular craft or grade—desire union negotiation on their behalf '. (*Fair Deal at Work*, 1968.)

Thus the machinery for promoting recognition by putting a squeeze on employers has to all intents and purposes become a political issue. But a final interesting, and operational, question in the controversy about a legal versus a gradual administrative approach to union recognition relates to the urgent question of union growth. Can the trade union movement, on Bain's thesis, afford to carry on the long and intensive grind associated with the gradual acquisition of bargaining rights for salaried employees? True, a case-by-case approach allows the unions to resolve jurisdictional and organisational questions in a pragmatic way, and this is the pattern which has been set and practised in the matter of inter-union relations in the past. There is no denying that these inter-union struggles for new members may be fierce when blue-collar supplies are drying up, and outside intervention via Courts of Inquiry (as in the steel dispute of 1968) provide a supplementary form of pragmatic pressure for the ' rational ' settlement of bargaining units and representation. By contrast, the legislative approach would initiate an almighty scramble and near chaos in organisational terms; but it might more expeditiously promote the surge of union membership among white-collar workers to which the unions now aspire.

In Sweden, the development of white-collar unionism after 1936 was promoted through the establishment of a new central white-collar organisation—T.C.O. (The Central Organisation of Salaried Employees). There is no doubt that this has enabled Swedish white-collar workers to organise without feeling that they were at the same time deserting the bourgeois ranks and joining the class-conscious blue-collar union movement. T.C.O. has made a virtue out of its avowed political neutrality. So far there has been no overt suggestion in Britain that a separate central organisation should be established to promote white-collar unionism outside the T.U.C. But the T.U.C. has not yet found satisfactory machinery for catering for the special economic and ' status ' aspects of white-collar organisation. The annual conference for non-manual workers, which embraced 57 unions and close on 2 million members in 1968, has all the appearance of a one-day talking shop, no doubt useful as a sounding board, but by no means a coherent focus for distinctively white-collar problems. (T.U.C., 1969.) This may be a wise strategy on the part of the T.U.C., not least in the light of Swedish experience; but it means that the T.U.C. may be seeking to promote white-collar membership by stealth rather than by a policy which is positive and vigorous in its search for this promising new life blood. A stealthy approach is likely to be a slow one. The question is whether the present trade union movement can afford it. The opportunity cost may be on the high side. Moreover, the T.U.C.'s domain does not extend to some of the strongest professional groups, such as the British Medical Association, which have been willing and able to go their own way and develop their own particular bargaining strategy by doing and learning. Such groups appear to need the solidarity and support of T.U.C.-model trade unionism less than it may eventually need them.

IV

SUMMARY

It is easier to discern future developments of white-collar activity in the public sector than in the private. Because it is already heavily unionised, the main problems in the Civil Service may prove to be stress on the existing hierarchy of staff associations once the class system is replaced by a comprehensive grading scheme. Something akin to industrial unionism may emerge. The other problem in the public sector will be the introduction of flexible pay incentives which can be controlled and do not perpetuate the difficulties that have arisen through salary drift and grade creep in many public sector activities.

In the private sector the main issue is how to promote white-collar unionism in an environment in which management is, in many instances and at best, neutral to salaried employee unionism and where pay and job analysis techniques are being developed, privately and under the aegis of the P.I.B., which provide a proxy for collective bargaining solutions.

Organisationally, we have opted in Britain for a gradual administrative approach to promoting white-collar union recognition. The main problem then will be to develop orderly arrangements for bargaining representation between exclusively white-collar unions and those blue-collar unions that have white-collar sections. It is questionable whether this gradual approach will promote unionism faster than a legal codification of the right to organise.

Heriot-Watt University,
Edinburgh.

REFERENCES

BAIN, G. S. (1967). Trade Union Growth and Recognition, Research Paper No. 6, Royal Commission on Trade Unions and Employers' Associations 1965-68. HMSO, 1967.

BARNES, SIR DENIS (1967). Technological Change and the Occupational Structure, *in International Conference on Automation, Full Employment and a Balanced Economy,* Foundation of Automation and Employment Ltd., London, 1967.

CHEMICAL EDC (1967). *Manpower in the Chemical Industry,* London, HMSO.

CIR (1969a). The Associated Octel Company Ltd., Commission on Industrial Relations, Report No. 1, Cmnd. 4246, London, HMSO.

CIR (1969b). General Accident, Fire and Life Assurance Corpn. Ltd., Commission on Industrial Relations, Report No. 2, Cmnd. 4247, London, HMSO.

CIR (1969c). W. Stevenson & Sons, Suttons Cornwall Ltd., Commission on Industrial Relations, Report No. 3, Cmnd. 4248, London, HMSO.

COURT OF INQUIRY (1955). Interim Report of a Court of Inquiry into a Dispute between the British Transport Commission and the National Union of Railwaymen. Cmnd. 9352, London, HMSO.

DONOVAN COMMISSION, EVIDENCE (1967a). Royal Commission on Trade Unions and Employers' Associations, Minutes of Evidence No. 22, witness The Confederation of British Industry, London, HMSO.

DONOVAN COMMISSION, EVIDENCE (1967b). Royal Commission on Trade Unions and Employers' Associations, Minutes of Evidence No. 36, witness The Draughtsmen's and Allied Technicians' Association, London, HMSO.

DONOVAN COMMISSION, EVIDENCE (1967c). Royal Commission on Trade Unions and Employers' Associations, Minutes of Evidence No. 60, witnesses The Associations of Local Authorities in England and Wales, the Greater London Council and the Local Authorities' Conditions of Service Advisory Board, London, HMSO.

DONOVAN REPORT (1968). *Report* of the Royal Commission on Trade Unions and Employers' Associations, Cmnd. 3623, London, HMSO.

Fair Deal at Work (1968). Conservative Political Centre No. 400, London.

FULTON COMMITTEE (1968). *The Civil Service, Report* of the Committee 1966-68, Cmnd. 3638, London, HMSO.

JOHNSTON, T. L. (1962). *Collective Bargaining in Sweden*, London.

KASSALOW, EVERETT M. (1968). Canadian and U.S. White-Collar Union Increases, *Monthly Labor Review*, U.S. Dept. of Labor, July 1968, pp. 41 *et seq.*

LOMBARDI, V. and GRIMES, A. J. (1967). A Primer for a Theory of White-Collar Unionization. *Monthly Labor Review*, U.S. Dept. of Labor, May 1967, pp. 46-9.

LOCKWOOD, DAVID (1958). *The Blackcoated Worker*, London.

MILLS, C. WRIGHT (1956). *White Collar*, Galaxy Edition, New York.

PIB (1966). *Productivity and Pay during the Period of Severe Restraint*, National Board for Prices and Incomes, Report No. 23, Cmnd. 3167, London, HMSO.

PIB (1967a). *Productivity Agreements*, National Board for Prices and Incomes, Report No. 36, Cmnd. 3311, London, HMSO.

PIB (1967b). *Salaries of Staff Employed by the General Accident, Fire and Life Assurance Corporation Limited*, National Board for Prices and Incomes, Report No. 41, Cmnd. 3398, London, H.M.S.O.

PIB (1967c). *Pay of Chief and Senior Officers in London Government Service and in the Greater London Council*, National Board for Prices and Incomes, Report No. 45, Cmnd. 3473, London, HMSO.

PIB (1968a). *Payment by Results Systems*, National Board for Prices and Incomes, Report No. 65, Cmnd. 3627, London, HMSO.

PIB (1968b). *Agreements relating to Terms and Conditions of Employment of Staff Employed by the Prudential Assurance Co. Ltd., and the Pearl Assurance Co. Ltd.*, National Board for Prices and Incomes, Report No. 74, Cmnd. 3674, London, HMSO.

PIB (1968c). *Job Evaluation*, National Board for Prices and Incomes, Report No. 83, Cmnd. 3772, London, HMSO.

PIB (1968d). *Pay of Staff Workers in the Gas Industry*, National Board for Prices and Incomes, Report No. 86, Cmnd. 3795, London, HMSO.

PIB (1969a). *Pay of Salaried Staff in Imperial Chemical Industries Ltd.*, National Board for Prices and Incomes, Report No. 109, Cmnd. 3981, London, HMSO.

PIB (1969b). *Productivity Agreements*, National Board for Prices and Incomes, Report No. 123, Cmnd. 4136, London, HMSO.

PIB (1969c). *Salary Structures*, National Board for Prices and Incomes, Report No. 132, Cmnd. 4178, London, HMSO.

PIB (1970). *Hours and Overtime in the London Clearing Banks*, National Board for Prices and Incomes, Report No. 143, Cmnd. 4301, London, HMSO.

PRANDY, KEN (1965). Professional Organization in Great Britain, *Industrial Relations*, Vol. 5, University of California.

PRIESTLEY COMMISSION (1955). *Report* of the Royal Commission on the Civil Service 1953-55, Cmnd. 9613, London, HMSO.

ROUTH, GUY (1965). *Occupation and Pay in Great Britain 1906-60*. Cambridge.

TASK FORCE (1968). *Canadian Industrial Relations*, The Report of the Task Force on Labour Relations, Ottawa.

TREASURY (1965). *Staff Relations in the Civil Service*, London, HMSO.

TUC (1969). *Non-Manual Workers*, 32nd Conference Report, Trades Union Congress.

DISPUTES PROCEDURES

A. W. J. THOMSON

It was for a long time an article of faith of the British industrial relations system that there was a 'tendency in the British system for the parties to rely for their relationship upon mere frameworks of substantive rules and to improvise their detailed joint regulation upon procedural handling of grievances'.[1] This procedural basis was desirable because it provided a degree of voluntarism and flexibility which a more tightly structured system could not achieve; the values supporting it were those of economic freedom and industrial peace. The role of the state was limited to providing ancillary procedural systems when the voluntary ones broke down, but these involved no compulsion. Indeed, in its heyday of intellectual respectability in the early 1950's, Kahn-Freund claimed that the system's emphasis on procedural rather than substantive norms, which he designated as 'dynamic' as opposed to 'static' bargaining, was associated with 'the most highly developed forms of labour-management relations' and even verged on the mystical when arguing the irrelevance of law after the development of a 'higher community'.[2] Of course, neither Kahn-Freund nor anyone else could claim universal satisfaction with the British system, but his tone did reflect a general acceptance of its basic principles.

Since then discontent with the system has grown rapidly, and inevitably, in view of their importance, procedures have come under heavy criticism. It has thus become something of a ritual to lay most of the blame for difficult situations on poor procedures, as can be seen from the courts of inquiry of recent years. A milestone in their fall from respectability was marked by the TUC's attack on procedural inadequacy in its investigation into disputes and workshop representation in 1960 (T.U.C., 1960, pp. 126-7). But the main investigation was left until the appointment of the Royal Commission in 1965. The two research papers by Arthur Marsh, the second of them with McCarthy's assistance,[3] provided the first real analysis of the application of disputes procedures, of procedures in general, and of five major industry-wide procedures in particular. Their examination, using the criteria of acceptability, appropriateness and the public interest, destroyed the myth of the current industry-wide procedures as ideal problem-solving mechanism and discovered that they caused many problems on their own account. The ensuing Donovan Report charge that there had been a

---

[1] Marsh (1966, p. 17). Indeed, Marsh noted that procedures are little used in the interpretation of substantive agreements; rather they deal with grievances raised about matters outside the agreement (p. 16).

[2] Kahn-Freund (1954). It is interesting to note that recent analysis of the period at which Kahn-Freund was writing rejects his contentions. Indeed Fox and Flanders (1969, p. 170) have argued that: 'The post-war period thus inherited a situation which was more or less guaranteed to produce disorder on a major scale'.

[3] Marsh (1966) and Marsh and McCarthy (1968).

failure to develop adequate institutions in changing circumstances was in large part directed at procedural defects, to whose redress the Report gave a high priority. Indeed, the Report went a long way towards sympathising with those who felt themselves obliged to take unconstitutional action in the absence of effective procedures and argued that they 'should not be threatened with any disadvantages imposed by law until new procedures have been put into operation, procedures which are clear where the present procedures are vague, comprehensive where the present procedures are fragmentary, speedy where the present procedures are protracted, and effective where the present procedures are fruitless' (Donovan, 1968, p. 136). Donovan strongly advocated comprehensive company or factory agreements with concomitant domestic procedures. While not specifically ruling out industry-wide agreements or procedures, the Report suggested their limitation to matters which could effectively be regulated. But the primary point was that for most matters effective regulation was possible only at the level of the firm; hence the need for a much more formal local institutional structure.

The wheel, in fact, has turned full circle; there have inevitably been arguments that it has turned too far, that the present chorus of dissatisfaction with procedures is as unrealistic as the earlier supposition that procedural forms could adequately compensate for the absence of substantive norms in a full employment economy. It is true that the strictures of the Donovan Report were not immediately relevant to all industries; in those where fragmentation of bargaining from the national to the local level has not developed as far as in the engineering and building industries, the present procedures still perform satisfactorily by Marsh's criteria. Those public service industries with long established bargaining mechanisms, most of the nationalised sector, including the coal industry, and many private industries such as textiles, rubber and chemicals have either found their existing procedural forms satisfactory or have found it possible to develop new ones in tune with changing circumstances. Furthermore, although little is known about the subject, there are undoubtedly many examples of more or less informal procedures which have grown up at company, plant and even shop floor levels parallel with the development of informal substantive bargaining and which in practice work extremely well.[4] Indeed, the most informal of arrangements may deserve the title of procedure if it is understood and complied with; the British industrial relations system would have collapsed long ago if it had had to depend only on formal industry-wide dispute procedures.

[4] The Government Social Survey (1968) did give some numerical indications of the extent of and satisfaction with the grievance procedure at the place of work. 67 per cent. of stewards had no complaints, while 96 per cent. of managers and 93 per cent. of foremen thought such procedures worked well on the whole. When stewards were asked whether there was a written domestic procedure or whether they relied on a national procedure, 51 per cent. did not have a written domestic procedure, while 38 per cent. did and the rest gave other answers or did not know. There was also evidence of increasing use of procedures within the plant.

Yet for several reasons the main burden of the Donovan case stands, that procedural forms and norms have not been able to accommodate the shift in emphasis from the formal system of industry-wide bargaining to the informal system of plant bargaining. A greater or lesser degree of informal local bargaining, which is the starting point for a re-examination of procedures, already exists well beyond the boundaries of the engineering and construction industries by which the Royal Commission was held to be unduly influenced.[5] If procedural ineffectiveness is greatest where the shift has been most marked, it seems only a matter of time until the advice has a wider application. This is particularly true for those industries where full collective bargaining is only now becoming a reality; in cases such as the Durham teachers dispute of mid-1969 the lack of relevance of the formal procedures may be decisive in causing or not resolving a dispute.[6] Again, Marsh and McCarthy pointed out that the parties do not necessarily know the procedures which are best for them and that procedures adequate at their inception may well not remain so (Marsh and McCarthy, 1968, p. 88). Moreover, procedural changes must be seen as complementary to other desirable changes in the industrial relations system: a particular case in point is the extension of collective bargaining.

To be more specific, an analysis of the defects of current procedures might include the following points:

1. Procedures are frequently slow or indecisive or both. The engineering industry is perhaps best known for these faults; it was severely castigated by the Royal Commission and its research papers for its long delays and poor record of eventual solution. But if engineering is the worst, other national procedures have similar faults, and the same is also true if less so of domestic procedures. In one strike jointly investigated by the CBI and the TUC, the convener had to go through five stages in order to reach the personnel officer, and on some occasions the whole procedure took six or seven weeks. Such situations, at whatever level, are clearly frustrating and put a premium on less formal means of settlement, either by short-circuiting the procedure to go straight to the final decision-maker (a frequent complaint of supervisors), or by increasing pressure through industrial action.

2. Present procedures, not having been brought up to date, frequently reflect a situation now long past. One aspect of this is that the subjects which can be raised are often very narrow in scope, covering wages and little else. The TUC's *Programme for Action* particularly noted that under some procedures dismissals and redundancy could not be raised. Another aspect is

---

[5] See Donovan (1968), Appendix 5, for the best available analysis of the extent of informal bargaining. Both the CBI and the TUC accused the Commission of this undue concentration on particular sectors, the TUC in its pamphlet *Action on Donovan* (1968a) and the CBI in a Press statement on November 5, 1968. They also made the same criticism, if less explicitly, in a joint statement.

[6] Department of Employment and Productivity (1969). The individual contracts of service supplied the only procedure by which the dispute could be handled. This was strongly criticised by the Committee as quite inappropriate for dealing with a 'militant' trade union.

that some procedures do not mention key actors such as shop stewards, even though informally they are very prominent. Similarly, the procedure may have no provisions for giving facilities to stewards, or may give them the right only to negotiate with the lower levels of supervision. Thus, as McCarthy argues, ' the more restricted the *de jure* rights are, and the more the steward is in consequence forced to insist on *de facto* privileges, the greater the chance that he and his members will come to have little respect and regard for such a procedure, together with its peace clauses ' (McCarthy, 1966, p. 64).

3. Some procedures have, in the eyes of one party, a built-in bias towards the other. Employer conciliation, in which the employers' association plays the dual and potentially incompatible roles of defending employer interests and mediating between a particular employer and his employees, is much resented by the unions. This is especially the case in engineering, where the unions remember that it was imposed on them after the lockout of 1897-98. Another area of discontent is that of managerial prerogatives, whereby the status quo operates to management's advantage. In engineering this is known as the management functions clause, reading ' work shall proceed under conditions following the act of management '. In instances such as those following dismissals, this is clearly unsatisfactory, although in most instances modifications are made. It is also unsatisfactory to the extent that management might use the delay to its own advantage. Points such as these tend to bias the peace obligation, which is for both sides the major consequence of the procedural rules.

4. Even allowing for a desire to avoid undue delay, procedures are not used consistently by either side. As Munns observed of employer associations, which might seem to have a vested interest in maintaining procedural regularity: ' The use of informal methods is not regarded by association officials as an indication that the procedure requires revision, since the procedure is simply a means of reaching agreement and not the only way ' (Munns, 1967, p. 9). This is even more true of domestic procedures insofar as they exist. As Marsh noted: ' But investigation shows that, even where procedures are written, they seldom operate strictly " according to the book ", partly because the issues to be dealt with are too varying and complex to make this easily practicable, and partly because most managements are too little concerned about the letter of procedures to administer them consistently or invariably ' (Marsh, 1966, p. 24). It is therefore perhaps less easy for officials or other employers to claim that the procedure must be followed rigorously when it suits their book. Employee irregularities are of course epitomised in unconstitutional strikes, but there are many other less absolute ways of circumventing all or part of the procedures. It must therefore be questioned whether Kahn-Freund's characterisation of British collective bargaining as ' a very firm procedural framework for a very flexible corpus of substantive rules ' is any longer valid, if indeed it ever was (Kahn-Freund, 1959, p. 263).

5. Inconsistent observance of procedures is explicable in that they are

seen not only as a mechanism for problem-solving, but also as an integral part of the bargaining process. There is no doubt that a lot of hypocrisy, posturing and tactical manoeuvering is involved in invoking procedures, with short-term gain rather than long-term stability the prime consideration. Sometimes claiming procedural merit amounts to a considerable twisting of logic. McCarthy noted that some shop stewards justified unconstitutional stoppages by arguing that management had itself broken the agreement by ' refusing to negotiate '. What this sometimes meant was that management had refused to make what the stewards considered to be a ' reasonable ' offer (McCarthy, 1966, p. 25). Employers, for their part, are usually happy to avoid making decisions for themselves by pushing complaints to higher stages of the procedure in the hope that the problem will go away, whilst at the same time depending on the peace obligation to prevent trouble. Unfortunately, the structure of procedures encourages these attitudes.

6. Perhaps the most telling criticism concerns the unitary nature of British procedures, at least in their formal aspects. Even where there is some restriction in scope, the present structure assumes that procedures are capable of solving a wide range of issues which come before them. Very little if any attempt is made to distinguish between problems according to their susceptibility to resolution by different kinds of treatment. While the system as it stands does give the parties full control of their own affairs, it is arguable that it does so at the loss of some desirable specialisation of function. The question is whether a single forum can decide equally well issues as disparate as the extent of recognition, substantive negotiations over the major conditions of employment, and petty differences which might arise at the most local level. Taking an analogy from political science, the procedure must perform the constitutional function of setting the parameters to the relationship, the legislative function of settling the rules under which the parties will live, and the judicial function of interpreting those rules. It is hardly surprising that there must often be a Procrustean cutting or stretching of the dispute to make it fit the forum.

The Shape of the Future

The main trends for procedures in the 1970's might be termed decentralisation and differentiation. Decentralisation was of course Donovan's main theme; differentiation is a natural outcome of its recommendations, although its extent and implications have been less generally recognised. On the other hand, neither trend can be regarded as a fait accompli. The future of procedures is intimately tied to that of the bargaining structure; indeed the two complement and interact upon each other. Here lies much of the difficulty of initiating change, particularly with respect to the decentralisation of formal decision-making. One of the main functions of procedural rules is, to ' define the bargaining unit and the structure of relationships between the bargaining parties ' (Flanders, 1968, p. 572). Thus change in the procedural rules would seem to precede changes in bargaining structure. But major changes in procedural rules would destroy the continuity with the past which is the main means of effectuating and legitimising the relationship between the parties. Marsh and McCarthy emphasised the premium placed on formal procedural stability even when joint regulation seemed to the outsider to have collapsed, and suggested that to challenge the procedural rules, being analogous to challenging a political constitution, is 'to invite accusation of subversive or revolutionary behaviour' (Marsh and McCarthy, 1968, p. 90). Thus the extent of the dependence on procedural rules is a major bulwark against change both in procedures themselves and in the bargaining structure. In recognition of this, the Commission for Industrial Relations has been set up to create an impetus towards change; whether it, and the other forces tending in this direction, will be sufficient to achieve implementation of the Donovan recommendations is a question we shall return to. Creating the dynamics of change within a still voluntarist system promises to be the major problem of the 1970's; at the very least the process will be piecemeal and unsystematic.

The process of procedural differentiation assumes implementation of the basic Donovan recommendations. While the extent to which this is achieved may render some of the following arguments rather hypothetical, it is nevertheless worth examining their implications. Differentiation means simply the evolution of procedural forms which are better suited to solving particular types of problem than the unitary procedural mechanism which exists now. Foreign observers have suggested that this development is a vital *sine qua non* if the degree of control over the labour-management relationship is to be increased (Garbarino, 1969). This increased specialisation does not only apply to the narrow private labour-management relationship; it includes public and inter-union procedures as other potential fields of development. Indeed, the best example has already been set by the TUC which in *Programme for Action* set out to identify different categories of disputes and thereafter different means of solving them by its division of inter-union disputes into those concerning recognition, membership, demarcation, and wages and conditions (T.U.C., 1969, pp. 15-18).

The major area of concern, however, is that of issues now dealt with by the industry-wide procedure. Here, it can be argued, Donovan has two fundamental implications. The first is the creation of certain public rights by means of legislation. The rights concerned, notably those of membership of a trade union, recognition and appeal against dismissal, would merely bring Britain into line with standard practice in many other countries, to say nothing of ILO conventions. Nevertheless, the creation of public rights will necessitate public procedures to effectuate them, and will take some considerable part of the burden of dealing with these issues away from private procedures.

The second and even more important implication of Donovan concerns the nature of the agreement, its change from being a nebulous, industry-wide document, legally 'void through uncertainty', to a 'formal, comprehensive and authoritative company or factory agreement '.[7] The current argument is whether or not such an agreement should be legally enforceable. While this has some importance, it is not as significant as what derives from the nature of the agreement itself. British agreements are intended to become increasingly codified, contractual, and based on substantive rather than procedural norms. Therefore issues, both substantive and concerning rights and obligations, which were previously dealt with informally or through the procedure, will in future be spelled out in the agreement; the more the present voids caused by 'custom and practice' and 'gentlemen's agreements' are filled in, the more important interpretation of the language of the agreement will become and the less important negotiation over the individual grievance. Again, there is little use negotiating a detailed contract if it has to undergo a process of continuous negotiation every time there is a quibble about it; it therefore follows that there will be a need of fixed-term or at least minimum-term agreements. By the same token the negotiation of the detailed terms of the agreement will become a much more important event on its own, an event with wide repercussions rather than one creating only a very few basic rules. It, rather than a procedure agreement several decades old, will become the basis of the relationship, and will need to develop its own specialised procedure of how, where, and when bargaining takes place. In other words, a comprehensive agreement means the development of issues of rights and issues of interest, requiring separate procedures to resolve them. An acceptance of this distinction, which is already accepted as natural and obvious everywhere in the world except Britain, together with that of fixed-term agreements does mean, of course, that Kahn-Freund's demarcation between 'dynamic' and 'static' bargaining would no longer hold true. On the other hand, it fits in with the theory of convergence expressed elsewhere in this issue.[8] Under the new taxonomy of disputes, there will thus be three categories: public rights, private interests, and private rights, forming a much more complex matrix of procedural forms than hitherto. We shall now examine each of these categories in turn.

Public Rights

The creation of certain public rights raises questions both of the substance of the rights and of the machinery required to effectuate them. Here we are concerned only with the latter. It might appear at first sight as though there would be little difficulty in creating the necessary public procedures to enforce the fairly limited rights which Donovan, *Fair Deal at Work* and *In Place of Strife* have suggested. In fact, however, the machinery recommended is so complex as to amount to a sort of Parkinson's Law of the proliferation of public procedures. Under *In Place of Strife,* which admittedly is selected because it proves the point, a wide range of bodies is involved in enforcing the rights. The recognition proposals involve the CIR as the

[7] The form of words is taken from *In Place of Strife* (1969), pp. 11, 18.
[8] See the contribution by J. W. Garbarino.

primary investigating body, the Industrial Court to perform unilateral arbitration, the TUC initially to investigate inter-union recognition issues, the Secretary of State to give effect by order to the CIR's recommendations, and the Industrial Board to impose fines on recalcitrant parties. Appeals against unfair dismissal would be handled by the Industrial Tribunals, which would also expand their jurisdiction into interpreting individual contracts of employment and additional statutory claims to those already covered. On the other hand, there have been suggestions that those private procedures which already have satisfactory provisions for handling dismissals will be allowed to contract out of the statutory machinery. If this is so, the choice of procedure could itself provide some interesting points for bargaining in the future. Complaints by individuals against unions would be examined in the first instance by the Registrar of Trade Unions and Employers' Associations and secondly by the Industrial Board, although in this instance it would have a different composition from that in the recognition situation. These three rights alone therefore involve at least eight differently constituted bodies or individuals in their enforcement. And these do not take into account two other rights in the White Paper. The right of belonging to a trade union is to be established by making any stipulation preventing or obstructing membership void in law, while the provision enabling unions to obtain certain kinds of information was not backed at the time by any particular machinery, although there have been suggestions that the Industrial Court may perform the function. Some of the means of enforcement mentioned have already been discarded, but the main point, that apparently simple rights may require complex administration, still stands.

Part of the reason for this profusion in *In Place of Strife* was undoubtedly the desire to maintain as much informality as possible and to ensure, wherever attainable, enforcement through persuasion rather than coercion. *Fair Deal at Work,* with its more formal approach, would leave most of the effectuation to the new multi-faceted Industrial Court. Even under its proposals, however, there would also be specific functions in this area for the Registrar, the DEP or its Conservative equivalent, and the Productivity Board.

Disputes of Interest

The typical situation in this category will be the procedure for the negotiation of the substantive collective agreement. The parties themselves can of course develop private procedures which will minimise the chances of ultimate conflict; such might be an agreement to have the company's books examined by a third-party neutral; a pact to apply for government mediation or conciliation if no agreement is reached during some specified time period; or indeed, a common acceptance of arbitration for issues in dispute. Procedures may also be necessary within the parties, especially on the union side. The composition of the negotiating team, the development of bargaining demands, the ratification of the agreement all require procedures. To take only one example, if the Ford strike in February 1969 proved anything, it was that some form of proportional representation is vital if a negotiating team is to have the confidence of the workers. Also in the private sphere, there can be procedures—it is perhaps better to call them rituals—in the bargaining itself.

The state will probably have a more important role to play in resolving disputes of interest than in the past, if only because some clashes will be real tests of economic strength such as rarely occur under the present system. Its role in collective bargaining has hitherto been to provide facilities and procedures for helping to resolve disputes after the parties have either asked for help or shown themselves unable to make progress. There are few signs at present that this aspect of its role will change in principle, although because bargaining will be more comprehensive and intensive, it may be presumed that the services will be used more often. There is general agreement that the conciliation functions of the DEP are excellently carried out but both *In Place of Strife* and *Fair Deal at Work* propose that the present system whereby conciliation officers must wait to be invited into a dispute should be replaced by one giving more freedom of intervention. One of the interesting issues which may emerge is whether Department officials will be more willing to enter a situation where procedure has not been followed. Hitherto they have been most reluctant to do this, but now that the TUC has grasped the nettle of intervening in unconstitutional and unofficial strikes, the DEP may well do likewise.

Similarly, voluntary arbitration through the Industrial Court or a board of arbitration or a single arbitrator will continue, with its main functions, as in the past, lying in the public service field. So will the system of Courts of Inquiry and Committees of Investigation, if only to generate the power of public opinion behind recommendations, something in which they have generally been very successful. In the same general category may be placed the initiatives the TUC has declared itself willing to take in investigating troublesome situations, and any similar role which the CBI may decide to play in the future either by itself or in conjunction with the TUC. These are all acceptable procedures in a voluntarist system because they have no powers of compulsion. Even the ultimate resort of a declaration of a State of Emergency is acceptable because of its extreme rarity of use and because of its carefully developed safeguards for the rights of strikers and the industrial status quo.

The question is bound to arise, however, of the need for procedures giving the state more active powers in a dispute situation. This is a separate question from state control of the end result of bargaining under incomes legislation, an issue which lies outside the scope of this article. Given a dispute of some national importance, there are various possibilities involving varying degrees of intervention and compulsion. In its mildest form, intervention might involve selective compulsory conciliation, as in the abandoned conciliation pause of *In Place of Strife*. A more interventionist role would be an equivalent of the Taft-Hartley Act for national emergency disputes, a fact-finding Board of Inquiry followed by an 80-day injunction with a ballot on the employer's last offer after 60 days. This procedure has been advocated by the Conservatives in *Fair Deal at Work,* but with the additional stage that after the fact-finding Board of Inquiry, the Minister could refer the dispute to the Industrial Court for arbitration. The Conservatives call this compulsory arbitration, but it is compulsory only in the sense that the dispute could be taken to the Industrial Court against the wishes of the parties, not that the findings of the Court could be enforced against their wishes. Another possibility concerned with arbitration would be the reintroduction of Order 1376, whereby on a unilateral application the Minister could submit a dispute to the Industrial Disputes Tribunal for arbitration, the results of which would then become an implied condition of employment. Reintroduction of this procedure has been suggested by many unions and the TUC itself, but strongly opposed by employers, who feel that the procedure worked in a one-sided way in the past, in that awards could be enforced against employers but not effectively against unions or employees. But given that some strikes would be intractable, with or without a national emergency procedure, it seems probable that there will be calls for the introduction of full compulsory arbitration, whereby the state not only takes the parties to arbitration but enforces the results afterwards. Its deceptive attraction is that it seems to offer a way out of the jungle law of conflict over income distribution. In practice, of course, the struggle would be merely one stage further removed to the political arena.

The problem with all these suggestions is that, with the exception of the reintroduction of Order 1376, they suspend the right to strike. Whether this can be justified, or even more importantly enforced, is highly dubious. For this reason, state intervention and compulsion is likely to be a blind alley which might detract from the much greater need of the state to do everything it can to foster effective private procedures. If the latter are sufficiently improved, occasional protracted strikes can be accepted as a necessary price for collective bargaining.

Private Rights

In predicting the future perhaps the most difficult problem is that of private rights, or contract interpretation. It is also in the British context the most important, since our main difficulties arise from an inability to handle the relatively petty grievance. The Americans have always argued that the grievance procedure is the heart of the collective agreement, because unless it operates smoothly the relationship is bound to be bad. The grievance procedure is a predominantly judicial and administrative process and only secondly an additional bargaining mechanism. If either side uses it primarily as a means of exercising bargaining power to gain strategic advantages, it loses credibility. To coin another favourite American saying, 'Grievances must be regarded as problems to be solved and not arguments to be won'. The development of adequate grievance procedures raises a number of difficult issues, although those which attract so much current attention, such as the desirable number of stages or the time period between each, are not the most important factors in a good procedure.

The question of level will be one important issue for grievance procedures. There are three basic choices. The first is plant level. Jack Jones has gone on record as saying that dispute procedures must end at the place of work.[9] There is much to be said for this as a locale for settling grievances, but since most of the medium and large size plants where this is likely to be feasible are part of multi-plant companies, there is more to be said for the company level as a finishing point, especially for issues concerning wages or other direct economic costs. The third possibility is of course the industry level or at least some level higher than the company. The problems of the industry-wide procedure have already been discussed; it is difficult to see how comprehensive company agreements can adequately be interpreted at the industry level. It follows that grievance procedures should be foreshortened to the level at which the comprehensive agreement is made. There may, on the other hand, be a case for maintaining the industry procedure for the small company without the facilities to negotiate a comprehensive agreement.

Another critical aspect will be the final step in the procedure. Here there are almost too many options. Employer conciliation is unlikely to be acceptable to unions in the future. Either joint conciliation or, more probably, the development of third party arbitration on the American model, looks much more likely. Alternatively, if the parties agree, interpretation by the courts is a possibility mentioned in both *In Place of Strife* and *Fair Deal at Work*. Some again would make contracts enforceable whether the parties want it or not; others with the same basic viewpoint would differentiate between the substantive and the procedural provisions. It is also possible that workers could have a choice of public or private forums such as exists in France or Germany if the idea of using the Industrial Tribunals to interpret personal contracts is developed, since a more comprehensive agreement would encourage Tribunals to read more of the collective agreement into the personal contract.

Of these possibilities, arbitration looks the best for the longer term as being most in keeping with voluntarist traditions and yet avoiding the problem of any hiatus through inability to come to a decision. It is by no means a new idea in this country and has been recommended more recently by the Donovan Report, *In Place of Strife* and, more forcefully, by Jack Jones before the Institute of Personnel Management. Moreover, as procedures are shortened to end at the level of substantive bargaining, the independent element which constitutes the main justification for joint con-

[9] In a speech to the Institute of Personnel Management, 11 October 1969. He offered either local arbitration or the right to take industrial action as possible conclusions to such procedures, but it was not clear whether one or the other was to be specified or whether they were to be free alternatives. Employers saw this primarily as a tactic to permit a strike to be declared constitutional and official much sooner than previously.

ciliation will disappear. The closer the issue is to the place of work, the greater the likelihood that there will be an emotive content in the position taken by the two sides and the greater the likelihood of conflict if resolution is left to them alone. There is no doubt that the long drawn out nature of British procedures was designed to, and has often succeeded in, cooling down tempers. The problem is that its bluff is now being called. It might well be, therefore, that the only way to get independent judgment whilst not taking the decision far from the persons involved is to call in a third party arbitrator. This system only just falls short of being universal in the United States. However, three apparent misconceptions about the way grievance arbitration works in the United States could profitably be cleared away. In the first place, there is no direct connection between arbitration and legal contract enforceability; arbitration was introduced as a purely voluntary procedure long before contracts were legally enforceable. Secondly, it is not the case that arbitration requires the highly complex formal documents which are the present American collective agreement. Many of the early American contracts were every bit as nebulous in the substantive sense as present British ones. Thirdly, it is not the case that managements have always, or even typically, seen arbitration only as a *quid pro quo* for a no-strike clause.[10] Unfortunately there are not statistics to show how many legal strikes took place during the life of the agreement but it is nevertheless wrong to equate arbitration with a denial of the right to strike.

Sanctions is a further area sure to raise important issues under contract interpretation. The American system of arbitration operated for at least twenty years using only social sanctions, and still depends for its acceptability on the control of the parties over the conditions under which the arbitrator operates. But assuming this is considered insufficient, the law could, as in America since 1960, stand behind the arbitrator's decision by enforcing whatever ruling he made. In spite of this, it is noticeable that American employers rarely take unions to court for breach of the contract. In Britain a popular solution, included in *Fair Deal at Work,* is for employers to be able to sue unions if they do not do sufficient to persuade recalcitrant members to go back to work. This indirect remedy, made necessary by employers' unwillingness to take legal action against individuals, seems likely to lead to either increasing union sophistication at equivocation, or an increasing division between unions and members. In either case, little is likely to be gained. As for the hope that an automatic penalty could somehow be imposed on individuals without dirtying the employers' hands, that was exploded by Donovan. The problem of sanctions therefore remains the Achilles heel of the reorganisation of British collective bargaining. Penalties on individuals are likely to be those which are most resented and most

---

[10] An examination of 1,717 major agreements by the U.S. Department of Labor showed that only 757 had an absolute ban on strikes (Department of Labor Bulletin No. 1425-6, 1966, p. 83). The possibility that some issues need not be arbitrable also detracts from the argument against arbitration that at least some decisions must be kept in the hands of the parties.

difficult to put into operation yet at the same time most needed. Ultimately, there is no substitute for firm but fair action by the employer. Yet the history of the Ford penal clauses is likely to give employers pause before incorporating them into an agreement. The TGWU has in any case given notice (at its Douglas Conference, 1969) that it will refuse to accept any penal clauses and will demand that the watered down version left in the Ford contract should be removed. In saying this so boldly, the union may well be creating trouble for its own officials, who may find it increasingly difficult to utilise the social and moral sanctions which have always been the main means of controlling members. With this sort of attitude towards discipline, it will be difficult to make even local procedures credible. Yet if militancy is permitted to be successful, it will tend to become the norm, whatever the procedures. Joint rule-making breaks down and rules cease to be rules if there are no sanctions for breaking them. Voluntary rule-making means that the parties must be able and willing to impose sanctions themselves. If they cannot do so both sides are likely to lose their legitimacy.

More specific characteristics of grievance procedures, needed to counter-act some of the defects described in the earlier part of this article, may be briefly listed as follows. All points of issue under the contract must be capable of being raised as a grievance; the procedure must also make arrangements for points not previously negotiated. The participants in the procedure must have the facilities to carry out their roles; this goes for foremen as well as shop stewards. The procedure must make provision for participation by higher levels of management. There should be a degree of formality in the procedure, both to avoid delay by management and short-circuiting by unions. In spite of the last point, consideration should be given to accelerated resolution on particular issues such as discipline. Lastly, procedures must be joint; this may appear simplistic, yet one of the most profound comments on the loss of managerial control was Flanders' that: ' The paradox, whose truth managements have found it so difficult to accept, is that they can only regain control by sharing it.' (Flanders, 1968, p. 555.) This means, for instance, that the open-ended management rights clause will disappear; sacrificing the shadow of total control for the substance of partial control would be no bad bargain.

Issues of private rights do not only refer to the employer-union relation-ship. Indeed, some of the most important rights procedures may well prove to be in the inter-union area. The Bridlington procedures have now been supplemented by the decision of the special congress of the TUC in June 1969 to give the General Council greater powers under Rule 12 and by the TUC's promise to the Government of active intervention. Moreover, outside the aegis of the TUC but with its strong encouragement, there are numerous bilateral working agreements between unions. Of these, the recent demarca-tion procedures involving the shipbuilding unions are among the most interesting and hopeful, involving as they do third party arbitration of very much the kind which is advocated for the employer-union relationship. Even so, the problems of inter-union conflict, whether or not there are rights involved, will be sharpened when unions must operate at the level of the plant rather than being able to obscure their differences through national negotiating. However, this problem belongs more properly to the following section.

The Lag in Practice

We must now return to the supposition postulated earlier that the implementation of Donovan is far from complete, or at least that the transition period takes a considerable length of time. There will thus be a lag between the theoretical outcome just described and actual practice. Viewed from the vantage point of late 1969, some eighteen months after the Donovan Report was issued, this portent looks all too accurate. There has been nothing of the revolution in attitudes, institutions or procedures which Donovan recommended. This should not be too surprising, since Donovan was from the start acclaimed with much more enthusiasm by outside observers than by the participants themselves. If change has its advantages to them, it also creates new possibilities of conflict, and conflict of a potentially dangerous sort since, as noted, procedural changes go to the very heart of the relationship. As a generalisation, however, it is fair to say that unions are much more enthusiastic than management about both procedural and substantive decentralisation; they feel that for too long they have been called on to do management's disciplinary work. Although Donovan pointed to management and particularly to boards of directors to take the initiative, few managements want to leave the protection of the industry association. It is understandable that employers wish to avoid the whip-sawing which they see as an inevitable concomitant of independent bargaining, but the absence of any procedural institutions for handling the problems of the shop floor is allowing this to happen in any case. There might well be a case for a rewidening of bargaining structures once such local institutions are created, but the present danger is that adherence to the industry-wide system does appear to be having this inhibiting effect. Procedural initiatives are lacking even where there would seem to be most incentive to introduce them; thus although a tremendous amount of effort has been invested in productivity bargaining, relatively little thought seems to have been given to procedures to implement and adjudicate the results.[11] Again, there is virtually no experimentation with arbitration; indeed the National Coal Board, hitherto the most important adherent of grievous arbitration, has now largely discarded it.[12]

[11] The chemical industry, which was taken as a prototype by the Donovan Commission, has separate procedures for negotiating productivity bargains and for interpreting them.

[12] The circumstances were perhaps rather special in this case, since the move away from arbitration was a result of the National Power Loading Scheme and the virtual end of piecework. Moreover arbitration remains as before at the District and National (as opposed to the Pit) levels. Nevertheless, third party arbitration was not found to be altogether satisfactory since it involved a subjective analysis of the work/wage relationship in a particular situation, and problems of relativity inevitably arose.

Some companies, notably the American subsidiaries, have always bargained outside the employers' associations, and consequently have better developed company procedures. This has not necessarily meant a Donovan-type situation; the agreements have still been very loosely drawn compared with what is suggested. Even so, it is these companies which have made most progress since Donovan. Unfortunately, the example of Ford, which tried to move its bargaining structure and procedures towards the Donovan mould, has obviously not been very encouraging to other employers. In any case there has been no rush away from industry-wide bargaining and industry-wide procedures. Cadbury and Rootes are probably the only large companies which have recently decided to go it alone; otherwise companies seem content to follow the lead of the industry associations.

It is therefore at the industry level that there has been most action, although for the most part skirmishing and jockeying for position. Donovan, the incomes policy, wage drift, and productivity bargaining have between them caused a great deal of discussion of the need for change, but since much of the discussion has revolved around modifications of the present framework, there is an obvious danger of *plus ça change, plus c'est la même chose*. The engineering industry, always the chief target of criticism and the one to which the Donovan recommendations most obviously applied, provides perhaps the best example of the problems since talks to reconstruct the industry's procedure have at the time of writing deteriorated to the point where the unions have threatened to abrogate the procedure completely after twelve months of discussions. The Engineering Employers' Federation, recognising the need for some changes, initially proposed modifications in the procedure which on their face went some way towards Donovan. There would be a new local institution, the works council, which would act as the final stage of the domestic disputes procedure and the primary body for factory bargaining; there would be a re-examination of the facilities for and functions of shop stewards. Outside this, however, the current procedural structure would still govern. Admittedly, domestic wage issues, which now comprise between two-thirds and three-quarters of the questions going to central conference, would be cut short at local conference, but the decision would still be out of the hands of the bargaining parties.[13] With respect to other important topics, the EEF suggested central conference would still be the ultimate place of decision; such topics would include the activities of shop stewards, disciplinary questions, and changes in methods of work. The Confederation of Shipbuilding and Engineering Unions, for its part, has argued that the final decision should be made at the place of work, without going to any external stages, for a wide range of topics and has insisted that the managerial functions clause should be abandoned. The EEF has given way on the range of disputes to go before

---

[13] It is very difficult to envisage the operation of formal, comprehensive and authoritative company or factory agreements if the procedure for solving grievances presupposes the continuous negotiation of wage issues with the key decisions being taken outside the company.

central conference and has modified its stand on the management functions clause, but the two sides are still far apart. The possibility is thus that a breakdown of procedural negotiations will leave a vacuum which the official parties to the relationship cannot fill. Powerful, if unofficial, groups will unilaterally create new procedural forms for their own benefit; indeed, this is one of the primary manifestations of the breakdown of the old order. If such a collapse did no more than force the parties to reappraise their position, it might be no bad thing; on the other hand, it might lead to a situation without a formal structure or procedure at any level; this would be the worst of all worlds.

The procedural struggle in the engineering industry may be the most visible, and perhaps also the most intractable, but it is likely to be repeated in many other industries. If so, the full implementation of Donovan may take a long time indeed, although unions elsewhere also would prefer a decentralised and very much speedier procedure. It should be noted, however, that if employers' associations seem especially reluctant to decentralise, they have the willing support of many managements who still want procedures which will help them find external solutions to their internal problems. To be fair to such managements, unions have shown little sign of accepting the responsibilities which would come from more formal plant agreements and procedures; merely leaving things to the shop stewards is not a recipe for a constructive outcome. Moreover, even at higher levels the unions are by no means enthusiastically embracing all the implications of Donovan. The TUC in its pamphlet 'Action on Donovan' had the following to say :

> In many industries (notably of course the motor industry) the almost continuous change in production processes means that the question of interpretation of the terms of the contract is impossible to separate from the question of considering an amendment to the contract . . . It may be possible to differentiate ' rights disputes ' and ' interests disputes ' theoretically, but they cannot readily be distinguished in practice (T.U.C., 1968a, pp. 17-18).[14]

If the TUC insists that each and every change should be a subject of *de novo* negotiation, then rights disputes are by definition excluded. Yet it can hardly be argued that the rate of change is any slower in foreign industries, particularly the motor industries, and it occurs without the disruption currently inherent in the British system. Even where piecework is prevalent, as in Sweden, bargaining is minimised by a greater acceptance of work study

[14] It is not without significance that the TUC, in its evidence to the Royal Commission, was able to distinguish rights and interests disputes with apparent precision. In an analysis of the operation of Order 1376, it was noted that out of 1,270 awards by the Industrial Disputes Tribunal, 1,070 related to differences of interest and 200 to questions of rights (TUC, 1968b, para. 324). It should not however be assumed that in view of this inconsistency on the part of the TUC, the differentiation will be easy, especially under the present system of continuous bargaining, merely that it is feasible.

and like techniques. Both unions and employers, in fact, have taken refuge in the argument that there are great variations between industries, and hence that general solutions are not relevant. While this obviously contains a good deal of truth, it also means that change is seen as being desirable only where it is tactically advantageous.

The Government naturally recognised the problems of change and set up two agencies, the CIR to examine ways of improving and extending procedural arrangements, and the Manpower and Productivity Service of DEP to examine and advise on registered procedures up to the point at which a reference to the CIR is desirable. *In Place of Strife* also offered financial assistance in training for unions. Although received with little enthusiasm by unions, there is a great need for improvements in this area, since the problem of finding the extra qualified manpower to operate the new procedures will not be easy.

Although a policy-making role was assigned to the CIR and the MPS it is in fact far from explicit. There are no more than general guidelines as to what constitutes a good procedure. Nor is it at all likely that a model procedure could be devised with applicability to a wide range of situations. The two agencies are therefore going to have to feel their way. Principles can emerge only with experience, and a good deal of investigation by the CIR and collation by the MPS will be necessary before this happens. For the time being the MPS has sent out a checklist of factors which may appear in procedure agreements and arrangements to employers. Insofar as it does push employers into stating whether they have supplementary arrangements to those provided by the industry procedure, and whether they already differentiate in practice between procedures for settling terms and conditions of employment and those for handling grievances, this will bring to light an area of procedures about which little is known. But it seems likely that many companies will merely register their industry procedures whilst waiting for their employers' associations to take more positive action. The CIR has had a difficult first year; although the dearth of assignments has now been overcome and a general reference (on facilities for shop stewards) has been accepted by the CBI and the TUC, it is as yet too early to say what the Commission will be able to achieve. One thing seems certain, it will not be as positive an agent of change as Donovan would have liked; the CBI and the TUC have been given too strong a veto for that. It would be inconceivable, for instance, that the CIR should be given the task of advising on the reconstruction of procedures in the engineering industry.

Conclusion

Much of the argument contained in this article presupposes a fairly radical attitude to change in the structure of the British industrial relations system. This follows from the pattern laid down by Donovan, but whether that pattern can be achieved is obviously open to doubt. Only time will tell whether the CIR and the MPS are sufficiently positive agencies of change or whether employers will be willing to break away from their associations or whether the associations will be willing to decentralise control sufficiently to permit comprehensive company and factory agreements to become a reality. Two possible models of the future have therefore been put forward: one static, but neat and definitive, the other dynamic, but groping and backward-looking; it is likely that there will be elements of both in existence by the end of the 1970's. The balance between the two, however, is very difficult to predict. The larger companies will in all probability have accepted change, but the smaller companies in the more competitive industries will probably continue to be dominated by the national associations.

It must also be pointed out that the negotiation of new procedures will be no easy task. Each side will battle for procedural just as for substantive gains since both realise that the nature of the process contributes greatly to the end result as does the status conferred by procedural recognition. Difficulties will be created, moreover, by the differential rate of change between industries and between firms, since problems remaining in the less progressive industries may affect others. Nor of course will the problems of industrial relations cease as soon as better procedures are created. A degree of conflict must be expected whatever the procedural mechanisms. 'Fractional' bargaining within the agreement through the grievance procedures is a well established habit in America, as Kuhn (1961) showed, and would undoubtedly continue here. It is one of the peculiar characteristics of the British economy that we assume that 'institutionism', i.e. the reconstruction of the institutional framework while leaving the underlying economic forces untouched, will solve all our problems. It will not. Better procedures may answer some of the sociological causes of worker dissatisfaction, namely those emanating from a felt inability to control one's environment; they can be of only limited help in solving the basic economic issues of distributing the national income. Nevertheless, the importance of procedures cannot be overstressed; in the words of Fox and Flanders: 'For the keynote of the age is unquestionably continual and accelerating change, and a congruent order must therefore embody, above all, agreed procedural norms which provide for its accommodation and orderly regulation' (Fox and Flanders, 1969, p. 180).

University of Glasgow

REFERENCES

DEPARTMENT OF EMPLOYMENT AND PRODUCTIVITY (1969). *Report of the Committee of Inquiry into the Dispute between the Durham Local Education Authority and the National Association of Schoolmasters.* Cmnd. 4152. London, H.M.S.O.

DONOVAN (1968). *Report* of the Royal Commission on Trade Unions and Employers' Associations. Cmnd. 3623. London, H.M.S.O.

FLANDERS, A. (1968). Evidence to the Royal Commission on Trade Unions and Employers' Associations. *Selected Written Evidence submitted to the Royal Commission.* London, H.M.S.O.

FOX, A. and FLANDERS, A. (1969). The Reform of Collective Bargaining: From Donovan to Durkheim. *British Journal of Industrial Relations,* July 1969.

GARBARINO, J. W. (1969). Managing Conflict in Industrial Relations: U.S. experience and Current Issues in Britain. *British Journal of Industrial Relations,* November 1969.

GOVERNMENT SOCIAL SURVEY (1968). *Workplace Industrial Relations.* Enquiry undertaken for the Royal Commission on Trade Unions and Employers' Associations. SS402, March 1968. London, H.M.S.O.

In Place of Strife (1969). Cmnd. 3888. London, H.M.S.O.

KAHN-FREUND, O. (1954). Intergroup Conflicts and their Settlement. *British Journal of Sociology,* 1954.

KAHN-FREUND, O. (1959). Labour Law. *in* Ginsberg, M (ed.). *Law and Opinion in England in the 20th Century.* London, Stevens and Sons Ltd.

KUHN, J. W. (1961). *Bargaining in Grievance Settlement.* Columbia U.P.

MCCARTHY, W. E. J. (1966). *The Role of Shop Stewards in British Industrial Relations.* Royal Commission on Trade Unions and Employers' Associations. Research Paper No. 1. London, H.M.S.O.

MARSH, A. I. (1966). *Disputes Procedures in British Industry.* Royal Commission on Trade Unions and Employers' Associations. Research Paper No. 2 (Part 1). London, H.M.S.O.

MARSH, A. I. and MCCARTHY, W. E. J. (1968). *Disputes Procedures in Britain.* Royal Commission on Trade Unions and Employers' Associations. Research Paper No. 2 (Part 2). London, H.M.S.O.

MUNNS, V. G. (1967). The Functions and Organisation of Employers' Associations in Selected Industries. *in Employers' Associations.* Royal Commission on Trade Unions and Employers' Associations. Research Paper No. 7. London, H.M.S.O.

T.U.C. (1968a). *Action on Donovan.* Trades Union Congress, November 1968. London.

T.U.C. (1960). *Annual Report.* Trades Union Congress. London.

T.U.C. (1969). *Programme for Action.* Trades Union Congress, June 1969. London.

T.U.C. (1968b) *Written Evidence to the Royal Commission on Trade Unions and Employers' Associations.* London, H.M.S.O.

THE FUTURE ROLE OF THE LAW

CYRIL GRUNFELD

Labour relations in this country will not be legally regulated in the future, but the law will play a role in labour relations of increasing importance.[1] If the latter statement is greeted with incredulity, it is, in my opinion, because of two fallacious assumptions which have been allowed to gain wide currency.

The first is that, in Britain, unions and workers want nothing more of the law than that it should leave them alone. This is very far from the truth of the matter. The truth of the matter may be expressed as being that, on the one hand, unions and workers are opposed to law which enlarges managerial bargaining power or diminishes union bargaining power and autonomy or which holds back advantages for individual employees, while, on the other hand, they warmly favour and will press hard for law which maximises union bargaining power and autonomy or which maximises advantages for individual employees, including especially union members. This, of course, is only natural but it is important for an understanding of future legal development that the true position should not be camouflaged and should be precisely understood.

The second fallacious assumption is that judges and lawyers are intrinsically unfitted to deal with labour relations issues. This is sometimes phrased even more tendentiously by saying that the trade unions and industrial relations must not be made the plaything of the legal fraternity. This sentiment, like that of being left alone by the law, may stem from a selective historical memory of the over-identification with employer interests of magistrates and courts in the nineteenth century as well as, possibly, the hundreds of cases on workmen's compensation in this century in which the phrase, 'arising out of and in the course of employment', was made the subject of lengthy and expensive litigation.[2] This latter development was not, however, the deliberate intent of lawyers but the result of a system initiated by Parliament which nevertheless laid the foundation for the present comprehensive social security arrangements in the establishment and running of which lawyers have played and continue to play a substantial part. On the other hand, this historical memory is selective in that it invariably excludes any recollection of how the judiciary and other lawyers liberalised the common law of industrial accidents and the Factories Acts and other

[1] The trend towards extending and improving legally guaranteed minimum standards, the increasing concentration of power in organisations, whether industrial or trade union, the escalating power of work groups through rapid technological changes and their consequences, and the increasing repercussion of industrial conflict on society as a whole make an enlargement of the legal role inevitable, in my opinion.

[2] The 48 volumes of Butterworth's Workmen's Compensation Cases are an imperishable monument to this experience.

protective legislation[3] or of how they preserved the Trades Disputes Act 1906 from being undermined in its early days[4] and established a regime of legal neutralism throughout the struggling days in this century of British trade unionism.[5] In my opinion, the danger today is not that industrial relations may become the plaything of the legal fraternity but that the law may become the plaything of industrial relations.

Not only are lawyers capable of playing a vital, *supportive* role in labour relations, as the work of American labour arbitrators amply shows, but the clear-headed analysis and even-handed judgment which are the marks of the good lawyer are, I believe, deeply needed elements in defining and making effective for both employees and management an important range of rights and responsibilities. This article will be concerned with the lines along which the role of the law may enlarge in the remainder of the present century, the basic principles which should direct this enlargement and the manpower requirements it implies.

There are three areas of labour relations, not entirely insulated from each other, to consider: individual labour relations, internal union relations, and management-labour relations. In these areas, two broad policies, which unfortunately do not have the attractive simplicity of extremism, should be pursued. The one policy is to raise the standards of employment terms and conditions and social security and increase the legal protection of the individual employee while maintaining the conditions of managerial efficiency. The other policy is to encourage the development of collective bargaining in sympathy with the aspirations and interests of both managers and managed while substituting, wherever possible, the public interest in law and orderly procedures for private power and industrial battle.

INDIVIDUAL LABOUR RELATIONS

The protection of individual employees and the nature of their terms and conditions of employment depend, in part, on the law and, in part, on

---

[3] From about 1890, the courts created an entirely new action for damages for breach of any statutory duty contained in safety and health legislation, neutralised the defence of consent (*volenti non fit injuria*), greatly mitigated the defences of contributory negligence (until it was abolished as an absolute defence by the L.R. (Contributory Negligence) Act 1945) and common employment (until abolished by the Law Reform (Personal Injuries) Act 1948, and steadily enlarged the scope of liability of employers and their insurance companies. The backpedalling which began in 1952 appears now to have ended and a new liberal phase to have been inaugurated as, for example, most recently in *Millard v. Serck Tubes Ltd.* [1969] 1 All E.R. 598 and *Boyle v. Kodak Ltd.* [1969] 2 All E.R. 439.

[4] The prevention by the Court of Appeal of an emasculating interpretation by the High Court of the pivotal concept of a 'trade dispute' in the Trade Disputes Act 1906 is never recalled in any historical review of the relationship between the trade unions and the judiciary. The judicial preservation of the 1906 Act took place in *Dallimore v. Williams* (1914) 30 T.L.R. 432; *Hodges v. Webb* [1920] 2 Ch. 70; and *White v. Riley* [1921] 1 Ch. 1.

[5] The highlights were *Reynolds v. Shipping Federation Ltd.* [1924] 1 Ch. 28; *Crofter Hand-Woven Harris Tweed Co. v. Veitch* [1942] A.C. 435; *Thomson v. Deakin* [1952] Ch. 646; *Scala Ballroom (Wolverhampton) Ltd. v. Ratcliffe* [1958] 3 All E.R. 220.

autonomous collective bargaining and private collective power whether derived from trade union organisation or from organised ' shop floor ' action, generally, of trade unionists. British trade unionists account only for about 40 per cent. of the labour force divided roughly between 50 per cent. of blue collar and 30 per cent. of white collar employees. Nevertheless since collective agreements bargained by trade unions or shop stewards are normally applied also to non-unionists, the terms and conditions of employment established by collective bargaining have been estimated to govern the jobs of about 65 per cent. of the labour force. (Donovan, 1968, para. 38.) But, the protection afforded individual employees as a whole by private collective power is deficient in three important respects and in considering them reference will be made to possible future developments in the law of individual labour relations.

Limits of private collective power

First, collective bargaining and collective agreements constitute processes which are incapable of creating or maintaining a comprehensive system of duties and rights and a national administrative structure to protect the safety and health of employees generally. In the vitally important area of safety and health, the role of the trade union or of unofficial action is at best supportive only. Equally another inherent limitation of organised labour is that it is by itself incapable of creating or running a comprehensive social security regime, not to speak of a national health service. Again, the trade union role can only be ancillary, though trade union funds and energy are very properly poured into the political sphere in order to press governments to introduce the needed law or amendments to it and to make sufficient public funds available to protect employees comprehensively. The hollowness of the claim that private collective bargaining supported by private insurance can confer adequate social security on the members of a labour force, not to speak of people at large, has been well demonstrated in the United States. The instrumentality of the law backed by the power of the State is the sole instrumentality capable of establishing adequate safety, health and social security standards for employees as a whole. For this reason, in these spheres, British trade unions and workers have wanted nothing of the law save that it be brought into being and strictly enforced.

Sectionalism of collective agreements

The second inadequacy of private collective power lies in the content and area of application of collective agreements. Collective agreements cover about 65 per cent. of the members of the national labour force but they cover them overall with a substantial degree of imperfection and unevenness. This is only to be expected, though perhaps insufficiently noticed, given the substantial variation which exists among the different sectors of industry in standards of professional competence of management and union officials and shop stewards in dealing with the crucial problems and issues of labour relations. Variations in ability, skill and awareness in the labour relations sphere, in part a hangover from the earlier amateurism in this respect of British industry, is compounded by variations in power and wealth generated directly by the different sectors of employment, whether in productive or extractive industry, service trades, including entertainment, central and local government, higher education, health and other administrative and professional services. Only the law can establish and enforce equal minimum standards among all classes of employees.

Redundancy is a good illustration. Before the Redundancy Payments Act 1965, a survey by the National Joint Advisory Council[6] revealed, subject to certain notable exceptions, a remarkable indifference in industry to the consequences of making employees redundant; and this indifference was not confined to management. A great mitigation of hardship was introduced by the 1965 Act and that mitigation was further enhanced by the inauguration of earnings-related unemployment benefit in the National Insurance Act 1966. Between these two statutes, the standard of financial provision for redundant employees is now better than it was under the best voluntary collective agreement which previously dealt with this problem, and all employed persons enjoy these benefits, not merely those who happened to have management and unions aware of the need to deal with the problem and sufficient bargaining skill and power to produce a sectional solution.

The new law of redundancy also illustrates the capacity of the judiciary and members of the legal profession to administer a not always perfectly drafted statute in the interests of those for whom it was passed, namely, redundant employees. In the limited space at my disposal, I shall confine myself to the one example of the interpretation by the industrial tribunals and the courts up to the House of Lords of the phrase, ' temporary cessation of work '.[7]

This phrase is relevant to the question of the length of a redundant employee's continuous employment. The importance of determining the length of continuous employment lies in the fact that a redundancy payment is calculated in accordance with a formula consisting of three major factors: age, continuous employment and ' a week's pay '. The longer a redundant employee's period of continuous service is, up to a maximum of 20 years, the greater will be his redundancy pay. Consequently, it is a matter of considerable importance in individual cases to decide whether, when an employee has had to be laid off temporarily for one reason or another, the break in his employment breaks his continuity of employment or, on the contrary, not only does not break his continuity of employment but is itself to be added to his total length of continuous service.

The latter effect occurs where the employee had been ' absent from work

<hr>

[6] Ministry of Labour (1961), updated in Ministry of Labour Gazette of February 1963.

[7] Contracts of Employment Act 1963, Sch. 1, para. 5 (1) (b), incorporated in the new redundancy law by Redundancy Payments Act 1965, s. 8(2).

on account of a temporary cessation of work '. Initially, the industrial tribunals themselves gave the statutory phrase a rather restricted interpretation, namely, that a temporary cessation of work was a cessation for a period which, at the time it began, was regarded by both employer and employee as intended to come to an end within a foreseeable period of time.[8] Clearly, this interpretation afforded considerable opportunity for avoidance of the full effect of the 1965 Act by giving foremen instructions not to indicate to employees laid off that it was intended to re-engage them when, for example, trade picked up again or supplies of raw materials were resumed. The Divisional Court of the High Court liberalised the interpretation of the phrase in *Hunter v. Smith Dock Ltd.* ([1968] I.T.R. 198.) The applicant had been employed by the dock company as a rivetter in ship repairing work on and off for 40 years. Over the period he had been from time to time laid off as work in the ship repairing industry fluctuated. In 1967, some three years after his last lay-off of 32 days, he was finally dismissed as redundant. The High Court held that his periods of lay-off did not break the continuity of his employment but, on the contrary, were to be included in his total length of continuous employment in accordance with the 1965 Act. The criterion of ' temporary ' previously adopted by the industrial tribunals was erased and replaced by the High Court with the decision that the temporary nature of a cessation of work had to be considered retrospectively from the time when the employee returned to his work and in the light of all the circumstances of the cessation, including how it began, its duration, how and why it ended, as well as the nature of the employment; and, applying this ' hindsight test ', the court held that Hunter's period of continuous employment had not been affected by his successive periods of lay-off, lengthy though some of them were.

Subsequently, the Court of Session in Scotland gave a rather restricted meaning to ' cessation of work ', while accepting the interpretation of ' temporary ' in *Hunter's* case. The Court of Session held that ' cessation of work ' referred only to a total cessation of work in a plant or clearly defined section of a plant and did not extend to the temporary cessation of the particular employee's job.[9] In its turn, this interpretation, which the Court of Appeal in Northern Ireland had also adopted,[10] was overruled recently by the House of Lords[11] to the effect that ' cessation of work ' was to be understood as including the cessation of a particular employee's job in isolation as well as an employee's cessation of work as part of a more general stopping of work in his plant or section thereof.

[8] In *Wilson v. Courtaulds Ltd.* (1966) I.T.R. 442, 443; *Minards v. Courtaulds Ltd.* (1967) 219; *Houston v. Murdoch MacKenzie Ltd.* (1967) I.T.R. 125; *Burrows v. Cheall, Knowles & Co. Ltd.* (1967) I.T.R. 533.
[9] *Fitzgerald v. Hall, Russell & Co. Ltd.* (1969) S.L.T. 169, (1969) I.T.R. 32.
[10] *Monarch Electric Co. v. McIntyre* [1968] N.1 163.
[11] *Fitzgerald v. Hall, Russell & Co. Ltd.* [1970] I.T.R. 1, so belying the alarm originally expressed that the stop-go conditions of work in the construction, ship-building and ship repairing industries ·would deprive employees in those industries of the benefit of the new redundancy law.

Other equally striking examples have occurred in the administration of the Redundancy Payments Act 1965 which demonstrate the modern awareness of both the courts and the members of the industrial tribunals, legal and lay, concerning the realities of industry. Not least among these illustrations has been the insistence both by courts and tribunals on deliberate informality of procedure, including a refusal to apply to redundancy proceedings the strict rules of evidence normally applied in common law actions.[12]

Possibly now a code of good practice issued by the Department of Employment and Productivity in respect of pre-planning and carrying out the dismissal of employees for redundancy, quite apart from financial provision, might be considered for inclusion in the next round of redundancy legislation as compulsory guide lines for all management and union officials. Such legally enforceable standards, I would emphasise, do not reduce the influence of trade unions, they merely modify and elaborate their role. The influence of the unions will only be reduced by legal developments if they prove incapable of adapting their role and the services they provide to the new law. But autonomous bargaining in the strategic areas of wages, hours, disputes procedures, etc., remains valid and irreplaceable in our kind of democratic society.

Discrimination against non-unionists

I turn to the third inadequacy, from the viewpoint of individual employees, of private industrial power. This is that, although collective agreements are normally applied also to the non-unionists in a labour force, non-unionists are not protected in practice by the unions' collective power in respect of any matter for which the collective agreement does not itself expressly provide, like unfair dismissal or unjustified denial of promotion.

True, the withholding of such protection by a union may be regarded as a useful recruitment factor, but this is cold comfort for the individual concerned who may wish to live his life and earn his living independently of a labour organisation and who should have this choice in a society in which private power is kept in its due place. The preservation of individual freedom of unionists as well as non-unionists in the midst of industrial power relations is one of the most intractable problems posed for the law by modern labour relations. The individual in industry finds himself at the point of intersection of managerial and of trade union and shop floor power. His adequate basic protection must depend on developments in the law of individual labour relations and also on a civilised legal framework for the closed shop, if the latter is not to be wholly outlawed. The closed shop issue will be postponed to the next section on internal union relations.

The law governing individual labour relations is now teetering on the threshold of a major enlargement of scope and application. The Industrial

---

[12] See, e.g., *Douglas v. Provident Clothing & Supply Co. Ltd.* (1969) I.T.R. 15.

Relations Bill, which it is proposed to introduce in the present parliamentary session, contemplates a new law to protect individual employees from ' unfair ' dismissal and the transformation of the industrial tribunals into a national system of labour courts with jurisdiction over not only redundancy payments, industrial training levies, selective employment tax, written particulars under the Contracts of Employment Act 1963 and certain statutory odds and ends but also all disputes arising from breach of contract of employment together with administration of the new unfair dismissal provisions. (*In Place of Strife,* 1969, paras 103-6; Donovan, paras 520-86.)

As its shape begins to emerge, the law of unfair dismissal appears likely to stigmatise as unfair reasons for dismissal, trade union membership, participation in legitimate union activities outside working hours or within working hours with the permission of the management, acting as shop steward or other workers' representative, being of a certain race, colour, sex, nationality or social origin, being married or being of a particular religious or political persuasion; otherwise, dismissal will not be unfair if connected with the capacity or conduct of the employee or if based on the operational requirements of the place of work unless, presumably, the employee is able to satisfy a tribunal on the merits that he was in fact unfairly fired. Conciliation machinery, reinstatement as a remedy with the possibility of back pay, and adequate if not punitive compensation (in contrast with the inadequate existing common law remedies) may possibly figure among these revolutionary proposals. There will also have to be co-ordination of collectively agreed dismissal procedures with the new jurisdiction. Plainly, the industrial tribunals will have an important discretion vested in them to determine the issue of fairness of dismissal. Conditions of managerial efficiency, the danger of authentic ' disruptists ' within British industry, and the protection of individual employees from the abuse of managerial power will all be among the guide line policies which the tribunals and, on appeal, the courts will need to take into account. The implications of a new law of this kind for the at present unfettered use of trade union or shop floor bargaining power will be considered later.

Equally important from the point of view of enforcing rights and responsibilities in industry is the proposal to extend the industrial tribunals' jurisdiction to embrace all breach of employment contract disputes. In one of the outstandingly important documents produced by the T.U.C. after publication of the Royal Commission's Report, the T.U.C. General Council disagreed that the industrial tribunals' jurisdiction should be extended to cover all disputes arising from the individual contract of employment ' because this would necessarily involve interpretation of collective agreements ' (T.U.C., 1968, para. 70). This is, with respect, so thin a reason that, if it is not an objection for the sake of bargaining with the Government, it must rest on a deep unreasoned antagonism to law in management-labour relations save so far, of course, as the law provides unions or their members with a 22 carat guarantee of exclusive benefit.

However, if the unions want their members to enjoy the protection of a law of unfair dismissal and are willing to allow the other 60 per cent. of the labour force to have the same protection, then, they must be persuaded to allow a generalisation of the tribunals' jurisdiction or go without, since a law of unfair dismissal cannot in practice be fairly split off from the general law relating to the termination of employment.

For example, at present, if a tribunal discovers that an employee has been wrongly dismissed, or has not been given the holiday money to which he was entitled, or has not been made any payment in respect of holiday entitlement under his contract, or has not been repaid his contributions to an occupational pension scheme, or has not even been paid the wages accrued due to him before his dismissal, the tribunals can do absolutely nothing about it. Their jurisdiction is confined strictly to the question of redundancy pay and to only the least important part of the Contracts of Employment Act, namely, merely to settling what an employee's written particulars ought to have contained. The tribunals do not even have the power at present to enforce the statutory minimum periods of notice under the 1963 Act by being able to award damages in the form of net wages due for the notice period which a dismissed employee should have been given. This particular lack of power on the tribunals' part will be aggravated if the Government extends the statutory notice periods for longer service employees if only to align our own individual labour law more closely to that of West European countries. Furthermore, if an employee is absent from work owing to sickness, unless his contract of employment expressly or impliedly provides otherwise he is entitled to receive his full wages. If he does not receive his wages, he is more than likely to fail to pursue the point at the present time in the county court. Breach by his employer of the common law obligation to pay the employee during sickness should be actionable before the industrial tribunals.

Of course, a tribunal may have to interpret and apply a collective agreement in determining whether an employer or, indeed, an employee was in breach of his contract of employment. But, the industrial tribunals do this already in connection with calculating dismissed employees' redundancy pay, and the only complaint made has been that they ought to interpret and apply not only national but also plant and site agreements.[13] The T.U.C. might argue that the express reason they gave in opposition to conferring on industrial tribunals a general jurisdiction was not the true reason but was to be taken as indicating their deep-seated fear lest management might take advantage of the speedy, inexpensive and informal procedure of the industrial tribunals to bring employees to court for damages for breach of

---

[13] Especially in deciding what were the 'normal working hours' fixed by the redundant employee's contract of employment: e.g. *Turriff Construction Ltd.* v. *Bryant* [1967] I.T.R. 282; *Pearson and Workman* v. *William Jones Ltd.* [1967] I.T.R. 471; *Pioli* v. *B.T.R. Industries Ltd.* [1966] I.T.R. 255; cp. too, *Sylvester* v. *The Standard Upholstery Co. Ltd.* [1967] I.T.R. 507; *Duff* v. *Taylor Woodrow Construction* [1967] I.T.R. 258.

their contract of employment.[14] But, management may do this already in the county court and the fact that proceedings before the county court are rather slower and more formal and expensive than they would be before an industrial tribunal does not have the same weight on management's side as it necessarily has on the side of the employee. And the same considerations apply to the argument that management might be tempted to sue before industrial tribunals unofficial, unconstitutional strikers. Even so, if transfer of jurisdiction to the industrial tribunals in respect of all breaches of contracts of employment led management on occasion to bring an employee before a tribunal, for example, for breach of a binding obligation in respect of manning or even for breach of procedure, it would certainly not sound the death knell of the trade union movement and might even remind individuals that obligations freely entered into by themselves or their representatives ought not in fairness to be regarded as breakable at will.[15]

If the new law and new jurisdiction of the tribunals prove capable of meeting fully the labour relations problem of unfair, arbitrary or wrongful dismissal, one may be certain that ultimately the question will be raised of whether the use by the unions of their private collective power to protect their individual members against such dismissal ought not to be barred in the presence of an adequate but peaceful substitute. This particular bridge, however, should be crossed only if and when it is reached. It has yet to be demonstrated that the law and legal procedures are able to cope with all the possible forms of unfairness which may occur in the exercise of the managerial power to dismiss while bearing in mind the conditions needed for the effective and efficient discharge of the function of management.

Assuming the transformation of industrial tribunals into a system of labour courts concerned with disputes arising out of individual labour relations (other than industrial accidents), the question of supply of personnel for the tribunals will have to be considered. The present tribunal members including the lawyer Presidents and chairmen[16] have made a notable success

[14] Another unexpressed reason might be that grievances satisfactorily settled through the industrial tribunals would mean reducing trade unions' and shop stewards' power and influence insofar as this may be derived from the fact that at present the individual employee can look only to his union or shop steward to attend to his grievance. If this were the true reason, it would indicate a disturbing fear of and resistance to change by British trade unionists. A new law beneficial to all employees in theory would require skilled servicing by the unions to ensure that its benefits were enjoyed in practice. The needed change in the law described above involves not a diminution in union or shop steward power but a change in and adaptation of their role. While unions and shop stewards serve employees beneficially, they will not lose an iota of their present power and influence.

[15] The fact that agreements are and can be thrown overboard in important sectors of industry when employees are displeased with their terms in the light of experiencing them creates a positive disincentive to many unions to attend to the training and competence of officials and shop stewards in order that the agreements they negotiate will stand up to the subsequent test of experience.

[16] These may be either barristers or solicitors, including university law teachers. The first generation of chairmen have included a number of ex-colonial and ex-county court judges.

7

of the existing redundancy legislation. Many more members would be required in the future and, if and when the new law is enacted, serious consideration ought to be given to the organisation of conferences and short training programmes in the fields of both labour relations and labour law for existing and potential tribunal members and legal practitioners.

INTERNAL UNION RELATIONS

I would submit that it is a just and necessary corollary of continuing the lawful standing of the closed and union shop that the protection afforded to individual employees against the abuse of trade union or shop floor power should be strengthened.

The proposals of the present Government, which the T.U.C. is adamantly resisting,[17] are in brief to make union registration compulsory, extend the list of compulsory union rules at present required by the Trade Union Acts 1871-76, greatly to strengthen the supervisory power of external adjudicators in the shape of a new Industrial Board in respect of admission to and exclusion from union membership, and to make trade unions liable for non-trade dispute torts (*In Place of Strife,* 1969, paras 107-118; Donovan, 1968, paras 587-727, 751-808).

At present, roughly 340 out of a total of 540 trade unions are voluntarily registered. Compulsory registration of all trade unions is designed by the present Government, in part, to enable all unions to be capable of suing and being sued in their own names but, mainly, to ensure that all trade unions include the minimum statutory content in their rule books. The content additional to that required by the 1871-76 Acts would be an admission rule giving a rejected applicant a right of appeal to a higher committee within the union, clearer disciplinary rules including a full statement of the procedural requirements of ' natural justice ', a grievance or disputes procedure to process internal union disputes other than disciplinary questions, clear rules governing candidacy, voting and the fair conduct of internal union elections, fuller rules specifying the functions and responsibility of union officials and a definition of the place and role of shop stewards within the union structure. Compliance with these compulsory rule stipulations would be secured by the need to register the union and its rule book under the scrutinising powers of a new Registrar of Trade Unions and Employers' Associations.

In addition, certain substantive provisions would be enacted. Apart from the new tort liability outside the area of trade disputes, these substantive provisions would be principally concerned with safeguarding the individual union member from loss of union membership especially in the crucial situation of a closed shop where loss of union membership involves loss of livelihood. The additional safeguards proposed are, in a sense, the counter-

---

[17] See, generally, the T.U.C. documents, *Action on Donovan* (T.U.C., 1968) and *Programme for Action* (T.U.C., 1969b).

part in internal union relations of the proposed new law of unfair dismissal within the sphere of individual labour relations.

Building on the new compulsory admissions rule and internal appeal machinery against a rejection of admission to a union together with the new clearer compulsory rules concerning the disciplining of a union member, administration of the new substantive provisions would be based on a new adjudicatory tribunal, called the Industrial Board, whose personnel would be the lawyer-chairman of the present Industrial Court together with two other members both drawn from the Court's panel of trade union representatives. The Board would have jurisdiction to take appeals from the internal appellate machinery of a union against its support for the rejection of admission to a union and, furthermore, would have jurisdiction with regard to the imposition of a penalty and, more especially, of expulsion on an existing union member. Thus, assuming that a union member were expelled in accordance with the union rules as well as the rules of natural justice and his domestic appeal (if any) was unsuccessful, the member would be able to appeal to the Industrial Board not only on the interpretation and application of the rule book and rules of natural justice but, in addition, on the penalty of expulsion itself. The Board would have jurisdiction to decide whether *on the merits* the expulsion was unfair or arbitrary and on this ground might either vary the penalty (e.g., reduce expulsion to suspension or a fine) or order that the penalty be a suspended one conditional on the good behaviour of the union member concerned.

Trade unions are naturally suspicious of a jurisdictional power of this kind and their suspicion is, in my respectful opinion, a legitimate one insofar as the Board might force upon the union a member whose true motives were of a disruptive character. However, given the composition of the proposed Board, it should not be impossible for the Board members to discern on the evidence the authentic if relatively infrequent disruptist and decide accordingly. It is to be hoped that, if the new provisions are enacted, there will in addition be enacted a provision securing an expelled union member in his employment, subject to his continuing to pay his subscriptions, until such time as the expulsion is confirmed or otherwise by the appellate bodies whether inside or external to the union.

The T.U.C. has endeavoured to counter the above proposals by proposing that union registration should not be made compulsory, that there should not be an extension of tort liability, that the Industrial Board should not have the jurisdictional power described above, but that the T.U.C. should itself draw up a set of model rules along the lines indicated above and persuade its member unions to incorporate these model rules in their rule books as soon as they are able to do so under their own rules amendment provisions (T.U.C., 1969b, paras 63 ff.). In my respectful submission, this counter proposal is both inadequate and lacking in credibility. It is inadequate because it would apply only to the approximately 155 unions affiliated to the T.U.C. and would not require the other 400 or so unions to incorporate in their rule books the rules which the proposed legislation would make compulsory. It lacks credibility, not because the sincerity of the members of the T.U.C. is in the least in doubt, but because the T.U.C. is virtually powerless to enforce any suggestions it wishes to make concerning rule books upon its member unions. The T.U.C. may propose, but its member unions dispose. This impotence was strikingly illustrated in the case of the model rule which the T.U.C. asked its member unions to adopt after *Spring's* case (1956).

In *Spring v. National Amalgamated Stevedores & Dockers Society* ([1956] 1 W.L.R. 585) the court held that the plaintiff had been unlawfully excluded from membership of the defendant union when the latter sought to expel him and others in pursuance of an award of the T.U.C. Disputes Committee based on the poaching of members belonging to another T.U.C. affiliated union by the defendant union in contravention of the Bridlington Agreement. The ground of the decision was that the defendant union's rule book contained no explicit expulsion rule empowering exclusion from membership in order to carry out an award of the Disputes Committee. Thereupon, the T.U.C. at the Annual Conference of 1956 recommended affiliated unions to incorporate in their rule books a model rule empowering the appropriate body of the affiliated union to terminate the membership of any member ' if necessary in order to comply with a decision of the Disputes Committee of the Trades Union Congress '. An examination of the rule books of the unions affiliated to the T.U.C. has revealed that many have not yet incorporated the recommended rule, and this after nearly 14 years. This abysmal response to a request to amend rule books to incorporate a relatively simple rule is unlikely to be bettered in response to a new request to member unions to adopt a far more complex set of model rules; and a poor response would be virtually guaranteed once the threat of impending legislation disappeared.

The closed shop is relevant to the issue of freedom to join and not to join a trade union, to the issue of entry into employment, to trade union bargaining strength and to the protection of union members from arbitrary or unfair decisions within the union power structure whether at national or local levels. I would suggest that a continuance of the closed shop must in the interests of the protection of individual citizens be made to depend upon a reinforcement of the protection which the law affords to individual union members. The fear of the T.U.C. that, if it accedes to compulsory union registration, this will pave the way to future Conservative legislation designed to reduce trade union bargaining power by making de-registration part of a scheme of anti-union sanctions is, in my opinion, misconceived. If a future Conservative Government is determined to introduce crude legislation to restrict the private collective power of trade unions, the absence of compulsory union registration will be the last consideration to deter it. A civilised legal framework for the closed shop will be part of an intelligent and fair extension of the future role of the law in labour relations.

MANAGEMENT-LABOUR RELATIONS

The existence of conflict is not a problem peculiar to British management-labour relations. Conflict is endemic wherever there is human organisation and a division of labour irrespective of what the national economic structure may be. The problems of British industry are those of industrial efficiency and, in certain key sectors, industrial disorder, i.e., disorder in the way in which industrial conflict is from time to time temporarily resolved.

The role which the law can play in raising the general level of industrial efficiency is minimal. Efficiency depends on the quality of those concerned, management, including supervisors, employees generally, union officials, shop stewards, and their education, training and high standards of professional competence. The role of the law is related to the quality of management-labour relations. Having dropped its ill starred and ill conceived proposals for a compulsory conciliation pause and secret strike ballot, the Government's more constructive proposals in the White Paper are about to be issued in an Industrial Relations Bill. In the course of the discussion that follows, I shall suggest that the present proposals may be excessively one sided, while the Conservative Party's proposals in *Fair Deal at Work* as supplemented by the recent statement of Mr. Robert Carr at the Conservative Party Annual Conference are both excessively crude and excessively one sided.

Broadly speaking, the ends served by management-labour relations are the creation of national wealth, both by production and investment, and its distribution in the form of remuneration including fringe benefits, interest and dividends. The adequate and fair distribution of the wealth so created, not only among its producers, but through the community at large in the form of education, housing, health services, pensions etc., constitutes a vital dimension of the productive process. On the distributive side, the law plays a substantial role, if only because distribution of wealth involves in a sense its redistribution, and this requires compulsion; but the principal concern of this paper is with the law's role in management-labour relations as a primary component in the production of national wealth. Its sensible and just distribution will not be further mentioned, but it would be wise not to forget it.

In what ways may the law be relevant to improving the quality of management-labour relations and so helping to raise British industrial productivity and competitiveness? The law means sanctions, sanctions mean coercion. The role, or roles, which coercion, sanctions, and law may play in management-labour relations can never contradict but must reflect the way in which social and human relations are ordered in the wider national society which forms the context for industrial relations. In British society, in my opinion, the law in the major area of management-labour relations may stimulate or may dampen or may ease but cannot directly regulate. It may be used as a light accelerator or light brake or a lubricator of some parts but it cannot be used to drive the entire vehicle. And it can perform these functions only if the agreements, procedures and conditions in industrial relations are in their nature, objectives and fairness such as to make the sympathetic administration of legal standards and sanctions generally acceptable.

Labour law may be regarded as consisting of an extended 'agenda' of basic problems or issues of legal policy in the area of labour relations. The particular items on this notional agenda which I want to examine in connection with the problem of raising the quality of management-labour relations are: freedom of association, recognition of unions for bargaining purposes, especially white collar unions, the legal basis of union bargaining capability, and the legal enforceability of collective agreements in general and of procedure agreements in particular.

(1) FREEDOM OF ASSOCIATION

Freedom of association involves two separate issues: the freedom of the individual employee to belong to a trade union, and the freedom of the individual employee not to belong to a trade union.

The question of whether this second freedom should be guaranteed by the law is, of course, pre-empted once one decides as a matter of general policy to support the closed shop. But the policy of supporting the closed shop is unbalanced and unstable unless it includes a policy of strengthening the protection of the individual employee both in his employment and within his trade union and to these corollaries of the closed shop policy should also be added an escape route for those employees who, on grounds of conscience, do not wish to belong to a trade union. It should not be impossible with the help of the outside adjudicatory services of the Industrial Board to identify such employees and grant them exemption both from the rights of union membership and from all its obligations with the exception, I would suggest, of payment of the union's general subscription, since they will benefit from the bargaining and consultative activities of the union. Such a proposal is not included in the White Paper, while the Conservative Party's proposal in effect to outlaw the closed and, to a substantial degree, the union shop, does not strike a reasonable balance between protection of the individual and support for strong legitimate unions. (*Fair deal at Work*, 1968, pp. 24 ff.) But, I hope that the minds of the politicians will be applied to this particularly acute problem of reconciling organisational needs with individual freedom and independence.

Freedom to belong to a trade union is fundamental to the establishment of voluntary collective bargaining. At present, managerial resistance to freedom of association has to contend with the 1946 Fair Wages Resolution of the House of Commons in the case of contracts with Government departments, the majority of local authorities and the nationalised industries, as well as with trade union power including the use of the secondary boycott. In addition, the anti-union condition in the constitution of the Foremen and Staff Mutual Benefit Society has now been deleted, apparently, under pressure. The Government White Paper proposes to guarantee freedom of association in law by two proposals, the one minor, the other of major significance. The minor proposal is that 'yellow dog' contracts shall be void, while the major proposal is that dismissal for union membership or legitimate union activity should be unlawful because 'unfair', and that the remedies for unfair dismissal shall include reinstatement or punitive damages.

Unfortunately, it would seem that the proposals contained in the Government White Paper, as indeed in the Conservative Party's *Fair Deal at Work*, have been put forward without consideration being given to their repercussions on a fair and rational balance of power in industry. Thus I would suggest, in accordance with the policies which I originally proposed might be pursued, that, if an employee may be richly compensated or reinstated because he was dismissed for joining a trade union, then, the use of the private power of a trade union for the same purpose ought not to be encouraged. Accordingly, the proposals in the White Paper expressly to legalise the secondary boycott should be reconsidered in respect of, to begin with, the use of the secondary boycott for the purpose of countering managerial resistance to freedom of association. This is one sector of labour relations in which effect might be given to the public interest in replacing industrial battle by law and orderly procedures.

(2) RECOGNITION

The issue of recognition affords one of the vital gateways to the future of British trade unionism and industrial relations. If present trends continue, in a mere 15 years' time, the majority of the labour force in this country will be white collar employees, i.e. technical, clerical, supervisory, professional and administrative employees. At the present time, white collar employees number $8\frac{1}{4}$ million of a total $23\frac{3}{4}$ million in the labour force. Unionisation in the public sector of central and local government, nationalised industries and higher education is relatively high at 75 per cent. but in the private sector of industry and trade it is significantly low at 15 per cent. (T.U.C., 1969a, paras 23 and 24). It is in the private sector of industry that a major opportunity for the future lies as well as a major source of trouble. Before looking at the role of the law in the area of recognition disputes, it is necessary to sketch the law of the secondary boycott which in recent years has loomed fairly large in recognition disputes.

Legality of the Secondary Boycott

The secondary boycott is a strategem of industrial conflict used where the embattled union lacks sufficient strength in the plant of the employer in dispute to bring effective pressure to bear through those of its members employed there. The union in dispute may, therefore, try to sharpen the bargaining pressure by having recourse to sympathetic union action in the form of a secondary boycott, i.e., by cutting off supplies to the employer in dispute or by sealing off outlets of distribution of the product of the employer in dispute or by both of these tactics together. The secondary boycott it will be seen involves procuring breach of a commercial contract between the employer in dispute and his outside suppliers or customers. It is for this reason that the law governing the secondary boycott is exclusively common law and that section 3 of the Trade Disputes Act 1906, which refers to breach of the contract of employment only, is irrelevant.[18]

In recent times the utility of the secondary boycott has been in evidence in respect of freedom of association, already referred to, and recognition. It is not merely a coincidence that the three reported cases on the secondary boycott decided since 1964 have all been concerned with recognition. *Square Grip Reinforcement Ltd. v. Macdonald* ([1968] S.L.T. 65) was concerned with a straight employer-union recognition dispute in Scotland. The two major decisions of *Stratford v. Lindley* ([1965] A.C. 269) and *Torquay Hotel Ltd. v. Cousins* ([1969] 1 All E.R. 522) involved inter-union recognition disputes, in the former, a small union challenging the exclusive bargaining rights of the Transport & General Workers' Union, in the latter, the Transport & General itself muscling in on the territory of the National Union of General & Municipal Workers.

Liability in tort for organising a secondary boycott will arise in two principal situations: where the union officials directly induce the external supplier or customer to break off dealings with the employer in dispute in violation of their commercial contract with each other, or where the union officials induce the employees of the supplier or customer to commit unlawful acts which cause their employer to break his commercial contract with the employer in dispute. Such unlawful acts by the sympathetic employees may be disobedience to orders to deliver goods, withdrawal of labour without due strike notice, or withdrawal of labour in breach of procedure whether or not due strike notice is given. Thus, the desirable spread of procedure agreements increases the chance that a secondary boycott will be unlawful.

The law of the secondary boycott as laid down in *Thomson v. Deakin, Stratford v. Lindley* and *Torquay Hotel Ltd. v. Cousins* implies that such a boycott would be lawful only in limited circumstances and only if restraint is exercised, i.e., only where the pressure used is a complete withdrawal of their labour by sympathetic employees after due strike notice and no procedure agreement was incorporated in their contracts of employment to make their stoppage a breach of those contracts. It should be emphasised that whether an application is made to the courts for an interlocutory (emergency) injunction on the basis of affidavit evidence for an allegedly unlawful secondary boycott is exclusively a matter for decision of the management in dispute.

---

[18] The Government's proposal in the White Paper is to extend s. 3 to cover secondary boycotts by, in effect, deleting ' of employment '.

Union-Management Recognition Disputes

Take first the straight recognition dispute between union and management, which the rise of the white collar employee and his unionisation is likely to make increasingly prevalent in the private sector unless management takes prudent forethought. There are now two organisations which officially include among their concerns recognition disputes between management and union. They are the Department of Employment and Productivity and the Commission on Industrial Relations. The powers of the Industrial Relations Officers of the D.E.P., though it is proposed to extend them in practice, are very limited in this sphere as has been demonstrated by the history of the National Union of Bank Employees' fight for recognition in the banking industry.

But now the Commission on Industrial Relations has come on the scene with the concurrence of the C.B.I. and T.U.C. Established by Royal Warrant, it has no statutory basis as yet and no statutory powers. References to it can be made by the D.E.P. only with in practice the consent of both the C.B.I. and the T.U.C. A number of relatively minor references have already been made but, if present control by the C.B.I. and T.U.C. persists, there is a real danger that the Commission will be slowly stifled into insignificance. It is disturbing that such a potentially valuable invention as the C.I.R. should be subject to the veto of the two main interested parties. The White Paper proposes to place the Commission on a statutory basis and to give it a reserve power to hold a secret ballot among employees to determine whether they wish a particular union to act as their bargaining agent. The Government further proposes to confer on the Secretary of State for Employment and Productivity power, where management refuses to comply with a C.I.R. recommendation to recognise a particular union for bargaining purposes, to confer on that union the right to take management to the Industrial Court for legally binding arbitration in each dispute arising between them.[19]

Assuming that these statutory powers are conferred on the C.I.R. and Secretary of State, as they undoubtedly should be if we are to develop a system capable of making informed and rational decisions about the spread of collective bargaining, the legal freedom of a union to try to force recognition by a strike of those of its members employed by the employer in dispute should be left untouched notwithstanding the fact that the union may have had conferred on it by statute the power of recourse to compulsory arbitration, since these powers would not go the whole way to enforcing full recognition. On the other hand, the capability of the union to have recourse to a secondary boycott should be left subject to its present legal restriction at management's option. A union ought not, in my opinion, to be given the green light to have recourse to secondary boycott action by expressly legalising the secondary boycott in any trade dispute situation, as appears to be the

---

[19] *In Place of Strife* (1969), paras. 56-61: this will be a return to the compulsory arbitration procedure before the Industrial Disputes Tribunal but on a case-by-case basis.

Government's present intention. The outlawing of the ' yellow dog ' contract and, above all, the enactment of an unfair dismissal law should enable a union to organise in sufficient strength either to compel recognition by direct action or to secure recognition through the orderly procedures of the C.I.R. and the D.E.P. The Government should not go out of its way to encourage dislocation by secondary boycott in such situations, not to speak of under-cutting the services of the C.I.R. and D.E.P. In other words, the common law of the secondary boycott should be left where it is enabling a lawful secondary boycott to be imposed with restraint in a limited number of situations. But, it cannot be too often emphasised that if a secondary boycott is unlawful at common law the enforcement of the law is exclusively a matter of management's decision.[20]

Inter-Union Recognition Disputes

This more complicated type of recognition dispute is likely to become more common and more acute in the years ahead. As events in the steel industry in the latter half of 1969 have indicated, the blue collar unions too have seen the writing on the wall and are beginning to make strenuous efforts to diversify into the growth sector of the labour force, even if it means colliding violently with existing white collar unions.

On June 5 1969 a Special Congress of the T.U.C. met in Croydon and unanimously adopted the proposals contained in the very important docu-ment entitled, *Industrial Relations—A Programme for Action.* One proposal adopted was for the amendment of Rule 12 of the T.U.C. constitution to empower its General Council to intervene in the case of inter-union recogni-tion disputes, making use of its Disputes Committee if required, and to provide that the unions concerned comply with the Council's decision. But what if an affiliate feels strong enough to ignore the Council's decision and to be unmoved by suspension or expulsion or their threat? The White Paper proposes to support the Council with the services of the Commission on Industrial Relations together with ministerial power in the ultimate analysis to give effect to a C.I.R. recommendation by financial penalties against the employing organisation and, if need be, the recalcitrant union.

A combination of the work of the T.U.C. General Council and the supportive services of the C.I.R. and D.E.P. will form sufficient means of arriving at a fair and sensible solution to any inter-union recognition dispute. The use of outside economic power to impose one union's will by industrial dislocation should be discouraged when adequate peaceful means exist. My suggestion is, therefore, that careful reconsideration should be given to the proposal expressly to legalise the secondary boycott insofar as this industrial strategem may be resorted to for the purpose of dictating a solution to an inter-union recognition dispute. Again, it is worth stressing that the burden

---

[20] It may be that members of British management are too unaggressive and too concerned to avoid trouble to insist on the orderly use of industrial power even with the law's help: *sed quaere.*

of enforcing the existing common law relating to the secondary boycott must unavoidably rest on management.

Clearly, there are trade unionists who desire not only that special institutions exist to enable them to secure their bargaining rights vis à vis management or indeed vis à vis other unions but, in addition, wish to be totally free to deploy their own industrial power where that power appears great enough to secure success. It is highly debatable whether this is a reasonable or necessary attitude to adopt, at any rate if British management is skilled and imaginative enough to take advantage of working with trade unions rather than wage a relentless battle against them. But, if management's attitude is reasonable, then, in my opinion the law should be so adjusted as to assume a reasonable attitude on the part of trade union leaders and officials also. What I have suggested above, namely, to leave the common law of the secondary boycott where it is, at least so far as freedom of association and recognition disputes are concerned, is no more than a minor proposal to retain the present availability of the law as a very light brake on industrial disorder.

Bargaining Capability and the Law

For official as for unofficial industrial action, the principal legal basis of bargaining power is the right to strike lawfully, although in practice the less dramatic forms of lawful action of working to rule or a ban on voluntary overtime may be nearly as effective. Other forms of action less than a full strike, like go-slow or a ban on compulsory overtime, will involve breaches of contract of employment. Now, let us turn to consider the unthinkable.

The foundation of the right to strike as the law stands at present, is the power of each employee to withdraw his or her labour lawfully in concert with others. The orthodox view was that this power depended on the power of each individual employee to terminate his or her contract of employment lawfully by giving and working out the due period of notice. In *Rookes v. Barnard* ([1964] A.C. 1129), *Stratford v. Lindley* (1965) and *Morgan v. Fry at first instance* ([1967] 2 All E.R. 386), non-binding judicial dicta suggested that, since the industrial purpose of a strike was not to sever the employment relationship but merely to suspend it, the withdrawal of labour even after due strike notice was invariably in breach of contract, as suspension of a contract by one side only is not a recognised power in English law. However, in *Morgan v. Fry* on appeal ([1968] 3 W.L.R. 506) the Court of Appeal under Lord Denning, M.R. saved the legal foundation of the right to strike for the time being on the ground that withdrawal of labour after due strike notice suspends the employment contract by reason of an *implied* agreement to that effect between employer and employee. Davies, L.J. agreed with this while suggesting yet another possibility, but Russell, L.J. did not agree; and the views of the House of Lords are awaited. It is to be hoped that their lordships will appreciate the need to give formal recognition to the right

of employees to withdraw their labour lawfully provided only that the
orderly procedure is adopted of giving and observing due strike notice.

Meanwhile, throughout the period since 1964 when the very legal under-
pinning of the right to strike was in doubt, strikes, especially unofficial,
unconstitutional strikes, rose steadily in number but management had no
recourse to the courts against their individual employees even though their
contract was often doubly unlawful in that stopping work was in breach of
procedure as well as without due notice. The reason for management's self
restraint is too well known to spell out and was given by one team of
industrial management after another in evidence before the Royal Commission on Trade Unions and Employers' Associations.[21]

Why then trouble to establish that a strike may be called lawfully
provided due strike notice is given and worked out? The answer lies, if the
law of strike action is to be a rational one, in the legal pressure which may
be brought to bear upon the leaders of the strike, whether union officials
or shop stewards or others leading a strike unofficially. This pressure might
be in the form of management asking the courts for an interlocutory injunction to prevent the strike leaders either from threatening an unlawful strike
or from actually calling their rank and file employees out on an unlawful
strike. In other words, a rational law of strike action would, I suggest, lean
in favour of requiring that there should be a pause of at least seven days'
strike notice before work or production is brought to a halt.

But, at present, under section 3 (First Limb) of the Trade Disputes Act
1906 and under the provisions of the Trade Disputes Act 1965, leaders both
official and unofficial who threaten or call an unlawful withdrawal of
labour, are expressly immunised from liability provided only that they acted
in contemplation or furtherance of a trade dispute. Unthinkable though it
may be, I would suggest that for the law of strike action to be rational in the
sense of requiring minimum standards of orderly procedure, section 3 (First
Limb) of the 1906 Act and the whole of the Trade Disputes Act 1965 should
be repealed as one part of a carefully devised legislative pattern. Thus, it
would also be essential to establish seven days as the minimum strike notice
period whatever the period of notice which an employee is required to give
to terminate his own individual contract of employment, and, also, to
provide grounds of justification for calling or threatening to call a lightning
strike where the subject matter of the dispute or managerial conduct does
not brook delay or where the disputes procedure available is not a certificated one.

---

[21] One of the most serious aspects of present industrial disorder, at least from a
lawyer's point of view, is that the power to strike in practice is now utterly divorced
from the right to strike in law so that the controversy aroused by *Rookes v. Barnard*
in this respect and the solution proposed by the majority in *Morgan v. Fry* (C.A.)
and the keen anticipation with which the House of Lords' decision in *Morgan* is
awaited are all simply irrelevant to the present conduct of British industrial relations
—unless management avails itself of the conspiracy-to-break-a-contract liability which
logically stems from *Rookes v. Barnard;* but this would be an unsatisfactory substitute
for the statutory reconsideration suggested below.

So, to the present ground of justification for inducing breach of contract, namely, unreasonable moral risk,[22] might be added unreasonable physical risk (striking against dangerous work conditions, including risk of illness), unfair dismissal (subject to the availability of industrial tribunal proceedings with the possibility of reinstatement, etc.), and such other justifications as consultation and analysis might reveal. Where a procedure agreement would make a strike unlawful notwithstanding strike notice, the leaders would be liable to be enjoined for threatening or inducing breach of contract of employment only if the procedure had been duly certificated as fair and reasonable by an independent body like the Commission on Industrial Relations, as will be discussed later.[23]

If the Conservative Party, on returning to power, carry out their pledge in *Fair Deal at Work* to repeal the Trade Disputes Act 1965, they will only compound the present irrationality of the law of strike action. The repeal of the 1965 Act would mean that the strike leader will be exposed to liability for threatening an unlawful strike but will not be liable at all if he actually calls such a strike. It should be emphasised that repealing the 1965 Act and the relevant provisions of the 1906 Act will not render a strike leader liable to an interlocutory injunction in tort if the rank and file members themselves took spontaneous action, i.e., if the leader did not in fact lead. On the other hand, a strike commenced unlawfully, but unofficially, would involve the union officials concerned in tortious conspiracy if the unlawful strike were subsequently made official. But this possibility would direct the pressure surely in the right direction, namely, towards securing minimum standards of deliberate orderly procedure in industrial disputes. Today, with highly educated and well trained union officials and shop stewards, it ought no longer to be necessary to believe that they are unable to understand the simple legal position just described or know how to comply with it.

Since these proposals would make union officials or shop stewards liable to an injunction if, after a strike had broken out spontaneously, they then sought to jump in front of it in order to lead it (as opposed to negotiating to settle it), the repeal of the 1965 Act and of section 3 (First Limb) of the 1906 Act would help to reinforce the peace making role which the T.U.C. voluntarily undertook in respect of unofficial industrial action by its Downing Street Agreement of June 18 1969.

The anonymously authored proposals in *Fair Deal at Work* which the Conservative Party leaders continue to insist is their considered intention, are, in my respectful opinion, either obsolete because overtaken by events like the Downing Street Agreement, or unnecessary as in the proposal to outlaw sympathetic union action in apparent ignorance of the impact of what the judiciary has already done, or inadequate as in the law of unfair

---

[22] See *Brimelow v. Casson* [1924] 1 Ch. 302.

[23] Plainly, the legality of threatening or leading industrial action less than a strike, like go-slow or a ban on compulsory overtime, would need to be expressly established, e.g., by requiring a minimum 7 days' notice before *any* direct action might be started, again, subject to industrially sensible exceptions.

dismissal with its placement by the Conservative Party of the initial burden of proof that the dismissal was unfair on the employee, or irrational and even harmful as in the pledge merely to repeal the Trade Disputes Act 1965 and the proposals to introduce a sixty days cooling off period as well as to outlaw the closed shop and render the union shop unenforceable by direct industrial action.

In the area of British management-labour relations, the last five years have witnessed an historical break-through in knowledge and understanding. Merely to try by legal means to chip off a piece of union bargaining power at this point or at that or, indeed, to inflate the bargaining power of unions and the shop floor as if this were a good thing in itself, is to tackle a modern problem with the concepts of the past. To stimulate high quality management-labour relations, to dampen down industrial disorder, to substitute orderly procedures and adequate remedies for industrial battle requires a many sided and continuing process of industrial and legal statesmanship at every level. The *power* to strike or employ other forms of economic pressure cannot be absolutely prohibited nor can its exercise be effectively reduced, nor would this be desirable. But, if the English law of industrial conflict is to make sense and be a help to rather than an irrelevant excrescence on the British industrial relations system, its rules should be designed for the strictly limited objective of regulating the *manner* in which the power to have recourse to direct action is used by affording management the right to require leaders to employ deliberation, subject to reasoned exceptions, and to follow independently certificated procedures, and unions corresponding rights in respect of managerial good faith.

COLLECTIVE AGREEMENTS AND THE LAW

In *Ford Motor Company v. A.E.F.* ([1969] 2 Q.B. 303) the British judiciary in the person of Geoffrey Lane J. demonstrated to those prepared to see how much water has flowed under the bridge since the *Taff Vale* case.[24] The learned Judge in effect refused to thrust the law crudely into a vital area of management-labour relations without the thorough parliamentary discussion and consultation with both sides of industry, which ought prudently and properly to precede so great an innovation as making procedure agreements legally enforceable.

This does not mean, however, that the question of legal enforcement of disputes procedure provisions should be removed from the ' agenda ' of basic issues of legal policy in labour relations. It does mean that there is still a long way to go in raising the standards of such procedural provisions and in ensuring that an employing company too may be liable for bad faith or unjustified prevarication in following the agreed procedure. Furthermore, progress on the disputes procedure side of labour relations is bound to be uneven as between one industrial sector or another or among individual companies.

[24] *Taff Vale Rly. Co. v. Amalgamated Society of Railway Servants* [1901] A.C. 426.

There is unlikely to come a particular day on which it is fair to make all disputes procedures legally binding, like reaching a day when all traffic switches from the left to the right hand side of the road.

Certainly, the Conservative Party proposals should be given a second very hard look. First, the belief of the anonymous authors of *Fair Deal at Work* that repealing section 4 (4) of the Trade Union Act 1871 ' would put collective agreements on a par with any other type of contract ' is, with respect, utterly misconceived.[25] Section 4 (4) applies only to agreements ' between one trade union and another ' i.e., between trade union and employers' association, since the latter is at present included in the statutory definition of a ' trade union '. If employers' associations were taken out of the definition of a ' trade union ' so that section 4 (4) no longer applied to national agreements or other agreements to which an association is a party, this would merely place national agreements on a par with single company collective agreements, but not with any other type of contract. The sole effect would be that collective agreements both between unions and employers' associations and between unions and single employing organisations, both national, company and plant agreements, would be on the same legal footing, i.e., binding in honour alone because of lack of intention to create legal relations, as was held in the *Ford Motor* case.

That national and company agreements should be on a different legal footing has neither rhyme nor reason and the appropriate legal adjustment should be made despite T.U.C. opposition which at this point is, with respect, groundless. But the obvious Conservative Party intention to make all the terms of all collective agreements legally binding, subject only to an express contrary intention by the parties, is unsound (*Fair Deal at Work*, 1968, pp. 32 ff). In practice the question of legal enforceability of collective agreements arises for useful discussion in respect of two possible provisions only : the disputes procedure provision and a fixed term provision, i.e., a provision that the agreement shall remain in force for a fixed term like one, two or three years. What has been said about the procedure provision applies equally to the fixed term provision. There is still a long way to go before all collective agreements become detailed signed documents and indeed before the high professional competence on both sides, at present found only in certain sectors of industry, is sufficiently widespread to ensure that fixed term agreements whenever made will be such as to command the confidence of both negotiating sides and the employees on the job.

In developing disputes procedures which conform with the standards of modern labour relations, in developing collective agreements of consistently high standards, and in transforming the central area of the British system of management-labour relations by stimulating through recognition procedures collective bargaining between management and their white collar employees, the Commission on Industrial Relations should have a key role to play. This will not be the case in its present limited role when it is

---

[25] *Fair Deal at Work* (1968), p. 32. The T.U.C. apparently share the Conservative Party's misunderstanding: see *Action on Donovan* (T.U.C., 1968), paras. 123-125.

little better than a standing extension of the traditional Court of Enquiry procedure. Given an adequate statutory basis and adequate statutory powers, however, the Commission could spearhead the developments which it is increasingly becoming apparent must take place in the British system of industrial relations, since these developments can only validly take place stage-by-stage after thorough investigation and consideration.

Thus, the Commission on Industrial Relations should have power to certificate a disputes procedure as conforming with the requirements of modern labour relations, i.e., as being in effect a fair and reasonable piece of procedural quasi-law. This would then render strike leaders liable to be enjoined at the instance of management if procedure were not followed while the Employment and Productivity Secretary might be given power by Order to make that particular procedure legally binding in the sense that the employing company might be sued by the union for a limited financial penalty, e.g., for unreasonable delay in using the procedure, while management would have to elect between enjoining the strike leaders or suing the union in its turn for a limited penalty.

This pathfinding function will have to be vested in some such body as the Commission on Industrial Relations unless both sides of industry are themselves able to achieve the necessary goals. Experience, however, has shown that this is highly unlikely and it is improbable that history now has enough time left to pursue the experiment in *unfettered* autonomy any further. Nevertheless, whatever aid, support or stimulation is given from outside, the central area in which the necessary developments must take place is the area of autonomous management-labour relations. Here, today, lies a major opportunity for the initiative of management bearing in mind that the unionisation of white collar employees in the private sector of industry and trade is still only 15 per cent.

In the last two decades of the 19th century when trade unionism was a struggling youth, employers might have introduced an orderly and even legally regulated system of industrial relations, but most could think only of a negative resistance. When the General Strike collapsed, there was another historic opportunity for employers and management to be far sighted and establish a carefully thought out and fair structure of industrial relations. But the opportunity was not perceived. After World War II especially in the period of reconstruction, another moment for vision was let slip by both management and unions. Now, a further and perhaps final chance presents itself to management in the private sector of industry, finance and commerce. The opportunity resides in the present weakness of white collar employees in the private enterprise sector of the economy. Private enterprise management would do well to ask itself this serious question: is white collar unionism in private industry going to remain in its present relatively weak state or are white collar employees going to organise and, if necessary, organise militantly to try to extract by economic force what they regard as their rights from management?

My suggestion is that it would be wiser and safer to assume that the latter development will take place, to analyse the principles for a mutually equitable and orderly system of management-labour relations, to drop simple resistance, to encourage independent unions for white collar employees and to negotiate with them a labour relations structure based on those principles for which there are now many authoritative supporters within as well as outside the ranks of industrial management. Unbroken industrial peace is a fantasy; but orderly and efficient labour relations are not impossible if management can itself adopt and encourage in others constructive attitudes and reflexes based on adequate analysis and joint consultation. This will have special importance as increasing technological sophistication and industrial inter-dependence accumulates dislocative and therefore bargaining power for key groups of white collar employees.

We are already into the second industrial revolution. A corresponding revolution in managerial approach to relations with the employees of the future is indicated. For such an approach neither the law, nor the T.U.C., nor special legal machinery like the C.I.R., nor any other form of Government intervention can be an adequate substitute. The role of all these agencies will remain supportive only so long as our kind of free democratic society survives. What applies to management applies also to the unions and to all, like labour relationists, labour lawyers and industrial journalists, who make the concerns of industrial relations the main study and activity of their lives. It is insufficient for union leaders or management to mumble in their beards about fundamental issues concerning which the general public should be well informed, like the issue of the ' status quo ', the demand by unions and shop stewards for extensive information concerning the financial side of employing companies, or the issue variously called ' industrial democracy ' or ' workers' control '. For the sake of the future well-being of the nation, it will I believe prove to be vital that communications between the industrial relations system and the general public should be open and crystal clear.

In these fundamentally important activities and in this momentous debate, lawyers have a positive and substantial part to play. There is a great need for independent thought and analysis. My present tentative contribution to this urgent discussion may be broadly summed up as follows:

SUMMARY

1. All individual labour relations disputes arising out of breach of contract of employment including unfair dismissal should be capable of being settled by the relatively rapid, inexpensive and informal procedures of the industrial tribunals with further appeal on points of law;
2. The minimum condition of legal recognition for the closed shop should be the effective strengthening in law of protection for the individual union member or prospective member, subject to discretion concerning ' disruptists ';

8

3. In the central area of collective labour relations, the following policy suggestions are made:
   a) criminal or civil sanctions against individual employees are impractical and best forgotten. Sanctions can only be realistically considered in relation to leaders and organisations;
   b) the objective for a rational law of strike action (or other forms of direct action) should be limited if it is to be realistic, i.e., not the chopping down of managerial or trade union or shop floor power but insistence on a reasonable degree of orderliness and time for second thoughts in the run up to direct action;
   c) it is an ancient truth that only fair and reasonable laws will command respect. Disputes procedures are a kind of quasi-law. To command respect and to justify sanctions for its breach, a disputes procedure should be independently certificated as fair and reasonable in accordance with modern labour relations standards. The C.I.R. is at present the obvious body in which to vest this certificating power;
   d) where adequate procedures and principles are provided by the law to deal with an identified class of industrial dispute, the use of private power, including private collective power, to impose a solution should be legally discouraged.

London School of Economics and Political Science

REFERENCES

DONOVAN (1968). *Report* of the Royal Commission on Trade Unions and Employers' Associations. Cmnd. 3623. London, H.M.S.O.
Fair Deal at Work (1968). Conservative Political Centre, No. 44. London.
In Place of Strife (1969). Cmnd. 3888. London, H.M.S.O.
MINISTRY OF LABOUR (1961). *Security and Change*. London, H.M.S.O.
T.U.C. (1968). *Action on Donovan*. Trades Union Congress, November 1968. London.
T.U.C. (1969a). *Collective Bargaining and Trade Union Development in Private Sector —Non Manual*. Trades Union Congress, March 1969. London.
T.U.C. (1969b). *Programme for Action*. Trades Union Congress, June 1969. London.

WAGES AND LABOUR COSTS

GRAHAM L. REID

I

While a forward look into the 1970s can predict with reasonable certainty some developments in the evolution of the changing industrial relations system—with some qualifications on the exact timing of developments—it is much more difficult to make a quantitative forecast of the probable trend of wages and labour costs. Indeed, experts disagree even on short-run forecasts of wage trends, and at the end of 1969 there was no general agreement on whether 1970 would see (as it has) a 'wage explosion' with unions getting very large increases in wages, or whether the maintenance of a relatively restrictive economic policy would tend to hold down the rate of increase of earnings. Although the variety of economic and political variables affecting labour costs even in the short run would suggest that a forecast for the 1970s is impossible, some prospective view is essential. The history of the British economy since World War II emphasises the enormous importance of maintaining stable unit labour costs to preserve our international competitiveness, and much of the recent dissatisfaction with the industrial relations system and its collective bargaining methods also stemmed from the ill-effects on unit labour costs and prices. This brief survey therefore examines some of the factors which are likely to have an important effect on wages and labour costs in the 1970s. Section II considers the extent to which past trends give any guide to future performance, and Sections III and IV look in more detail at the major influences of the 1970s.

II

In discussing past and future trends, one is inevitably faced by definitional problems. Total labour costs, the aggregate amount spent by a company in connection with its employment of labour, comprise two major elements:

a) wages and salaries, which include certain payments for time not worked such as holiday pay and sick pay;
b) supplementary labour costs, including social security contributions and pension and welfare contributions made by the employer on behalf of his employees, expenditure on subsidised facilities, and the net effect of labour taxes or subsidies such as the Selective Employment Tax and Regional Employment Premium. This net effect may be a credit or a debit or be neutral.

Since we are interested in wages and labour costs from the point of view of their impact on prices and competitiveness, we must consider not simply the trend of money costs, but that of *unit* wage and labour costs. This means taking into account changes in output, and also changes in the proportion of time paid for but not worked: clearly, an extra week's holiday or a shorter working week may have no effect on money labour costs, but output would fall because of the reduced time at work, with a consequent rise in *unit* labour costs. The discussion which follows will concentrate on unit costs, and will deal with labour costs rather than simply wage and salary costs.

Table I

UNIT WAGE AND SALARY COSTS AND UNIT LABOUR COSTS (1960 = 100)

		1960	1962	1964	1966	1968
Manufacturing						
Industry	w&s	100	108·8	108·0	119·1	122·5
	LC	100	109·7	109·2	123·4	123·7
of which						
Metal Manufacture	w&s	100	115·2	114·1	129·6	135·2
	LC	100	116·4	115·3	134·1	137·5
Engineering etc.	w&s	100	105·8	105·9	114·7	116·7
	LC	100	106·7	107·1	119·0	118·1
Vehicles	w&s	100	110·2	108·0	112·9	118·3
	LC	100	110·8	109·0	116·6	119·8
Textiles	w&s	100	109·2	108·1	118·3	112·2
	LC	100	109·8	109·2	122·4	113·1
Mining & Quarrying	w&s	100	100·3	100·9	108·2	108·2
	LC	100	101·1	101·6	111·4	115·5
Gas, Electricity,	w&s	100	103·0	107·0	115·7	111·0
Water	LC	100	103·6	108·2	117·7	114·5
WHOLE ECONOMY	w&s	100	109·6	112·9	123·7	130·4
	LC	100	110·1	113·9	127·2	135·2

Source: Calculated from *Employment & Productivity Gazette,* November 1969, pp. 1090-1.

This latter point raises a statistical problem which makes it difficult to use past trends as a guide to what is likely to happen in the future. The movement of labour costs is dependent on both the increase of wages and salaries and the increase of supplementary labour costs, and while information on wages and salaries is plentiful, data on supplementary labour costs —and hence on total labour costs—are fragmentary. The Department of Employment and Productivity has carried out for productive industry two surveys of labour costs, one for 1964 and one for 1968, but the results of the 1968 survey are not expected until late in 1970: for 1964 results, see Department of Employment and Productivity (1968) and Ministry of Labour (1966, 1967). These surveys give a snapshot of money labour costs at points in time, but since 1968 the DEP has combined an index of money wage and labour costs (based on the 1964 enquiry) with an index of output per man to produce an index of *unit* wage and labour costs. This yields some useful information on the structure of labour costs throughout the 1960s in several industry sectors and the whole economy. Table I shows the increases in unit wage and salary costs and unit labour costs between 1960 and 1968.

In the whole economy, unit labour costs rose by 35·2 per cent. between 1960 and 1968, compared with 30·4 per cent. for unit wage costs. For manufacturing industry the difference was much smaller, at 23·7 per cent. and 22·5 per cent. respectively, while in each manufacturing industry sector the rates of increase of unit labour costs and unit wage costs were roughly similar, though there were substantial variations between sectors in the extent to which unit wage and labour costs had risen. The trends over time are interesting. In all sectors, unit labour costs, after moving at much the same rate as unit wage costs from 1960-64, had shot ahead by 1966, only to fall back again by 1968 in some sectors. The explanation for this is the introduction and phasing of the Selective Employment Tax. The tax began to be collected in 1966, so that in all sectors labour costs increased. SET rebates and Regional Employment Premium for manufacturing industry came into effect in 1967, and the net effect of these taxes and subsidies in manufacturing industry was to reduce unit labour costs below what they would have been in the absence of the taxes. Of course, unit labour costs did not actually fall in all industry sectors; in vehicles and metal manufacturing the 1967 increases in wages were such as to wipe out the advantage given by the SET rebates and premiums. In textiles and engineering, though, unit labour costs in 1968 were still below the 1966 level, as Table I shows. In mining & quarrying, which did not receive SET rebate, unit labour costs between 1966 and 1968 increased by almost 4 per cent despite stable unit wage costs.

Table II

SUPPLEMENTARY LABOUR COSTS AS PERCENTAGE OF TOTAL LABOUR COSTS

	1960	1964	1968
Manufacturing Industry	5·7	6·8	6·6
of which			
Engineering etc.	5·4	6·4	6·5
Vehicles	5·1	6·0	6·3
Metal Manufacture	5·4	6·4	7·0
Gas, Electricity, Water	8·5	9·6	11·3
Mining & Quarrying	7·1	7·8	13·0

Source: Calculated from Table I and DEP 1964 survey.

The data in Table I suggest two tentative conclusions which can be examined with the help of other evidence. First, since unit labour costs have in general increased by only a little more than unit wage costs, the proportion of supplementary labour costs in total labour costs has increased only slightly in the period since 1960. However, Table I only shows the relative change in wage costs and labour costs, and gives no information on how important supplementary labour costs were as a proportion of total labour costs. Table II shows this for manufacturing industry and a number of sectors in 1960, 1964 and 1968.

The manufacturing industry sectors were roughly similar with supplementary labour costs accounting for between 6 and 7 per cent. of total labour costs, while the two non-manufacturing sectors had proportions of 11·3 per cent. and 13 per cent. This difference is again explained by SET, which would appear as a net credit to the manufacturing sectors (i.e. supplementary labour costs would be reduced by virtue of the premium) and had a neutral effect on the non-manufacturing sectors. It should also be noted that the more complete view of supplementary labour costs which includes holiday pay (included in wages & salaries in Table I) would increase all the figures in Table II by about 5 percentage points. There is also the cost of employer-subsidised facilities, not included in Table II at all, but judging by their importance in the 1964 survey, these would be unlikely to account for more than one per cent. of total labour costs.

Table III

EMPLOYERS' CONTRIBUTION AS PERCENTAGE OF INCOME FROM EMPLOYMENT

	1960	1968
Manufacturing Industry	5·5	8·0
Gas, Electricity, Water	8·4	10·9
Mining & Quarrying	6·9	12·3
WHOLE ECONOMY	6·9	9·0
Social Security Contributions	(2·8)	(4·4)
Other contributions (pensions, etc.)	(4·1)	(4·6)

Source: Calculated from National Income & Expenditure 1969, Tables 17 and 19.

The second conclusion suggested by Table I is that any disproportionate increase in unit labour costs over the period 1960-68 has been largely due to the effect of the Selective Employment Tax. This in turn suggests that the other major components of supplementary labour costs may not have shown much variation, as a proportion of total labour costs, in the period 1960-68. As far as the two large items are concerned, legally required payments and private pension and welfare contributions, this is not borne out by other evidence, for as Table III shows, between 1960 and 1968 there were considerable increases in employers' contributions as a proportion of income from employment (roughly equal to total labour costs excluding the net effects of SET).

Employers' contributions showed a significant increase in all sectors, notably in mining & quarrying, and amounted to 9 per cent. of income from employment in the whole economy in 1968. It is interesting that whereas contributions to pension and welfare schemes increased by only slightly more than wages & salaries, legally required contributions rose very substantially from 2·8 per cent. of total income to 4·4 per cent., and were very largely responsible for the increased share of employer contributions.

This brief review of the scanty evidence on the growth and structure of labour costs contains two main pointers to the future. First, the components of total labour costs have changed relatively little between 1960 and 1968. The increase of wages & salaries has continued to be the main determinant of total labour costs. Although there have been suggestions in the past that 'fringe benefits' or supplementary labour costs will become a much larger proportion of total labour costs and will thus have an important influence on labour costs in the near future, the evidence of the period 1960-68 does not support this view. It indicates rather that supplementary labour costs will have a marginal significance, being more important in some sectors of industry than in others. Secondly, insofar as supplementary labour costs have been important, it has been through legally required payments— either payroll taxes or social security contributions—rather than through collectively bargained pension or welfare schemes. There are other significant points in the period 1960-68 which may have relevance in the future, but the problem is to know how far past and present conditions will persist into the future, and how far a new set of circumstances will influence labour costs in different ways.

III

It is at this point that we begin to indulge in speculation about what will happen in the 1970s, and though it is not difficult to list a number of factors likely to affect wages and labour costs, the exact importance of each is quite uncertain. Rather than simply cataloguing these factors and going through them one by one, we shall first deal in this Section with certain general issues of importance, and in the next Section we shall then discuss in turn factors affecting wages and factors affecting supplementary labour costs.

It is impossible in such a look into the future to rule out the effects of political decisions as to the development of the economy, and in the period up to 1975 there are four major political decisions which could have a very significant effect on wages and labour costs throughout the 1970s. First, there is the proposed legislation on *equal pay*. At the time of writing, the Government's proposals have been issued only as a Bill, but this states that the criterion will be equal pay for work of equal value, and that the full implementation of equality should be achieved by 1975 (Department of

Employment and Productivity, 1969, p. 935). The effect on unit labour costs will be both direct and indirect. The direct effect is simply that of increasing women's pay in relevant jobs to 100 per cent. of men's pay instead of the present 70-90 per cent. Insofar as companies can achieve a simultaneous increase in productivity unit labour costs will rise by less than the increase in money wages. But such an increase in productivity seems unlikely. The whole argument for equal pay rests on the assumptions that women have been exploited by being paid less than the wage a man would have received had he been producing the same amount, and that job evaluation can establish a wage equal to that in a male job of comparable productivity. After such a wage had been established, an increase in women's productivity without a corresponding wage increase could be and would be taken as re-establishment of the position of exploitation, and as evidence for a further wage increase.

As well as the direct cost effects, the indirect or secondary effects of equal pay through the wage structure could be important. For one thing, we have no knowledge of how lower-paid male workers will react to a substantial rise in women's wages. Will they accept this as being desirable in the interests of equality (an acceptance which would run counter to the decades of apathy shown by large trade unions towards the practical appli-cation of equal pay), or will they press for the re-establishment of the male-female differential? In this situation the employer cannot win : the legislation may prevent the differential being re-established, since any increase in male pay may by law have to be extended to female pay for comparable jobs, and this would also apply to any increases achieved by men in the course of normal collective bargaining. Clearly, the legislation will have to be most carefully drafted, for it would be undesirable for there to be a general link between male and female wage rates which was independent of the produc-tivity of the two groups and the different costs of employing them. The effect of equal pay legislation on unit labour costs will therefore be a compound of a number of factors, but in some companies employing women at a relatively low proportion of the male rate, it could be an important influence on unit labour costs, certainly in the transitional period. A DEP study (Department of Employment and Productivity, 1970, pp. 4-6) covering a number of companies estimated that in the period up to 1975, the median direct increase in the wage/salary bill would be 13 per cent. in retail distribution and 18 per cent. in clothing. There was, however, a very wide range of estimates among the companies surveyed, e.g. 0-18 per cent. in engineering, 0-21 per cent. in food, 0-31 per cent. in retail distribution, and 0-32 per cent. in hotels and catering. Thus, although the overall effect of equal pay on total direct costs was estimated to be only $3\frac{1}{2}$ per cent., the direct effects in some companies and industries could be quite substantial. This conclusion is reinforced by the fact that the DEP study adopted the simple ' equal pay for the same work ' definition, and not the much more far-reaching ' equal pay for work of equal value '. Under the latter definition, an estimate of the cost of equal pay would certainly be higher than that made in the DEP study, especially if full allowance were made for the indirect costs of equal pay, as a result of its repercussions on the wage structure.

The second political decision is Britain's proposed *entry to the Common Market*. There are three possible ways in which Common Market membership might affect unit labour costs. First, it seems to be generally agreed that under the Community's present agricultural policy, the price of food in Britain would rise as the transitional period progressed. The amount of the increase and the effect on the cost of living are matters of dispute, and since the ending of farm subsidies would permit tax cuts for hard-hit low-income groups, it is impossible to say what the effect on their standard of living would be. Nonetheless, a general increase in the Consumer Price Index would certainly lead to pressure for wage increases, especially from lower-paid workers. Secondly, the transitional period is likely to be difficult for marginally profitable companies and even whole industries as tariff protection disappears. Even presently efficient companies will find that the extension of markets is a two-edged weapon. The increased competition from European companies in the British market and the need to remain competitive in the larger European market will prompt companies to maintain tighter control over unit labour costs, not necessarily by holding down wages, but by securing an adequate productivity return for wage increases given. Of course, in large areas of the economy no international competition exists, and this influence will be less important. Thirdly, there is the effect of the various detailed provisions of the Treaty of Rome, especially on harmonisation of social security systems. During the 1962-63 negotiations for British entry, it was thought that the application of harmonisation would result in a massive switch of social security contributions to the employer, with a large unavoidable increase in labour costs. The next Section considers whether such an outcome is a likely consequence of British entry to the Common Market.

Both equal pay and entry to the Common Market are courses of action on which the Government had already embarked by the end of the 1960s. The other two major political issues are rather more contentious, and depend rather more on the outcome of the political contest. One is the fate of the *Selective Employment Tax*. The Conservative Party have pledged themselves to repeal SET, and the discussion of Section II suggests that this could reduce supplementary labour costs in some sectors of industry and increase them in others.[1] However, the problem of SET is bound up with the future structure of supplementary labour costs, and further discussion can be postponed until the next Section. Potentially much more important in its effect on unit labour costs is *the future of incomes policy* in the

---

[1] The 1970 Budget speech announced the Labour Government's intention of making SET a percentage of payroll tax rather than a *per capita* tax as at present. No rate has yet been announced nor is it known when the change would take place, but it would clearly affect the incidence of tax between industries and companies, and the economic effects would be different.

1970s. We must be quite clear on what the function of incomes policy is likely to be in the 1970s. The Prices and Incomes Board in their Third General Report suggested that during the three phases of policy 1948-50, 1961-62 and 1965-66 the rate of growth of money incomes had been reduced by about 1 per cent. per annum (National Board for Prices and Incomes, 1968, pp. 63-67). However, in these three periods the policy was of a stringency unlikely to be equalled in future. The Government's plans for 1970-71 envisage wage increases being delayed for a maximum of four months pending examination by the PIB, but no wage freeze or wage stop is likely to operate; indeed, since the Conservative Party seem to be opposed to even this type of incomes policy, there may be even less Government control over the size and timing of wage increases. But to assume that incomes policy is therefore likely to be ineffectual since it will not be able to hold down the rate of increase of wages or labour costs is really to misunderstand the potential contribution of incomes policy to the 1970s. The main aim of incomes policy has always been to change people's views on what constitutes a justifiable criterion for wage increases, and the continuing influence of incomes policy would therefore be not the existence of a numerical guideline, but rather the creation of a different environment within which collective bargaining took place. The question is simply this: will bargaining proceed in line with the PIB doctrine of efficiency, productivity and the control of costs, with the public interest entering where necessary to modify what have previously been considered private bargains between employers and trade unions; or will the expectation of high earnings stimulated by the experience of 1964-70 continue to mean wage demands well in excess of any possible productivity gains? One of the factors determining the answer to this question is whether the form of wage payment methods will change in the 1970s. Obviously, it would be advantageous for employers to introduce payment systems which related effort to income in such a way as to stabilise unit labour costs. Hopefully, one might see an extension of such systems as measured day work, and the revision of conventional payment by results schemes to remove 'drift' and improve their cost-effectiveness. This is only one wage issue: the next Section will briefly discuss some others, and then move on to consider the trend of supplementary labour costs.

IV

The Donovan Commission concluded that one of the main problems of the 'dual system' of industrial relations was the scope it gave for inflationary wage increases. Their conclusion was that an 'orderly' system of industrial relations would require changes in both the procedure and substance of collective bargaining. In considering the possibility of more stable wage costs in the 1970s, it is similarly important to ask at what level bargaining is likely to proceed, and what criteria are likely to be used by the parties.

The Donovan Report recommended that company or factory agreements should form the basis of a reorganised industrial relations system, and during

1968-69 there appears to have been a movement towards more important wage negotiations at the company level. However, the focus of bargaining moved to a more decentralised level for reasons other than those advanced by Donovan. The incomes policy of the period had as its chief exception agreements with a productivity content which were most easily negotiated at the company level. Associated with this was the effect of the engineering industry agreement signed in 1967, which allowed further increases in wages at the local level, provided there were measurable improvements in productivity. There also appears to have been a policy by some unions of encouraging local bargaining by shop stewards, again no doubt partly so as to move wage determination on to a level at which incomes policy finds it difficult to operate. It is difficult to know whether this greater power at the local level is likely to be a permanent feature of the 1970s, or indeed whether it must of itself result in more inflationary wage settlements. The answer to both these questions depends essentially on the control which trade unions wish to exert over local bargaining through a modernised and effective structure such as was recommended by Donovan, but does not presently exist. This control would, on the other hand, only contribute to stability of unit wage costs insofar as there was some reasonably direct link between wage increases and increases in output per man.

The best-publicised local agreements which have achieved this emphasis on a new criterion are the comprehensive productivity agreements such as those discussed in the PIB reports (see National Board for Prices and Incomes, 1967 and 1969a) but it would be grossly optimistic to suppose that such agreements will spread throughout industry in the 1970s. The detailed history of such agreements shows that their successful negotiation requires a technical environment, managerial expertise and an industrial relations climate which are present in only a small minority of collective bargaining situations. Indeed, even the apparent success of such comprehensive agreements can be misleading, for the granting of very substantial wage increases in return for major changes in work practices can give rise to differential problems and disappointed expectations of future large increases. Under the 1968/69 incomes policy, additions to the $3\frac{1}{2}$ per cent. maximum could be granted for 'agreements which genuinely raise productivity and increase efficiency sufficiently to justify' an exception. This raises a different set of questions about productivity, and allows bargaining about the fruits of productivity increases to which employees have contributed, though not necessarily through the major changes in work practices which were essential in a comprehensive productivity agreement. The major issue in wages policy in the early 1970s, which will largely determine the progress of unit wage costs, is whether productivity is to be the major criterion in collective bargaining demands, or whether the criterion of comparability, a major inflationary force in the 1960s, will be allowed to reassert itself.

It is not necessary to elaborate on the economic dangers of the extensive use of comparability, but there are three particular areas where the application of the principle is likely to occur in the 1970s. First, there is the general pressure by different groups to erode or maintain wage differentials. There is no sign that the Prices and Incomes Board's strictures against the use of comparability in this simple form have borne fruit. Secondly, there is the case of low-paid workers, whose poor wages are compared with wages of those in other occupations or with the average industrial wage. Unless these groups receive higher than average increases in wages, their relative position will not change for the better. Where the low-paid workers are in a low-paid industry, e.g. agricultural workers, pressure for substantial increases is certain to occur, but as the DEP survey of earnings showed, there are low-paid workers in all industries, and to increase their earnings would require differential increases within industries. The PIB comments that ' the improvement of the position of the low paid can be subsumed in the general problem of increasing efficiency ' (National Board for Prices and Incomes, 1969a, p. 21), and while this may well be true, it leaves unanswered the problem of whether the intra-industry differentials will be allowed to become narrower. Thirdly, many occupational groups in the public sector use comparability as the criterion for wage demands and in some cases, e.g. doctors and dentists, the principle has been accepted as valid by the Government. Also, in the public eye a kind of comparability of social worth has come to be used, under which wages in quite different jobs are compared. For example, the salaries of nurses and teachers are compared with those of dustmen or semi-skilled workers, and the conclusion drawn by many is that the wage relativities have gone wrong. The new militancy shown by some public sector employees during 1969 is certain to be continued into the 1970s, and the question is whether the employees' claims of comparability and equality are allowed to dominate in wage settlement.

The overall effect of all these influences on the total wage and salary bill, rather than the effect only in manufacturing or wage-earners' agreements, has to be estimated, but before considering this, we must discuss what seems to be the most likely trend of supplementary labour costs. One of the most important is increases in *legally-required contributions* on behalf of social security schemes. Table III showed that in 1968 employers' social security contributions were 4·4 per cent. of total labour costs, equal to 4·9 per cent. of civil wages & salaries. Because the contributions were very largely flat-rate, this percentage would vary inversely with the level of wages and salaries, so that in high-wage companies or industries social security contributions would account for less than 4·9 per cent. The proposals in the National Superannuation Bill and related legislation are that contributions should be increased and at the same time put on a proportional basis. By 1972 the employers' contribution would be 7·05 per cent. of earnings, made up as follows: superannuation 4·5 per cent., unemployment/sickness insurance 1·7 per cent, health 0·6 per cent., redundancy fund 0·25 per cent. The average increase of about 2 percentage points between 1968 and 1972 may not seem large, but it would amount to much more than this for many companies, and of course every increase in earnings would mean that a larger amount had to be paid by the employer to the social security agencies. It is impossible to say whether the long-term trend will be for employers' contributions to increase as a percentage of earnings. This could happen because the natural buoyancy of revenue may be insufficient to maintain the actuarial standards of the schemes as benefit levels rise, or because it has been decided as a matter of policy to increase the share of social security revenue contributed by the employer.[2] The existing reorganisation of the social security system and the higher employer contribution owes something to both these reasons, but it has been thought that British entry to the Common Market might give rise to pressure for even larger contributions from employers.

The reasoning behind this view is simply that one of the Treaty of Rome's objectives is to achieve a harmonisation of social security systems in an upward direction, and a literal interpretation would require a considerable improvement in British levels of benefit, which are in most cases inferior to the best European systems. This would require general contribution increases, and it has also been suggested that conformity with the European systems would require a larger share of social security revenue to be contributed by the employer, and a smaller share from general taxation. A very rough calculation is that in 1968 30 per cent. of social security revenue (including the Health Service) came from employer contributions and about 40 per cent. from general taxation. In Europe the lowest employer share in 1966 was 37 per cent. in Germany, and the highest share from general taxation was 22 per cent. in Belgium. However, the intra-European experience of harmonisation between 1958 and 1968 does not suggest that rapid changes in the British system will be necessary. European benefit levels continued to vary, and so did the financial structure of the schemes. In 1966 the employer share of revenue varied from 37 per cent. in Germany to 65 per cent. in France, and the inter-country variations were not much different from those in 1961 (High Commission of EEC, 1969, p. 298, and pp. 242-5). It is therefore unlikely that any transitional period before full Common Market membership would necessarily demand large increases in legally-required contributions. Nevertheless, the SET proposals and the financial methods proposed under the National Superannuation Bill are a pointer towards the future. A larger employer share of social security revenue would avoid the need for higher taxation to finance schemes from general revenue, and there is a belief that such a ' tax on the use of labour ' (more correctly, a tax on a high wage-bill) would lead to a more efficient use of labour and possibly improve the distribution of labour. There are, however, a number of questionable assumptions associated with this proposition.

Another area of supplementary labour costs where changes might occur is in ' fringe benefits ', particularly pension and welfare schemes and holidays

---

[2] It is a moot point whether an earnings-related contribution is less disturbing to employers than a flat-rate contribution which takes a sudden substantial jump upwards every now and then, as happened under the National Insurance system. But an earnings-related contribution which continually increases as a percentage of earnings is the worst of both worlds.

with pay. The discussion in the previous paragraph suggests strongly that if the National Superannuation plan comes into effect, *pension and welfare expenditure* is unlikely to increase and will probably decline. From the employer's point of view, the conditions of the new State scheme are such as to discourage occupational schemes, and it seems likely that some schemes will be abandoned. Certainly, given the financial arrangements for abatement and the additional legally-required payment falling on the employer in respect of the State scheme, it is difficult to see pension expenditure as a percentage of total labour costs showing an upward trend. It seems unlikely too that many unions would press for pension and welfare schemes as a substitute for wage increases, partly because they are complex subjects best suited to company bargaining which the unions are ill-equipped to do, and partly because there is no real evidence that manual workers prefer these fringe benefits to wage increases. The growth in occupational pension schemes in Britain since the war was not caused by collective bargaining pressure as it was in the United States, but by companies unilaterally choosing to introduce plans, especially after 1961 when there was a financial incentive to contract out high-wage employees. This might again occur in the 1970s, since the Conservative Party has announced its intention of abandoning the National Superannuation scheme and encouraging occupational pension plans. This would presumably lead to an increase in pension expenditure on private schemes as a proportion of total labour costs. It is doubtful, though, whether there would be any reduction of legally-required payments below the 1969 proportion, since the State scheme would need to continue for existing pensioners and for the 13 million workers who are not members of occupational schemes. Also, expenditure on other items of social insurance would continue to increase.

Paid holidays, on the other hand, are likely to become a more costly item on the employers' labour bill. The progress towards a basic three-week holiday has speeded up in the past few years, as Table IV shows.

Table IV

HOLIDAYS WITH PAY (EXCLUDING PUBLIC HOLIDAYS)

	Proportion of workers					
	1963	1964	1965	1966	1967	1968
Basic 2 weeks	96	75	70	60	56	52
Basic 2 weeks + extra days	4	25	30	35	34	33
Basic 3 weeks				5	10	15

Source: Incomes Data Services, *Report on Annual Holidays,* May 1969.

In 1970 it is estimated that up to 50 per cent. of workers will qualify for three weeks' basic holiday, and it would be surprising if this entitlement was not general by 1975 (Incomes Data Services, 1969, p. 6). Again, comparisons with European countries show Britain in an unfavourable light. In the Common Market countries, the statutory and negotiated holiday entitlement usually means at least three weeks' holiday plus between 6 and 13 public holidays. Even if we assume the minimum likely increase in Britain, to three weeks' annual holiday and six public holidays, the cost would probably be between 7 and 8 per cent. of total labour costs.

To sum up: though there may be offsetting factors in the repeal of the Selective Employment Tax and a decline in the cost of private pension schemes, it seems certain that money supplementary labour costs will be substantially above their present level, because of increases in legally-required payments, and in paid holidays. Any acceleration of the trend towards 'staff status' for manual workers would also tend to increase supplementary labour costs, insofar as the more costly staff sickness and holiday arrangements would apply more widely, but it seems unlikely that this would affect many manual workers in the early 1970s.

V

Having made some general observations about the likely trend of money wages and money supplementary labour costs, it seems desirable, if rather foolhardy, to conclude by making some kind of general prediction about what this means for *unit* labour costs. What is likely to be the effect of all these diverse influences on unit labour costs? The experience of the 1960s is again relevant in showing past performance and the relationship between year-to-year changes in wages and salaries, output per man, and unit wage and labour costs. Table V gives details.

Take first manufacturing industry. The average wage/salary drawn from aggregate statistics is greatly preferable to the use of data of average earnings or increases in basic wage rates, since official wage/earnings statistics are incomplete in coverage even of manual workers, and obviously do not cover salary earners. The interesting point about the Table is the movement of the figures from 1965-68. In this period, the average wage/salary increased very substantially at an average rate of over 6 per cent. per annum, but because of the trend of output per employee, these very large increases were not reflected in unit wage/salary costs. In fact, the year-to-year increases became progressively smaller from 1965 to 1968, and in 1968 the rate of increase of unit wage/salary costs was only 1·2 per cent. against 8·6 per cent. in the average wage/salary. A further paradox is that the rates of increase of unit labour costs showed quite a different pattern from those of unit wage/salary costs. As we have already seen, this was a result of the Selective Employment Tax and Regional Employment Premium, variations in which affected unit labour costs but not unit wage/salary costs. The experience of the period 1964-68 therefore leads to a cautionary conclusion: yearly variations in one of the aggregates is not necessarily a good guide to variations in the others. Thus, for example, the 1965-68 figures show that an increase in the average wage/salary need not be reflected in an increase

Table V

YEAR-TO-YEAR PERCENTAGE INCREASES IN WAGES AND SALARIES, OUTPUT PER PERSON EMPLOYED, AND UNIT COSTS: 1960-68

| | MANUFACTURING INDUSTRY | | | | | | | | | WHOLE ECONOMY |
| | Per cent change over previous year | | | | | | | | Average annual percentage increase 1960-68 | Average annual percentage increase 1960-68 |
	1961	1962	1963	1964	1965	1966	1967	1968		
Average wage/salary	5·9	3·1	3·3	8·0	7·7	6·2	4·4	8·6	5·9	—
Output per person employed	−0·9	1·2	5·3	7·4	2·0	1·6	2·7	7·3	3·3	2·6
Unit wage/salary cost	6·5	2·2	−1·2	0·5	5·6	4·5	1·7	1·2	2·6	3·4
Unit labour cost	7·0	2·5	−0·8	0·4	6·0	6·6	−2·2	2·5	2·7	3·8

Source: Calculated from *National Income and Expenditure 1969;* and *Employment and Productivity Gazette,* November 1969.

in unit wage/salary costs; nor will unit *labour* costs necessarily follow the trend of unit wage/salary costs, since the relationship between them depends on what happens to supplementary labour costs.

The point must be made that the annual average rate of growth of unit labour costs from 1960 to 1968, 2·7 per cent. in manufacturing and 3·8 per cent. overall, was far from satisfactory, in the sense that most of our international competitors did better. Is there any reason to expect an improvement in Britain's performance in the 1970's? The optimist might point to the below-average increases in manufacturing unit labour costs in 1967 and 1968 but each of these years was influenced by special factors, 1967 by the SET and REP rebates and premiums, and 1968 by a 7·3 per cent. growth of output per employee, more than twice the average rate. It is, unfortunately, easier to see adverse factors than favourable ones, whether one looks at output per employee or labour costs. One obvious point in Table V is the more rapid growth of unit labour costs in the whole economy than in manufacturing. This was not wholly due to the effect of SET— unit wage/salary costs also rose to a greater extent—but mainly to a slower growth in output per employee in the non-manufacturing sectors. As a higher proportion of the labour force comes to be employed in services and non-manufacturing industry, it will become increasingly difficult to maintain a rapid rate of productivity increase. The remedy, obviously, is to improve efficiency in these sectors, though not by increasing their labour costs and encouraging employment in manufacturing as SET was designed to do. Overall, even without taking this structural effect into account it seems unlikely that output per employee in the economy as a whole could rise at an average rate of more than 3 per cent. per annum in the early 1970's.

As far as labour costs are concerned, there are reasons to expect a growth rate not much below that of 1960-68, when total income from employment grew at an average rate of about $6\frac{1}{2}$ per cent. per annum. First, incomes policy has been relaxed, with the top figure of the permitted range $4\frac{1}{2}$ per cent., and as the PIB themselves acknowledge, the maximum tends to be regarded as the standard increase (National Board for Prices and Incomes, 1968, p. 19). Also, pressure from low-paid workers and public service personnel is likely to intensify. In early 1970, increases were running well above the $4\frac{1}{2}$ per cent. norm. Clearly the comparability principle is still far from dead, and claims based on maintaining or eroding differentials are likely to be a significant force leading to upward pressure on wage levels, especially in company bargaining where individual particularly generous settlements can have ill-effects on the local wage structure. Comparability within multi-plant firms, e.g. in the motor industry, is also important as a trade union goal. Secondly, there has been very little change since 1966 in the normal working week, and it seems likely that the period up to 1975 will see further attempts to gain shorter hours. Insofar as this happens without reductions in the actual working week, increases in overtime earnings will occur. Thirdly, the increases in legally-required payments and paid holidays seem certain to increase supplementary labour costs as a percentage of earnings, and these will constitute additional expenditures which improvements in productivity will have to cover if unit costs are not to rise.

In view of all these influences, it would be prudent to assume that perhaps even in the longer-term up to the mid-1970s, labour costs will increase by at least 6 per cent. per annum. Together with a productivity increase of not more than 3 per cent. per annum, this means an upward movement of unit labour costs of at least 3 per cent. per annum. Put this way, the forecast is optimistic by the standards of 1960-68, when the average annual rate was 3·8 per cent. However, the relevant comparison is not with Britain's own past, but with the current performance of her international competitors, and on the basis of the most recent data a unit labour cost increase of 3 per cent. per annum would seriously damage the international competitiveness of British exports. OECD figures published at the end of 1969 suggest that in the period from 1967 to the middle of 1969, unit costs in Britain had risen considerably faster than those of some of our major international competitors, Germany, Italy, France and Japan.[3] If this is a continuing trend, it has many serious implications of which only two will be mentioned here. First, as far as the general management of the economy is concerned, it may be necessary to avoid any relaxation of fiscal or monetary policy which might give the impression that larger wage increases are permissible without any basis in productivity improvement. This would mean that for the early 1970s at least, the level of unemployment could continue well above that which prevailed during the early and mid-1960s. Secondly, at the level of the individual firm, the demand for higher wages and shorter hours of work is bound to mean that increasing attention will be paid by the firm to the efficient management of its labour force in an attempt to get value for money. This could involve such apparently minor issues as improvements in supervision, control of absence, introduction of work measurement, more rational wage payment systems, and more importance being attached to the problems of motivating and controlling the workforce. It is as much through this kind of measure as through comprehensive productivity bargaining that better control of unit labour costs may come.

University of Glasgow

[3] The average annual increase in unit labour costs in 1967 and 1968 was 3·1 per cent., which suggests that a considerably lower rate than our 1970s forecast would have been necessary to keep pace with our foreign rivals.

REFERENCES

DEPARTMENT OF EMPLOYMENT AND PRODUCTIVITY (1968). *Labour Costs in Britain in 1964:* H.M.S.O.

DEPARTMENT OF EMPLOYMENT AND PRODUCTIVITY (1969). *Employment and Productivity Gazette,* October 1969: H.M.S.O.

DEPARTMENT OF EMPLOYMENT AND PRODUCTIVITY (1970). *Employment and Productivity Gazette,* January 1970: H.M.S.O.

HIGH COMMISSION OF EEC (1969). *Exposé sur l'Evolution de la Situation Sociale dans la Communauté en 1968.* Brussels.

INCOMES DATA SERVICES (1969). *Report on Annual Holidays.* May 1969. London.

MINISTRY OF LABOUR (1966, 1967). *Ministry of Labour Gazette,* December 1966 and March 1967: H.M.S.O.

NATIONAL BOARD FOR PRICES AND INCOMES (1967). *Productivity Agreements,* Report No. 36, Cmnd. 3311: H.M.S.O.

NATIONAL BOARD FOR PRICES AND INCOMES (1968). *Third General Report.* Report No. 77, Cmnd. 3715: H.M.S.O.

NATIONAL BOARD FOR PRICES AND INCOMES (1969a). *Fourth General Report.* Report No. 122, Cmnd. 4130: H.M.S.O.

NATIONAL BOARD FOR PRICES AND INCOMES (1969b). *Productivity Agreements,* Report No. 123, Cmnd. 4136: H.M.S.O.

EQUALITY AND INEQUALITY

K. J. W. ALEXANDER

Economists as a class have always been opposed
to inequality of income, and also to equality.
GEORGE J. STIGLER (1950).

I

The ambiguity to which Professor Stigler drew attention is explained by a number of factors, amongst the most important of which are semantic confusion and the difficulty of disentangling normative from positive influences in economic matters. In industrial relations as distinct from positive economics, however, the value judgements of individuals and interest groups are important in their own right, as determinants of behaviour and not merely as influences clouding the analysis of relationships. Although value judgements are not disallowed in industrial relations it is still necessary to try to distinguish their influence from that of more objective factors, usually a most difficult task.

Amongst the most powerful of normative influences in industrial relations are views on the desired distribution of income, on equality and inequality. Such views are not held in common; individuals and interest groups will have different value aims, and these help sustain competing ideologies within industrial relations. Semantic confusion, for example on the meaning of 'equal pay for equal work', can cause even greater confusion when it takes different forms with the different individuals and interest groups who are parties to an industrial relations situation.

The initial aim of this essay will be to reduce semantic confusion by distinguishing between the different meanings which can be given to 'equality' in industrial relations. Thereafter the sources of pressure for the different types of 'equality' and the factors influencing the strength of these pressures will be examined. The conclusion reached, that the pressures for equality are increasing and likely to continue, leads on to an examination of the extent of possible conflict between the goal(s) of 'equality' and other policy goals such as allocative efficiency. The final section will attempt to draw out the policy implications of the preceding analysis.

II

THE MEANING OF INEQUALITY

At their widest inequalities within industrial relations are part of a broader concept of social inequality which is an amalgam of class factors derived direct from the productive system, status which is concerned with

133

social estimation and prestige and power which is concerned with decision-taking. Of these three sub-divisions the one which most affects the extent of equality and inequality in industrial relations is class, derived from the productive system within which industrial relations exist. The other two also impinge upon industrial relations, however. Status considerations, for example, can explain the existence of non-competing socio-economic groups, and affect the elasticity of supply of labour to different occupations, and thus be influential in determining income structure. The desire to curb arbitrary managerial actions arise because of inequalities in the power structure. Thus inequalities of status, power and class may be complementary aspects of the same situation but they are not identical with each other.[1] In narrowing the focus hereafter to aspects of economic equality and inequality deriving directly from the productive process it is important to bear this complementarity in mind and to recognise that status and power considerations may also be influential in the area under consideration.

An attempt is made in Diagram I to distinguish between the different meanings which may be attached to equality in industrial relations.[2]

Equality of opportunity is strongly influenced by status factors, but also arises as an industrial relations issue in its own right, for example when trade unions require that all higher posts be open for competition between lower grades before being advertised outside the enterprise, or when entry to particular occupations require trade union endorsement not available to everyone thought capable of performing the required duties. In what follows equality of opportunity will not be treated as a separate issue, but only in relation to the effect of limitations on entry and income. The concentration on income is convenient because it removes from the discussion the non-quantifiable elements associated with comparisons of the net advantages attached by individuals to different jobs. The more subjective factors such as job satisfaction, status, etc., are taken into account the more tautological a theory of net advantages becomes. This is one reason why writers have focussed on money income, in some instances arguing that it could serve as a proxy for net advantages. Another reason has been that ' *changes* in money wage levels will give some guidance to changes in the net advantage of different jobs since many of the job-characteristics such as working conditions will remain constant ' (Hunter, 1968). Perhaps an even stronger justification for the concentration on money income is that this seems in accord with the attitudes of employees. This is not necessarily because money is thought to be more important, but because money differences are precise, calculable and capable of appraisal without working in a particular job, which is the only way in which most of the other attributes of the job which together make up its net advantages to an individual can be appraised. For this reason it is probably more appropriate to emphasise money at the

---

[1] These distinctions have been clearly delineated by Runciman (1966) and the paragraph above draws upon his book.

[2] The idea for this diagram comes from Carver (1925). The structure and scope of the diagram differ considerably from its orginal form.

expense of other job attributes when considering allocative efficiency than when considering motivation and efficiency of utilisation within industrial locations. Non-pecuniary attributes can also become more important in inducing application and in minimising voluntary labour turnover. One final

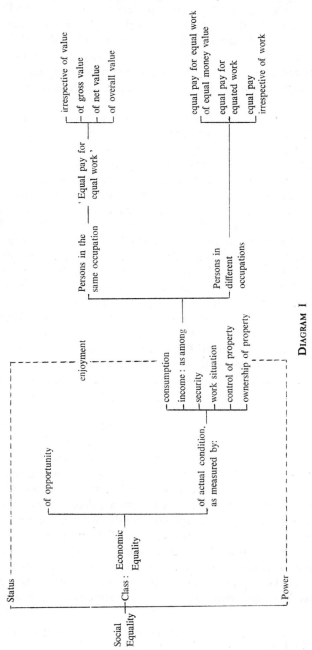

DIAGRAM I

justification for focussing attention upon income in this discussion is that this emphasis is shared by the principal bargaining agents, and in particular by the trade unions.

Inasmuch as we shall be concerned with pressures for greater equality it is clear that the major issues arise in relation to comparability between the remuneration of different groups of workers. The most obvious, and far-reaching, example is the demand for ' equal pay for equal work ' irrespective of sex. The main distinction which has to be made in comparison of pay levels is between those comparisons which are made between persons within the same occupation and those which are made between persons in different occupations.

Within the same occupation differences in the meaning attached to ' equal work ' can cause confusion. A broad distinction could be made between payment related directly to output (as when incentive schemes are in operation) and payment related only to the nomenclature of a job, and not directly related to variations in effort or output (at least within a band of acceptable performance, the narrower the band the less important being the distinction). The approach is illustrated by Article 119 of the Treaty of Rome which, in terms of the nomenclature of a job, lays it down ' that remuneration for work at time rates shall be the same for the same job '. In its approach to ' equal pay ' the C.B.I. has leaned towards this view whereas the T.U.C. has endorsed the approach of the I.L.O. Convention No. 100 which in 1951 laid down ' the principle of equal remuneration for men and women workers for work of equal value '. An inquiry by the T.U.C. in 1968, however, revealed that only nine unions (with $1\frac{1}{4}$m. female members) would not wish to go as far as to accept this apparently more demanding definition, and led the General Council to comment that ' attitudes towards equal pay, even of unions, still vary about the appropriate definition of equal pay, presumably according to whether their main aim is to safeguard the position of their male members or to gain parity for their women members ' (T.U.C. 1969a, p. 97).

When the basis of comparison is extended to include ' work of equal value ' the distinctions between overall, net and gross value become important in assessing the possible outcome in payment terms.[3] It arises when there are two individuals (or groups) producing the same gross output but one of them has required inputs of complementary factors of production costing more than the complementary factors required by the other. Examples frequently cited are of one group consistently using more raw material, or requiring mechanical help in lifting. This distinction can be refined and expressed in terms of work yielding ' equal net revenue ' to explain, for example, why workers with identical production but employed at different distances from the sources of raw materials and the markets for their end-product may have different worths to their employers, and accordingly be

[3] For an extended treatment of these distinctions see either Royal Commission on Equal Pay (1946), or Phelps Brown (1951) Chapter V.

paid different wages. An employer's estimate of the relative worth of employees can be influenced not only by the distance-factor and its influence on transport costs but can be influenced by the time-factor. The employment relationship is usually spread over months or years and the value of an employee can be influenced by the length of time spent with a particular employer and by the flexibility and interchangeability of the employee between jobs and work-cycles. The most frequently cited factors causing the overall value of one group of workers to be less than that of another group, even when the employees are in identical jobs of identical net value to employers, are different lengths (or expected lengths) of service and the existence of limitations on certain time-patterns of work applying to certain employees, such as shift-work limitations applying to females. Differences such as these, causing differences in the overall value of employees to employers were drawn attention to in the *Report of the Royal Commission on Equal Pay* and were advanced as argument against any unqualified application of the 'equal pay' principle: 'A rule of equal pay would be an injunction to ignore, in the pricing of wages, those considerations of over-all value.' When we move on to consideration of the remuneration of persons in different occupations we must drop the assumption that their output does not differ as to quality (i.e. it is homogeneous) but that it may differ as to quantity whether measured in gross, net or overall terms, particularly when the occupations are in different firms or industries. In such cases the 'equal work' element in the 'equal pay' concept must take one of two possible forms:

(i) First there is the possibility of comparing the money value of different physical outputs, the approach of marginal revenue productivity theory. This is very similar to the 'net value' approach applied to workers in the same occupation when comparisons of net value can only be made after translating physical inputs and outputs into money terms. The problem of imputing outputs to one of several complementary factors of production is greater when comparisons have to be made between two distinct production functions each producing distinct products. For this reason it seems very unlikely that wage determination for workers in different occupations would carry any conviction if based on statements regarding the equality or inequality of the marginal revenue products of the workers concerned. Marginal revenue productivity theory may nonetheless reflect real factors at work in the labour market, affecting investment decisions, the choice of production methods and the numbers employed in different firms and industries.

Even at the theoretical level if one assumes that the supply of labour to the two occupations is less than perfectly elastic the cases in which equality between wage and marginal revenue product will occur are limited in number and special in their assumptions. These special cases are illustrated below. Diagram II illustrates the case in which the two firms derive identical marginal revenue products from the employment of factor a in firm A and factor b in firm B (MRP_a, MRP_b) and when the supply conditions of a to A and of b to B are also identical (Sa, Sb) Diagram III illustrates the case where the supply of labour to the firms A and B is the same (Sa, Sb), MRP_a differs from MRP_b and Sa, Sb cuts where MRP_a and MRP_b intersect. Diagram IV illustrates a case in which the supply to the two firms is different, S_a and S_b, and when these supply curves cut the respective MRP curves of the firm at volumes of employment for which wage levels are the same, $W_a = W_b$.

If the equality of occupations is limited to cases occurring within one firm, Diagram II illustrates a situation in which jobs a and b, although

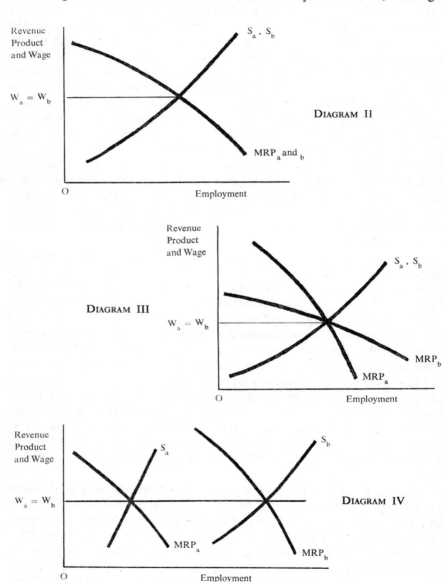

defined differently, have identical supply conditions (probably based on interchangeability of labour between them) and the same MRP. Diagram III illustrates a situation in which labour is freely interchangeable between the two jobs but its value in one differs from its value in the other according to the number employed in each. Only the coincidence of the triple intersection makes the payment of equal wages the optimising policy for the employer. Similarly in Diagram IV only the coincidence of the two intersections at the same level of wages and MRP makes the payment of equal wages the optimising policy. Thus Diagram II illustrates a case in which equal pay would most probably arise (for example by being the condition on which interchangeability was allowed by the union(s)), and Diagrams III and IV illustrate cases which are unimportant because of the singularity of the assumptions on which they rest. In all other cases with less than perfectly elastic supply and with less restrictive assumptions employers would optimise by paying unequal wages.

On both practical and theoretical grounds it appears that an approach to the concept of equal pay for equal work in different occupations through marginal revenue productivity theory can only be of very limited importance.

(ii) The second meaning which may be given to the ' equal work ' concept when applied to people in different occupations is based upon comparison of the qualities required to perform it. This approach, based on job evaluation, is that adopted by policy makers and industrial practitioners in determining whether or not work is of ' equal value '.[4] The distinction between this approach and that of assessing the value of work in terms of the value of its products is helped if the phrase ' equated work ' is used to describe cases in which job evaluation suggests that two or more different occupations are ' equal '. The existence of equated work can only be established when job evaluation has been applied and when the same system of job evaluation is used. If two occupations in different firms or industries are job evalued using, for example, different points rating systems the resultant job values will not be capable of meaningful comparison. Job evaluation emphasises some supply side characteristics in the labour market, and is only capable of taking account of demand side characteristics in a very broad and general way when particular weighting systems are adopted for use in a points rating system or by altering the money values given to the points rating of jobs. The supply side characteristics are those related to the qualities required to perform particular jobs, characteristics such as skill, effort, responsibility and working conditions.[5] If perfect knowledge and the absence of obstacles to mobility are assumed, two occupations having equal characteristics would also have closely similar supply conditions of labour. Whether this similarity of supply conditions would cover occupations with the same job values made up from different patterns of job characteristics would depend upon the extent to which the job evaluation

---

[4] See, e.g. Mepham (1969).
[5] For a discussion of job characteristics see, e.g. Lytle (1954).

system (the points attached to separate job characteristics and the weighting system applied to relate them and produce a job value) mirrors the subjective evaluation placed on the jobs by the relevant labour force. There is no place within a job evaluated system for changes in demand conditions. For example, two equally rated occupations can change in value to their employer(s) with changes in the demand for the different product each helps produce, but the occupations remain examples of 'equated work'.

In a diagrammatic representation of job evaluation the employer's demand will be represented at the wage level established by the job evaluation process. For example, in Diagram V, $W_{a,b}$ represents the willingness of employer(s) to hire employees capable of doing jobs a and b at an identical wage level $W_a = W_b$. The optimum employment levels in the two occupations will depend upon cost and revenue considerations within the firm(s), and it must be assumed that the wage levels arrived at by job evaluation are taken by the employer(s) as a reasonably close proxy for the revenue product of employees in these occupations. The firm(s) will only be able to optimise if the supply of labour to jobs a and b at $W_a = W_b$ equals or exceeds requirements. The maximum labour that can be attracted to each occupation is determined by the supply conditions S_a, S_b (which assumes similar subjective evaluations of the two occupations by the relevant labour force) at OM. If this supply is below that required by the firm(s) to optimise then either the wage level must be raised (perhaps putting the system of job evaluation in jeopardy) or the firm(s) must be content to operate at levels of employment and output which do not maximise profits. The possibilities of having to adopt sub-optimal policies as a consequence of 'equal pay for equated work' is increased when the supply conditions differ between the jobs being evaluated. The approach of equal pay for equated work through job evaluation is capable of wide application, but can result in problems of allocation and utilisation which will be considered in Section IV.

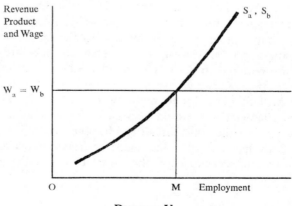

DIAGRAM V

III

FACTORS INFLUENCING INEQUALITY

We have seen that different meanings are attached to ' equality of pay ' in particular when this equality is related to ' equality of work '. Any consideration of the factors working for and against equality must take account of these differences of meaning. Some factors may operate against tendencies towards equal pay for jobs of equal gross value, yet may favour or at least be neutral in their effect on equal pay for jobs of equal net or equal overall value. Technological change will probably operate in these different ways.

The factors influencing the extent of equality and inequality may be classified under three headings: market influences; institutional influences; social influences. No such classification can be watertight, however. Market influences will reflect existing social factors, and in particular the effect of educational provision on the supply of skills and on manpower mobility. The market supply of labour to particular occupations will also be affected by status considerations and by established norms of reward in relationship to particular jobs.

These broad classifications can be broken down into more specific influences on equality and inequality. The more important influences at work in the market are technological change and the changes in the level and pattern of educational provision. In addition, changes in the availability of information about the labour market and in the extent of forward thinking on the need for adjustment (manpower planning) will also, by removing friction and easing mobility, work to reduce discrimination and inequalities arising from imperfections in the functioning of the market. The increasing professionalisation of management may also be listed as a market influence. Such market forces are most likely to work in favour of equality of pay for jobs of equal net or overall value, criteria which hamonise most with the optimising goals of the decision takers who respond to market forces.

Institutional influences include bargaining structures and the organisational basis of bargaining agents. Industry-wide collective bargaining will favour the cruder forms of equality of pay (e.g. for jobs with identical job titles or with equal gross outputs). Plant bargaining, on the other hand, particularly if it is geared to productivity criteria, will operate against the cruder forms of equality and in favour of the finer measures (e.g. of jobs of equal net overall value and of equated jobs). The effect of national incomes policy—which may be thought of as overlapping the institutional and social classifications—will depend upon the criteria associated with the policy and on the rigour with which these are applied. There will be a tendency to encourage cruder forms of equality, if only because national pressures favour the broad approach and nationally enunciated guide lines can be translated more easily into rules of thumb than into more sophisticated practice and policies. The one exception to this will be the encouragement which any national incomes policy is likely to give to job evaluation as complementary to work study measurement and a firmer foundation on which to emphasise productivity. The progress of the merger movement amongst trade unions is similarly likely to increase pressure for the cruder form of equality, but also to open out possibilities of equal pay for equated jobs using common standards and being applied over a much wider range than has occurred up to now. How far this process goes will depend to some extent on the attitude adopted by trade unions to job evaluation, an attitude recently assessed as 'suspicion and the lack of out-right rejection'.[6] We have already noted how the most efficient use of labour is frustrated if equal pay for equated jobs is applied over ranges within which the supply of labour to the equated jobs is not flexible and interchangeable. The trade union merger movement will probably increase the range of interchangeability and so encourage employers to favour an extension of job evaluation.

The influence of social factors on equality or inequality in wage/work relationships can, as we have seen, operate through market and institutional influences, in the form of educational policy and incomes policy respectively. These and other social influences will reflect social mores, and here the pressures for equality, with a preference for the cruder over the finer forms, will probably continue to build up. As one of the very few recent treatments of the topic by an economist puts it: 'The affirmative answer to the general question about equalization is so generally and so subconsciously given, so much a part of our culture-lore, that any further value-judgement statement seems redundant . . . the moving front of egalitarianism has carried us beyond the value-judgement level'.[7] Whereas it might be expected that egalitarianism would weaken as societies become richer and the standard of living of the low paid rises above that of subsistence and harsh poverty there is no evidence that this is so. If, as seems the case, the concept of 'low wages' is more relative than absolute there will be built-in pressure for 'equality' at all levels of national income. The pressure for 'equality' arising from the deprivation felt by low wage earners will also be exercised institutionally as the influence of collective bargaining is extended. The effect which the absence or weakness of collective bargaining can have in keeping wages low can be demonstrated by the fact that only 21 per cent. of males of 21 and over earning under £12 per week in September 1968 and only 17 per cent. of females of 18 and over earning under £7 were affected by national collective agreements.[8] The conclusion is that there will be a continuous build-up of pressures against inequalities and that of the various forms these pressures take that based on job evaluation will probably have the widest acceptability.

[6] Thomason (1968); and see T.U.C. (1964).

[7] Lampman (1957). See also Robbins (1963). Although Lord Robbins favours 'delevelling' he recognises that: 'Equality is a catchword of the day; the levelling spirit is a characteristic of the age.' (p. 73.)

[8] Employment and Productivity Gazette, October 1969.

IV

CONFLICTS BETWEEN EQUALITY AND ALLOCATIVE EFFICIENCY

Consideration of the possibility of conflict between equality objectives and other goals reinforces the view that the equality objective most likely to survive is that of equal pay for equated jobs. The two important aspects of efficiency are the allocation of labour between alternative uses and its effective utilisation in particular uses. The possibility of conflict between allocative efficiency and equality is least when payment is related to the net or overall value of employees, but such comparisons are limited by the practical difficulties of imputation and measurement and make very little concession to either the institutional or social pressures for equality. The possibility of such conflict is greatest with the cruder forms of equality. There is, however, a growing body of evidence indicating that re-allocation of labour depends very little upon widening differentials.[9] This accords with the observation that even at the level of the plant supply and demand considerations play little or no explicit part in the bargaining process. Expanding job opportunities are enough to attract labour into those occupations already enjoying higher levels of earnings. To attract additional labour to low paying jobs, however, it may be necessary to raise pay. Taken together this could mean that established differentials would narrow whenever changes in the pattern of demand involved expansion of the employment of lower-paid workers. Rising income in advanced economies would probably have this effect on the pattern of demand for labour,[10] thus encouraging a levelling-up process. A levelling-up in response to secular changes in the demand for labour must not be confused with an equalising process in response to institutional and social influences, however. In this latter case it is at least possible that the changes in differentials may work against the desired allocation of labour. This possibility can provide one reason for a wider adoption of job evaluation, with equality of pay being established for equated jobs. This approach, when associated with attempts to increase mobility between equated jobs, provides the most workable compromise between pressures for equality and the aim of allocative efficiency, although not necessarily optimising allocation.

Turning to the possibility of conflict between equality and the efficiency with which labour is utilised once in a given employment, again the risk is least if equality of work is measured in net overall terms and greatest if equality is determined by the gross value of work or irrespective of the value of work altogether. Wage differentials affect efficiency of utilisation in two ways, through their direct incentive effect and by the extent to which they create satisfaction or dissatisfaction. Amongst equality criteria only that of equal pay for work of equal net value will have a favourable direct incentive effect. All others will, by relaxing any clear relationship between effort and reward, tend to have an adverse or at least neutral incentive effect.

[9] e.g. Reddaway (1959), OECD (1965), and Routh (1965).
[10] See e.g. Raimon (1963).

Effective direct pecuniary incentives operate by differentiating reward according to measured effort and output, and most egalitarian trends minimise the capacity so to differentiate. It is possible, however, to graft individual or group incentive schemes on to various types of wage structure, so that an egalitarian base-rate structure for two or more occupations may be qualified by a system of direct pecuniary incentives producing a diverse earnings structure. The influence of the equalisation process *per se* on the efficiency of utilisation will then depend on its effect on employee satisfaction. It is not possible to generalise about the effect of any of the various approaches to equality other than that employees in those occupations which lose relatively as a result of any equalisation process are not likely to be more satisfied.

The approach to equalisation through job evaluation can increase satisfaction, however, both by removing inequalities and anomalies and by providing a rational explanation or justification of the wage inequalities which remain. Although it is difficult to distinguish ' rationalisation of pay structure ' from the benefit ' to increase the area of common ground between management and unions by establishing an agreed job hierarchy and thereby to reduce industrial conflict ' it is noteworthy that apart from ' rationalisation ' this second benefit was the most important one claimed by companies. (National Board for Prices and Incomes, 1968.) Reduced labour turnover, higher morale, lower absenteeism and better workplace relations generally were also claimed. Together these benefits would suggest that efficiency of utilisation need not be reduced and could be improved by the extension of equality to ' equated jobs '. Whether improvement is achieved would depend upon the extent to which the basis for job evaluation reflected the attitudes of workers regarding the relative worth of different jobs. Acceptance is more easily achieved in narrow areas within which the objective factors applying to different jobs can be known, but acceptance over areas larger and more complex than would allow such knowledge has been achieved. The importance of acceptability for the extent to which job evaluated wages structures will be compatible with supply side requirements in the labour market has already been noted. Further research is needed on the factors affecting acceptance of job evaluation systems and on the possibility of evolving systems which will win acceptance when applied widely.

The effect of the equalisation process on the pace of inflation will, of course, depend on the form the equalisation process takes. One general principle is that as moves towards equality will be made by ' levelling-up ' there will be a strong tendency for cost-push forces to increase during a transition period. Another general principle is that if the application of the principle of equality creates rigidities in the wage structure (the cruder criteria and job evaluation will create such rigidities, in contrast to net and overall job value criteria which involve fluctuations in response to labour and product market conditions) there will be a tendency for stronger cost-push forces to operate, as increases have to be applied more widely to induce a required increase in labour supply to a particular occupation.

This second general principle may be counterbalanced under job evaluation, however, by the reduction of cost-push induced by 'leap-frogging'. If wage structures based on job evaluation are accepted (e.g. as 'rational') then adjustments in wages can occur without the cumulative effect of comparability claims in which two or more rates are related to each other in successive negotiations without there being an agreed basis for 'comparability'. Coupled with policies designed to increase mobility in the labour market, wage structures based on acceptable job evaluation could probably withstand very considerable changes in the pattern of demand for labour without generating cost-push forces greater than those resulting from less formalised wage structures; and there is some possibility of easement resulting from a lessening of cumulative comparability claims.

Questions of equality and inequality in industrial relations cannot be confined within the wage and salary structure. Although in practice trade union energies in collective bargaining have been substantially engaged in a process of redistribution amongst employees in their joint roles as earners and consumers,[11] there can be no doubt that the intention has been to redistribute income from profits receivers and rentiers to wage and salary earners.[12] There are strong indications that trade union leaders are now looking at least as much towards fiscal means to achieve redistribution as to collective bargaining.[13] Despite the growing recognition that wage increases are not usually at the expense of profits[14] it is unlikely that redistributive aims will be surrendered within collective bargaining, at least at the ritualistic level. The issue is relevant to the consequences for the rate of capital accumulation of any move towards equality. If greater equality is achieved by a redistribtuion of the wage and salary bill alone no such problem arises. If a move towards equality were partly at the expense of profits the effect on saving and on the willingness to invest could not be predicted with any certainty. Much would depend on the social and political environment within which such a change took place. Experience suggests that the main circumstance capable of bringing about a substantial reduction in the share of profits is a combination of a depression sharp enough to induce price cuts and a trade union movement strong enough to resist

[11] See Phelps Brown (1968) Chapter II.

[12] In its evidence to the Donovan Commission the T.U.C. listed the reduction of 'gross inequality of income' as a trade union objective and collective bargaining as the most important trade union method: T.U.C. (1966).

[13] See, e.g. T.U.C. (1969b): 'The General Council have put to the Government and intend to pursue further with the appropriate Minister, ways of improving social equity . . . An advance in the living standards of lower-paid workers can be secured in a less cost-inflationary way by fiscal redistribution than by laying all the emphasis on increments to the wage bill' (para. 107). 'This' (the rise in equity prices and higher distribution of profits) 'clearly raises questions of social justice, and of the use of the tax system to redistribute more equitably both the benefits and social costs of dynamic growth' (para. 185). (This Review was accepted at a Special Conference of Executives by 6,395,000 votes to 2,239,000.)

[14] See, e.g. T.U.C. (1966) '. . . it is characteristic of the modern economy that administered prices in many industries can generally guarantee a "normal" rate of profit through cost increases being passed on to the consumer . . .' (para. 190).

10

equivalent cuts. (Phelps Brown, 1968, pp. 21-2.) Neither on practical nor on theoretical grounds could this be regarded as a combination of circumstances likely to increase equality.

If egalitarian tendencies are to make progress partly at the expense of the share of profits it seems reasonable to assume that this will be as the result of political influences, probably taking fiscal or legislative forms. This conclusion is in line with current trade union thinking, for example on the case for a legal minimum wage. The lower limit to the supply price of capital is set by conventional and subjective factors, and is capable of being depressed by political pressure. A combination of equalising forces within the wage and salary structure and a redistribution away from the share of profits and in favour of the share of wage and salary earners in the national product is therefore possible without reducing the rate of capital accumulation. What cannot be predicted with any certainty is the nature of the political changes necessary to make this possible, and the extent of the redistributive shift that would be possible without curtailing investment. Speculation on this would carry up further into politics. It is here that the traditional support of British trade unionism for public ownership impinges on industrial relations. As the T.U.C. (1969b, para. 187) has recently put it: '. . . the question of distribution involves wealth and property ownership, not simply the current flow of income'.

An approach to equality using job evaluation and the 'equated jobs' criterion provides the best compromise between efficiency and equality. If the increase in equality encroaches upon profits this need not affect the rate of capital accumulation. It may, however, affect the pattern of investment by reducing the willingness to take risks. This general conclusion does not controvert the conclusion reached by Professor Lampman (1957, p. 254) 'that the proposition relating income inequality with economic progress and efficiency has been seriously shaken'. The assertion that greater equality must be at the expense of progress and efficiency lacks both empirical support and the degree of acceptance which together *might* make these an effective brake upon equalising tendencies.

V

IMPLICATIONS FOR POLICY

The growth of sectional collective bargaining in conditions of full employment has weakened the operation of market forces in the labour market, and created something of a vacuum there. Without going as far as the Donovan Report (1968) or Fox and Flanders (1969) in characterising the contemporary industrial relations situation as one of 'disorder' there can be no doubt about the need for a few clear principles or guide-lines, widely accepted, as a basis for income determination. Greater equality has an obvious attraction as such a principle. The most effective way of establishing greater equality would seem to be by establishing a structure of jobs based upon job evaluation, within which equated jobs would be paid equal rates.

The determination of wage structures on the basis of job evaluation has the attraction of providing a means both for extending equality and for strengthening efficiency-oriented principles in a labour market from which supply and demand are in full retreat. Although wage structures based on job evaluation will result in wide differentials in pay, these will be related to explicit factors. If these factors enjoy wide acceptance the wage structures based upon them will be regarded as equitable. It is probable too that differentials based upon job evaluation will be narrower than those which have evolved as a result of the interaction of social and market forces and sectional bargaining. A clinical approach to job content and value can be a most effective form of attack on conventionally established differentials. In addition the process of job evaluation, by focussing attention on job content, sets in motion a number of tendencies which can narrow differentials. One by-product of job evaluation is the additional information available to the labour force; another is the increased possibility of using a combination of manpower forecasting, and training and retraining programmes to reduce gaps between supply and demand. In addition job evaluation encourages job enlargement and this can reduce differentials.

If job evaluation is to be given the key role which has been suggested a number of institutional and policy changes will be necessary. Some of these are already in train for different reasons, and this can help the equalisation process.

The essential role of institutional and political factors in any effective shift in the distribution of income in favour of wage and salary earners and at the expense of profit and rentier incomes has already been noted. To this can be added the finding of Turner and Jackson (1969) ' that deliberate change in the structure of relative wages is only possible, if it is to have more than short term significance, in the context of a comparatively central-ized wage-fixing system '. ' Equal pay ' legislation and the establishment of a national minimum wage could contribute to both of these necessary conditions. Additional and important contributions can be made by govern-ment and its agencies concerned with the reform and re-organisation of collective bargaining, manpower forecasting, the encouragement of job enlargement and the appropriate training policies. It is essential that govern-ment is clear about its distributive intentions. If acceptable criteria for income distribution are to be established these must build upon existing attitudes to equity, made more explicit by government and strengthened by successful operation in practice. This would bring income distribution openly into politics, probably initially as an issue of contention but with the possibility of a fairly broadly based consensus becoming established. It would be necessary for government to ensure that its economic and social policies were compatible with its distributive policy. All of these actions by government would be necessary to create a secure framework within which collective bargaining could establish more equitable wage and salary structures. The centralisation of the wage-fixing system which Turner and Jackson see as necessary need not be imposed by government, but could result from the increasing use within distinct collective bargaining structures of common guide lines and criteria, amongst which would be job evaluation. Any movement towards greater equity must be compatible with the results of free collective bargaining. A merger of the ' guide-lines ' function of the National Board for Prices and Incomes and the structural reorganisation function of the Commission for Industrial Relations would be necessary if the reform of the ' means ' is to make the most effective contribution to the achievement of the ' end ' of a more equitable wage system.

A major impetus for change would have to come from the trade unions. The union merger movement and the increasing interest of the T.U.C. in the character of wage claims lodged by individual unions both increase the possibility that common criteria will become more widely acceptable. Unless the trade union movement endorses broad principles for determining wage and salary structures and the individual unions seek to apply these principles in practice any progress towards greater equity will be limited and insecure. The translation of principles into practice requires agreement on specific criteria, and it is in this connection that the approach of the trade unions to job evaluation could be important. If there were agreement about applying job evaluation more widely within a framework of collective bargaining, it would be necessary to decide which job factors, weighting systems and methods of evaluation were in accord with the trade unions' aims for wage and salary structure. The National Board for Prices and Incomes (1968, para. 106) has argued that experience and expertise should be pooled in an attempt to prevent different systems of job evaluation in firms with similar economic and technological circumstances. With individual unions spanning several industries and the T.U.C. taking tentative steps towards a common policy the unions are in a strong position to contribute to and influence the character of any such spread and standardisation of job evaluation. The gathering of information on the different methods currently in use and the resultant wage structures would be necessary, and although very little research of this sort has been done there is considerable scope for it, by unions, employers (either jointly or separately) and by independent researchers.[15]

Widening the area of application of an acceptable methodology of job evaluation would be a gradual process. It could only come about by negotiation within collective bargaining machinery which itself will be in process of reorganisation. Such processes would have to be seen as part of a social trend towards greater equality if equalising trends were to make secure progress. The time-scale of such social evolution will be longer than that used by individuals, households and firms in their decision-taking. Hence

---

[15] The same suggestion is made by Fox and Flanders (1969, p. 126). An example of such research by a trade union exists in International Association of Machinists (1953).

the importance of political factors and the need for some institutions to set their targets in the middle distance and beyond. It is in the long run that we are all equal.

University of Strathclyde

REFERENCES

CARVER, T. N. (1925). The Meaning of Economic Equality, *Quarterly Journal of Economics*, Vol. 39, 1952.
DONOVAN REPORT (1968). *Report* of the Royal Commission on Trade Unions and Employers' Associations, Cmnd. 3623. London, H.M.S.O.
FOX, A. and FLANDERS, A. (1969). The Reform of Collective Bargaining: From Donovan to Durkeim, *British Journal of Industrial Relations*, Vol. VII, No. 2, 1969.
HUNTER, LAURENCE C. (1968). Income Structure and Labour Mobility, *in* B. C. Roberts (ed.) *Industrial Relations: Contemporary Issues*, London.
INTERNATIONAL ASSOCIATION OF MACHINISTS (1953). Distribution of Employees by Labor Grade in some Airframe Plants, *Research Bulletin of the International Association of Machinists*, Vol. VII No. 12, Washington, 1953.
LAMPMAN, ROBERT J. (1957). Recent Thoughts on Egalitarianism, *Quarterly Journal of Economics*, Vol. 71. No. 2, 1957.
LYTLE, C. W. (1954). Job Evaluation Methods (2nd ed.) New York.
MEPHAM, G. J. (1969). *Problems of Equal Pay*, Institute of Personnel Management, London.
NATIONAL BOARD FOR PRICES AND INCOMES (1968), *Job Evaluation*, Report No. 83 (Cmnd. 3772). London, H.M.S.O.
OECD (1965). *Wages and Labour Mobility*, Paris.
PHELPS BROWN, E. H. (1951). *A Course in Applied Economics*, London.
PHELPS BROWN, E. H. (1968). *Pay and Profits*, Manchester University Press.
RAIMON, R. L. (1963). Labor Mobility and Wage Inflexibility, *Proceedings of the Industrial Relations Research Association*, 1963.
REDDAWAY, W. B. (1959). Wage Flexibility and the Distribution of Labour, *Lloyds Bank Review*, October 1959.
ROBBINS, LORD (1963). Equality as a Social Objective, *in Politics and Economics*, London.
ROUTH, GUY (1965). *Occupation and Pay in Great Britain*, 1906-60, Cambridge.
ROYAL COMMISSION ON EQUAL PAY (1946). *Report*, London, H.M.S.O.
RUNCIMAN, W. G. (1966). *Relative Deprivation and Social Justice*, London.
STIGLER, G. J. (1950). The Economists and Equality, *in Five Lectures on Economic Problems*, New York.
THOMASON, G. F. (1968). *Personnel Managers' Guide to Job Evaluation*, Institute of Personnel Management, London.
T.U.C. (1964). *Job Evaluation and Merit Rating*, Trades Union Congress, London.
T.U.C. (1966). *Trade Unionism*, Trades Union Congress, London.
T.U.C. (1969a). *General Council's Report*, Trades Union Congress, London.
T.U.C. (1969b). *Economic Review, 1969*, Trades Union Congress, London.
TURNER, H. A. & JACKSON, D. A. S. (1969). On the Stability of Wage Differences and Productivity-based Wage Policies: An International Analysis, *British Journal of Industrial Relations*, Vol. VII. No. 1, 1969.

THE STATUS OF THE INDUSTRIAL WORKER

Tom Lupton and Robert Hamilton

I

If status is defined literally as 'standing' *relative* to other categories of occupation, and industrial worker is simply taken to mean manual worker, then the status of the industrial worker has changed little since World War II and is, in the nature of things, likely to change little in the future. This paper is an account of the reasoning by which we have reached this conclusion.

We have approached the matter at two levels. After having identified a number of dimensions of status, viz., income, hourly rate, overtime, holidays, family expenditure patterns, educational opportunity, and family structure we have used national statistics, and materials from other surveys where relevant, to compare manual workers with non-manual workers, to get a measure of their relative standing, and an idea of how this has changed or is likely to change. At this level we are dealing with the relative standing of gross occupational categories. Our conclusions about this are as good (or as bad) as the data available. We have chosen the particular dimensions we use for measuring status differences because they are the things to which people in one category refer when comparing themselves with those in other categories, and because numerical data are available.

The comparison of occupational categories on a number of dimensions using national statistics is an interesting starting point but not a particularly practical one. This is one reason why we have limited our detailed statistical comparisons for the most part to manual workers and the lower non-manual occupational categories. If, as we shall suggest, manual workers when making comparisons of status on the dimensions we have used, look only at other manual workers, and to adjacent clerical and technical workers, then we need not, if we are interested in the manual worker's subjective status, produce data on the whole spectrum of occupational categories. We hope to justify this decision when we move to the second level and examine the effect of status changes of manual workers on their behaviour in different social contexts.

The paper therefore falls into three parts. The first clarifies definitions and justifies the equation of industrial worker and manual worker, and supports the exclusion of a whole range of occupational categories from the analysis. We also explain the choice of the status dimensions we have used. The second part compares some manual and non-manual occupations on the status measures using national statistics, and draws conclusions about the relative status of manual workers. Finally, on much less plentiful evidence, we try to see how absolute and relative changes in the position of the manual worker on our dimensions of status have affected, or are likely to affect, his behaviour in different social contexts, e.g. the workplace and the family.

II

THE HIERARCHY OF OCCUPATIONS

In British society, a status hierarchy of occupations exists which is part of the culture and there is wide consensus about the ranking within it.[1] The consensus does not reach to details of the position of every possible occupational category, such as the Registrar Generals' list contains, only to a broad but comprehensive classification. The professions have higher status than the clerks, the clerks have higher status than the manual workers, and in each of these extensive groups the relative positions of, for example, doctors and teachers, of book-keepers and filing clerks, of skilled and unskilled manual workers, are widely agreed upon, and have deep historical roots.[2] The division between manual and non-manual has considerable historical inertia which will give it endurance in the cultural tradition over time; it cannot be expected to disappear as a force in British society as suddenly or quickly, for example, as is implied by the theory that a short post-war affluence has created a homogeneous middle class society in Britain.

The status hierarchy is a cultured norm learnt[3] in the socialisation process and reinforced by consensus used to order the unequal distribution of economic rewards in a legitimate way[4]; the higher an occupation's position in this hierarchy, the more economic resources are in general allocated to it for discretionary use. It is not a measure of importance in the sense of an occupation's functional relevance to the society[5]: modern society, at least, is so interlocked that an argument for the great importance of almost any occupational role is not difficult to adduce. Nor is the hierarchy a measure of sheer economic power; but it is related to the structure of economic power in two ways: it may legitimise now a social status gained by illegitimate power in the past; and it legitimises the use of economic power in the present; though it can be eluded sometimes in the short term, e.g. by the affluent car workers in the 1960s, and less frequently in the long term by the use of illegitimate power.

The influence of this hierarchy as a norm operates through two mechanisms: the socialisation process and public opinion, the one reinforcing the other. The first is present in reward allocating procedures, e.g. wage negotiations, because the individuals taking part are members of the same society

---

[1] The classic sociological investigation of this phenomenon was carried out by Hall and D. G. Jones (1950). Later studies have confirmed these findings; the most comprehensive study, in Denmark, is K. Svalastoga (1959).

[2] Reference to this hierarchy in the sixteenth and seventeenth century is made in Laslett (1965).

[3] Kriesburg (1962, pp. 238-44).

[4] Lenski (1966).

[5] Davies (1961). Ch. 3.

who will use that society's culture as an agreed frame of reference. The latter introduces influences from outside the immediate interpersonal relations into the allocating procedures. In contemporary society this external influence derives from three sources: data collecting agencies who distribute information on income levels to firms and unions, the mass media, and the government. The influence of the first is a direct application of hierarchical order for it explicitly makes the present a measure of the future. The second and third influences are alike in the publicising of wage and salary negotiations and their results. This discourages deviation from the accepted norms by threatening the condemnation of public opinion and the possibility of subsequent activity by others to conserve any differentials that are attacked: the familiar wages spiral.

Evidence of the informal use of the status hierarchy as a norm in wage fixing is available in the survey of Industrial Relations in the Workplace commissioned by the Royal Commission on Trade Unions and Employers Associations which found that arguments based on comparability receive a great deal of support from management and unions alike (Social Survey, 1968). Further evidence of the use of the argument of comparability is obtained in almost any report of the statutory wage fixing bodies such as the Review Body on Doctors' and Dentists' Remuneration.[6] But in recent reports, for example on the University teachers and on top salaries in nationalised industries the N.B.P.I. (1968, 1969) has attacked the doctrine of comparability and has supported the current government's emphasis on productivity as the only reason, apart from a few small exceptions, for wage increases. This principle, if applied widely, could lead to a considerable upset of the traditional status system. There is, however, opposition to its application, most vigorously on the grounds of the impossibility of measuring the productivity of non-manual jobs in any meaningful way. The maintenance of the clerical differential over the manual income levels in the 1960s suggests that the principle of comparability has not lost place to the principle of productivity.

Although there are profound economic and technological changes in contemporary society which will alter the balances of economic power, such as the ability of a small group of workers in the car industry to disrupt a large industry, the society has developed techniques for containing the use of this power—data collection, mass media and government control bodies which are conservative in their effects. We would not therefore expect that the distribution of rewards in British society will have changed much in the past or will change much in the future.

This study of the status of the individual worker takes the context of status to be the whole society. Such an extensive context blurs many status distinctions which are made in concrete interpersonal relationships, and considers only basic and crude characteristics. Basic in the sense that they are very important personal qualities in defining the behaviour of others

---

[6] The doctrine of comparability is explicitly defended in the 9th Report 1968, H.M.S.O. para. 40-43.

in an interpersonal relationship; crude in the sense that the behaviour defined by them is stereotyped, lacking the idiosyncratic qualities. The occupational characteristics which are important at the societal level of analysis are those of the traditional status hierarchy; professional, white collar, manual. We therefore focus attention in this study on the manual workers and, in assessing their relative status, groups adjacent to them: the clerical or lower non-manual worker. The dimensions of status we examine are in part determined by the data available; this is not a restriction because the data were collected within the theoretical perspectives of the social class and community studies which we are using.

First we consider the work situation as a focus for the allocation of rewards and look at income, hours of work, maintenance of income during sickness, holidays and the minor status measures of the methods of recording attendance, and the provision of canteens. Secondly, we consider the household situation as a focus of traditional sub-cultural patterns of living and look at household income, the ownership of houses, the purchase of expensive durable goods, and the extended family relationships. In the work situation we shall restrict the comparison to men and so avoid the aspects of status which are based on sex differences.

III

A. THE WORK SITUATION

1. *Income*

In our society, income is of great significance as an indicator of status. Levels of money income are themselves precise indicators of relative social position, but as money also gives access to economic goods, its very possession is a status indicator as well as the specific things possessed. Further, bargaining and other mechanisms for allocating rewards in society tend to use money as a measure because it gives precision and avoids ambiguity.

The manager uses money in diverse ways to motivate workers to high performance, to attract them from the labour market, to influence the number of hours they work, and the time at which they work them, and so on; this fact renders difficult the aggregated comparison of money income as a measure of status and this difficulty is compounded if payments in kind are included. The richness of the specific situation in which a manual worker's rewards are forthcoming is lost in the aggregation and we shall try to show in IV below the exact significance for the manual worker's status of the detailed structure of the pay packet. However, despite the difficulty, income is so significant that the attempt must be made to use it as a measure of the relative status of broad occupational categories. and particular occupations within them.

The survey of earnings in September 1968 by the Department of Employment and Productivity (1969) provides the most extensive and statistically reliable source of data of the income of various occupational groups. It differs in this from market research studies by professional societies and firms in the labour market; these are characteristically narrow in their subject and idiosyncratic in their design, whereas the D.E.P. has the advantage not only of a large sample, but of a consistent method for measuring income which provides reliable comparable data for the different occupations. We focus on the manual-clerical division in the status system, and here the survey classifies incomes in each of these broad categories into four sub-divisions which provide two hierarchies, a manual and a clerical, with comparable degrees of status within each hierarchy. The figures quoted by the survey are of gross earnings per week of men over 21 years of age defined to include basic pay, overtime, shift work pay, commissions, piecework, and all kinds of allowences, and exclude income in kind such as subsidised housing, free meals, transport, etc., Table I presents the data for these eight sub-groups giving median, quartile and decile levels of earnings. The Administrative and Managerial earnings figures are presented in order to give perspective.

Table I

MEDIANS QUARTILES AND DECILES OF EARNINGS OF MANUAL AND CLERICAL MALES OVER 21 IN 1968

	Nos.	Lower Decile	Lower Quartile	Median	Upper Quartile	Upper Decile	Decile Range
		£ p.w.	£ p.w.	£ p.w.	£ p.w.	£ p.w.	
Office Supervisor	144	£20·3	23·4	27·8	32·8	37·6	17·3
Clerk considerable responsibility	958	£18·4	22·1	25·6	30·8	35·8	17·4
Clerk with some responsibility	1,691	£15·4	17·6	20·6	23·5	28·5	13·1
Clerk routine	430	£13·0	15·3	17·4	20·6	24·7	11·7
Foreman	2,082	£20·0	23·7	27·6	32·4	37·9	17·9
Skilled	10,189	£17·2	20·0	23·9	28·8	34·8	17·6
Semi-skilled	5,004	£15·9	18·7	22·7	27·4	32·3	16·4
Unskilled	4,352	£13·6	15·8	19·1	23·4	28·2	14·6
Non-supervisory Clerical Group	3,079	£16·01	18·41	21·73	25·31	30·35	14·34
Non-supervisory Manual Group	19,545	£16·32	18·70	22·52	27·23	32·72	16·04
Administrative/ Managerial		£19·9	26·0	24·8	48·0	68·2	

Source: Employment and Productivity Gazette.

Within each occupational category, clerical and manual, and at each distributional level the earnings of each sub-group follows their status levels within the occupational category. There is, therefore, more opportunity for high earnings in a higher status job. Situations in which low status jobs earn more than higher status jobs, if they occur, will be very localised and deviant cases from an overall national pattern of close correlation between levels of rewards and level of status within the broad manual and clerical occupational categories.

A comparison across the manual and clerical categories reveals a slightly different pattern of rewards and status. In aggregate the non-supervisory manual workers obtain slightly higher incomes than the non-supervisory clerical workers, and because the manual range of income is wider than the clerical range, while both have the same income at the lower points of the range, the manual advantage increases as income increases, e.g. the manual advantage at the median is £0·8 per week and at the upper decile point it is £2·3 per week. This aggregate result is produced by three differences between the detailed structure of the clerical and manual earnings: (1) the clerical hierarchy spans a wider range of incomes than the manual hierarchy; (2) the two lower-status manual groups, unskilled and semi-skilled, have wider ranges of income than the two lower status clerical groups, routine clerk and clerk with some responsibilities; and (3) the respective earnings level of the six non-supervisory grades.

This aggregate manual advantage of earnings over the clerks is, therefore, a consequence of two disparate positions: higher earnings in the lower grades and lower earnings in the higher grades. The traditional manual-clerical positions on the dimensions of the level of earnings has been upset, but not unambiguously. The advantageous clerical position of 1924, when between 75 per cent. and 91 per cent. of clerks in different industrial groups earned more than the average earnings of the manual worker[7] (including those under 21 years of age) certainly has been eroded. In 1968 the percentages of clerks earning more than £24 per week, the median manual income being £22·4 per week, were 62 per cent. for clerks with considerable responsibility, 23 per cent. for clerks with some responsibility, and 12 per cent. for clerks with routine jobs.

In addition there are some manual jobs which provide opportunities for earnings considerably higher than the most responsible clerks: twelve of the manual occupations, classified in the D.E.P. Survey, representing about 12 per cent. of the manual workers, have higher levels of pay than the 5·2 per cent. of clerks with considerable responsibility with earnings over £40 per week. Two of these, printing press operator (skilled) and stevedore/docker, have 19·4 per cent. and 14·4 per cent. respectively of their members earnings over this amount. The clerks, therefore, have reasons to feel relatively deprived in 1968 compared with the 1920s. The upsetting of the traditional status positions is, however, far from complete, and the growing unionism and militancy amongst the clerks point to processes at work hindering any erosion of the clerical advantage.

2. Hours of Work and Income

So far, we have been comparing weekly income. From that comparison it appears that the manual workers have increased their status relative to

[7] Bowley and Stamp (1924).

the clerical workers. Yet this has been accomplished with a persisting relatively low hourly rate of pay for manual workers. 67 per cent. of ' clerks with considerable responsibility' earn more than 12 shillings per hour, compared with 56·4 per cent. of foremen and 30·5 per cent. of skilled manual workers. Manual workers have therefore attained equality of income with the clerks by working longer hours. Since the end of the last war the *basic* hours of both manual and clerical workers have decreased. In 1950 the basic manual hours were, on average, 45 hours per week and in 1969 they were 40·5 hours per week.[8] In 1946 the basic clerical hours were within the range 35 to 43 hours per week, with 67·8 per cent. of the clerks working less than 41 hours (Institute of Office Management, 1946). A survey by the Industrial Society (1966a) found the range for non-manual workers was 33·75 to 40·5 hours with 58 per cent. of non-manual employees working less than 36·5 hours per week. But these figures are not of actual hours worked. Since 1950 the average hours *actually* worked per week by manual workers has never fallen below the 46·1 of April 1967 or risen about the 48·9 of April 1955,[9] in spite of the decreasing length of the basic week.

An estimate of actual working hours can be made from the results of the D.E.P. survey of incomes by dividing median hourly rates of pay into median weekly earnings; the hourly rates consolidate overtime rates, shift premiums and other allowances.

Table II presents these computations listing the eight occupational groups in order of their hourly rate of pay. The broadly equal weekly earnings of manual and clerical workers in 1968 are concomitant with two related factors which differentiate the two occupational groups: a status factor, the length of the *basic* week; and a cultural factor, the persistence of a longer *actual* working week (averaging 47 hours) for the manual worker.[10]

In contrast to the clerks the manual workers seem to have had both the opportunity and the desire to use the shorter basic week as a means of improving their income rather than as a means of creating more leisure. The reasons for this are complex. Zweig (1961) has suggested that overtime is worked by young married men who are setting up home and starting families, so as to meet non-recurring calls on income. This is probably so, but it would hardly explain the increasing gap between basic hours and actual hours; and it is not only young manual workers who work overtime. Another reason might be that a reduction in basic hours probably does not signal a reduced demand for labour, and in conditions of labour scarcity and long order books the obvious way to meet production schedules would be to work overtime. Overtime would then tend to become regular, at the level of the previously worked weekly hours. This could explain why man-

[8] Employment and Productivity Gazette, November 1969.
[9] *Ministry of Labour Gazette,* February 1960 and *Employment and Productivity Gazette,* August 1968.
[10] The survey by the Industrial Society (1966a) asked firms if they had a policy of developing the same terms and conditions of employment for manual and non-manual employees: 35 per cent. of the firms had and 53 per cent. had not.

agers wanted workers to put in overtime, but it does not explain why workers are willing to work it, rather than go for leisure, and a lower income.

Table II
MEDIAN HOURLY RATES, MEDIAN WEEKLY EARNINGS AND ACTUAL HOURS WORKED FOR EIGHT OCCUPATIONAL GROUPS

	Median hourly rate Shillings (a)	Median weekly earnings Shillings (b)	Approx. hours worked
1. Office Supervisor	13·9	556	40
2. Clerk considerable responsibility	13·3	512	38·5
3. Foreman	12·5	552	42·5
4. Clerk some responsibility	10·5	412	39·1
5. Skilled	10·5	478	45·5
6. Semi-skilled	9·6	454	47·1
7. Routine	8·9	349	39·5
8. Unskilled	8·0	382	47·5

Source: Employment and Productivity Gazette.

There are obviously factors at work outside the workplace, other than those applying to young married men, to account for the desire to accept, and probably in many cases demand, overtime. Overtime is almost certainly in demand during periods before holidays, a likely reflection of the manual workers' traditional reluctance to save regularly for such occasions. But there is much regular overtime that cannot be accounted for in this way. Some researchers have suggested that the workplace, for the manual workers, is a source of much valued social relationships with mates, especially in these traditionally working class communities in which the division of labour of the spouses is sharp, and in which, apart from kin, they share few common friends and acquaintances. But, with the dispersal of many of these communities, these patterns are breaking up, so this can only be a partial explanation too.

The success of the advertisers in persuading manual workers that their expenditure should expand to meet or exceed their income, the temptations of hire purchase, and such things, must also play their part. The lengthening of the weekend and the annual holiday, and the increasing expense of weekend and holiday pursuits and household equipment and heating expenses might also add to the explanation. There might be an inclination to concentrate and intensify more expensive leisure pursuits, by means of long periods of hard and well-paid work—a style of life by no means confined to manual workers.

3. *Sickness Benefits provided by Employers; Maintenance of Income*

The Ministry of Pensions and National Insurance carried out a national survey of the broad characteristics of Employer Sick Pay Schemes in 1962

(M.P.N.I., 1964). The data in Table III have been reorganised from this source to compare the experience of manual and non-manual workers, and show the percentages in each group distributed according to qualifying period, number of waiting days, maximum duration of payments, and amount of payment. Each of these factors will influence the experience of a manual worker and his family during a period of illness: the amount of pay is the most important factor and the worker's access to this is constrained by waiting days and maximum duration of the benefits. A P.E.P. survey (1961) of a random sample of ' households with children ' in London and Nottingham inquired into the experience of households with a sick income earner and reported the percentages of families in socio-economic groups who considered that they had had a good deal of difficulty when living on sickness benefits (state and private) as: manual unskilled 31 per cent., manual skilled 21 per cent., supervisory, technical and clerical 19 per cent., and managerial and professional 6 per cent. The pattern of these results would be expected from the data shown in Table III, although the level of the P.E.P. figures is obviously a result of many factors in addition to the availability of benefits from their employers—other people in the family working, for example, or the possession of and willingness to use savings. It does support the proposition that the supply of sickness schemes by the employers is a reasonable measure of status within the work place which is reflected in a differential distribution of desired and needed resources.

On all the dimensions measured the data in Table III show the manual workers in a disadvantageous position; the traditional line between staff and non-staff is clearly drawn with the clerical workers enjoying a position little different from the higher status professional and managerial workers. Only one manual occupational group has a greater proportion of members covered by sick pay schemes than the clerical workers, the miners and quarrymen with 95·5 per cent. and, only one other has a proportion within 2C per cent. of the clerks, the gas, coke and chemical makers. The terms of the schemes for these manual groups are, however, much less favourable than the terms for the clerks. Both of these groups are, significantly mainly drawn from nationalised industries (M.P.N.I., 1964, Part I).

This difference between manual and non-manual provision of sick pay, coupled with the greater incidence of incapacity for work among manual workers, places the manual worker in a relatively insecure earnings situation (M.P.N.I., 1964). These different situations are reflected in the D.E.P. (1969) study[11], which collected data on the incidence of loss of pay during the week of the survey. Loss is measured here as being paid for less than the normal *basic* hours for the job, i.e. excluding overtime; this measure, therefore, will under-record loss to manual workers, for those workers customarily include some overtime in their normal working week. The percentage of the clerical and manual occupational groups who lost pay in that week because of sickness were clerical 1·5 per cent., skilled manual 4 per cent., semi-skilled manual 4·4 per cent., and unskilled manual 5·6 per cent.

[11] Employment and Productivity *Gazette*, September 1969.

Table III

PROVISION OF SICK PAYMENT SCHEMES BY EMPLOYERS,
BY OCCUPATIONAL GROUPS

	Manual	Clerical	Administrative Managerial	Professional
	%	%	%	%
Covered by a scheme	48	88	87	92
Length of qualifying period:				
none	11	50	56	64
0-6 months	18	18	12	15
7-12 months	18	11	7	6
more than 12 months or at discretion	1	9	12	7
Number of waiting days:				
1-3	29	83	85	89
more than 3	5	2	1	1
or at discretion	14	3	1	2
Maximum Duration of Payments:				
0-13 weeks	28	18	13	16
more than 13 weeks and at discretion	20	60	74	76
Amounts of Payment:				
Full pay				
a) without deduction	4·5	19	25	16
b) with deduction of N.I.	23	62	54	71
Half to full pay	2·3	1	1	1
Less than half pay and at discretion	18·3	6	7	4
Not covered by a sick pay scheme	52	12	13	8

Source: M.P.N.I. Enquiry into the incidence of incapacity to work 1964. Part II, H.M.S.O.
Note. The Manual Group is an aggregate of the 20 manual occupational categories used in the survey.

The differential coverage found in the 1964 survey by the M.P.N.I. appears therefore to have persisted through the sixties. Although these figures are influenced by the lower incidence of incapacity for work amongst clerks about half that for manual workers, this does not account for the three to one ratio, manual to clerical, of the results.

4. *Terms and conditions of work:*
   such as the amount of holiday entitlements and payments

Certain aspects of the work situation, holidays with pay, methods of attendance recording, canteens and guaranteed wages, have traditionally a status connotation of their own quite apart from their close relationship to the distribution of monetary rewards. The staff-non-staff division is an important reference in the allocation of benefits such as these, the staff obtaining a more favourable access to them, and there is evidence to suggest that this tradition is not dying. A 1966 survey by the Industrial Society, which asked firms whether or not they had different general practices in the treatment of manual and non-manual employees, shows that only 6 per cent. had the same terms.

The main beneficiaries of the Holidays with Pay Act of 1938, which gave one week's annual holiday to all employees, were the manual workers, since holidays with pay of a fortnight had been widely available to clerical workers well before this time (*New Survey of London*, 1934). In the late sixties, few employees had an entitlement of less than two weeks, ten working days, and many have fifteen or more days. The tradition of a longer holiday for clerical employees has, however, persisted in this general expansion of the holiday period both in the allotment of a basic entitlement and in the opportunity to increase this basic amount by service in the company. Two surveys by the Industrial Society (1966b, 1969) illustrate both the trend towards more holidays and the maintenance of the staff-non-staff differentials during the second half of the sixties. Table IV compares the two occupational groups in 1969.

The percentage of firms giving a basic holiday of more than 15 days to the two occupational categories in 1966 and 1969 rose from 17 per cent. to 47 per cent. between 1966 and 1969 in the case of manual workers, and from 38 per cent. to 76 per cent. in the case of clerical workers. Within a rising trend the ratio of 2 to 1 of the number of companies giving this longer holiday to clerks persisted. Figures given in Table IV of the maximum possible entitlement that can be obtained through service in the company show an even wider discrepancy between the two work groups, reflecting the greater opportunities of the clerks to extend their holiday period in this way. In addition to a longer holiday, the clerks have an advantage in the payments that are received during this period. According to the D.E.P. Survey of Earnings one half of manual workers are paid just over 60 per cent. of their average earnings during their holiday and nearly all clerks are paid 90 per cent. of average earnings (D.E.P. 1969).

The status significance of methods of recording attendances and the use of canteens is small compared with income levels, even though at times these matters have been elevated to positions of great emotional importance (Brown, 1960; and Marsh, 1963). The survey by the Industrial Society (1966a) included questions on these topics and provides some evidence of the extension of these practices. The results are mixed, providing support, in methods of attendance recording, of a persisting difference in the experience of clerical and manual employees, and support, in the use of canteens and the provision of a guaranteed weekly wage, of a narrowing of status differences. The data are summarised in Table V.

11

Table IV

LENGTH OF HOLIDAYS OF MANUAL AND CLERICAL WORKERS IN 1969

	Days Holidays 1969				
	10	11-14	15	16-19	20
	Basic Entitlement				
Manual	23	30	41	6	0
Clerical	11	14	53	20	3
	Maximum Entitlement				
Manual	9	23	45	12	11
Clerical	2	4	41	22·5	30·5

Source: Industrial Society.

B. THE HOUSEHOLD SITUATION

5. Household income

The family and household situation is a second significant context in which we can consider manual-clerical differences. Habits of life within the household are, of course, closely linked to the circumstances of the work situation which provides money, determines leisure hours and introduces behavioural reference points important in understanding those habits. However, traditional, culturally-learnt behaviour dominates this situation rather than the status expectations which dominate in the work situation. This is because in family living patterns and consumption behaviour, the status differences minimally intrude: the family lives within the environment of families of similar status and contact with families and individuals of different status is small. In the purchasing relationship, the possession of money is the supremely important variable and few distinctions can be, or are, made about the type of money. There is, however, some intrusion of occupational status in the consumer market, insofar as credit is more readily and cheaply available to persons of a high occupational status and, consequently, a higher income, and insofar as the buyers' occupational status is reflected in their style of interpersonal behaviour, some of which the seller favours and some of which he rejects, e.g. the innkeepers who refuse to serve coach parties, and the high and low class stores who consciously or unconsciously provide an atmosphere in which high and low status purchasers respectively feel at ease. Generally, however, the money nexus predominates and the use of economic resources, already earned, by households is patterned according to the personal and cultural preferences of the purchasers.

Table V

PERCENTAGE OF FIRMS WHO SUPPLY CANTEENS, A GUARANTEED WEEK AND WHO RECORD ATTENDANCE; 1966

	Manual	Non-Manual
Canteens		
Are supplied	94%	94%
Are not supplied	6%	6%
Manual and non-manual share	60%	60%
Attendance Recording		
Clock	93%	33%
Sign a line book	3%	16%
Recorded by officials	3%	6%
No recording	3%	46%
Guaranteed Week		
Provided	77%	N.A.
Not provided	22%	N.A.

Source: Industrial Society.

The long historical division of society between those who rule and those who do not rule, the privileged and the non-privileged[12] has produced two distinct sub-cultural patterns of living in British Society. The manual-clerical division is an important boundary of these two sub-cultures; so we should still expect to find today a difference in patterns of behaviour of households headed by manual and clerical workers. To examine this we focus on education, general expenditure preferences, the ownership of houses and consumer durables, patterns of extended family living, and the make up of the household income.

The household's income rather than personal income, is the support for consumer spending, since certain costly and fundamental items such as houses, furniture, kitchen equipment and motor cars are common to all members of a household. Some data on household incomes derived from the Family Expenditure Surveys are presented in Table VI.

The slightly higher clerical household income shown in Table VI is achieved by fewer earners contributing to it; and the manual families having a large number of children will have on average more wage earners. In 1968 the average number of earners in manual households was 1·82 and in the clerical households was 1·70. This difference is highest at the high levels of income £35 or more per week, where the manual households have on average 0·35 more earners per household. This pattern of income does not only imply a clerical advantage in income at the aggregated household level, but also that

[12] Cf. Lenski (1966).

Table VI

HOUSEHOLD INCOME RANGES AND NUMBERS OF EARNERS PER HOUSEHOLD:
MANUAL AND CLERICAL, 1962, 1963, 1968.

	Manual		Clerical	
Mean Household Income 1962 1968	£ 20·7 p.w. 30·7 p.w.		£ 22·7 p.w. 32·3 p.w.	
	1963	1968	1963	1968
	£	£	£	£
Lower Decile Income	11·4	15·9	11·7	16·4
Lower Quartile Income	15·4	21·5	16·03	23·9
Median Income	20·6	28·5	21·8	29·2
Upper Quartile Income	27·2	37·3	29·4	38·5
Upper Decile Income	35·3	44·4	39·1	44·3

Source: Family Expenditure Surveys 1962, 1963, 1968. H.M.S.O.

the manual household incomes are less consistently at high levels overtime. Any contribution other than from a husband or wife will have a temporary quality, at least potentially, because it will be derived from a child on the brink of leaving the household, or less frequently, from a relative who has ties to the household which can be broken more readily than the husband-wife tie. The more enduring contribution from the wife as a second earner is not less frequent in clerical households: in the 1966 Sample Census, both manual and clerical families had approximately 44 per cent. of wives working. The very high manual household incomes, therefore, result in the traditional working class pattern of larger families having, for a short period in their life cycle, many earners simultaneously contributing to them.

6. *Education*

In general, the education and training for an adult worker will be strictly vocational, and the higher his present status the more likely is it that the training will be for promotion. The Open University offers a non-vocational education to the adult, but it has yet to prove itself as a ladder for occupational mobility.

However, in his children, the adult becomes involved in the educational system and vicariously is substantially influenced by the structure of this system.

The social class differences in educational experiences have been recorded in a number of studies[13] during the 1950s and 1960s. The data show an increasing equality of educational experience measured in terms of oppor-

---

[13] Little and Westergaard (1964) provide a useful survey of these studies.

tunities to obtain the crucial paper qualifications of G.C.E. and University degree since the 1920s, but, in spite of this, there is still a severe inequality. In 1961 still only five per cent. of children of skilled manual workers stayed in the Grammar school to age 17, compared with 15 per cent. of children from clerical families and 41 per cent. from professional and managerial families; and 1 per cent. of children from manual families enter universities compared with 12 per cent. from non-manual families. Douglas's study (1968) of a national cohort of children confirms these findings. The educational success of his subjects, defined as the attainment of a good G.C.E. at O level, is influenced not only by the social class of their parents but by the parents' position within the social class measured mainly by their own educational experience. In Table VII, which reproduces some of Douglas's results, the upper part of each class has a relatively better education than the lower part. A child's ability is obviously an important influence on his performance, but it cannot completely overcome an unfavourable home background: the lower manual child in the 50-55 ability range would, in fact benefit as much from a change in home background to upper non-manual as from an increase in his ability to the next higher level.

Table VII

PERCENTAGE OF SUBJECTS AT VARIOUS I.Q. LEVELS OBTAINING A GOOD G.C.E.

Social Class	Ability level at 15 years				
	60 and more	59-55	54-50	49-45	44 and less
Non-manual Upper Lower	77 60	33 18	11 6	4 —	— —
Manual Upper Lower	53 37	15 9	2 3	1 —	— —

Source: Douglas (1968).

The school situation can be analysed into three interdependent variables: the children's interest in education, the teachers' ability and interest in educating the children, and the socio-physical learning environment at the school. The three are positively correlated, so that lack of one will encourage lack of the others and vice-versa. The Plowden Report (1967) focussed on the socio-physical environment and charted the interrelationship between the local catchment area, the type of pupil this provides and the type of school in terms of amenities, staffing and academic texture that these encourage. The Report pointed out that some of these variables could be adjusted directly by the input of financial resources which suggestion the educational administration of this country is well able to process. A second variable, the teachers' quality, is amenable to improvement and adjustment, through a highly organised training system in the universities and colleges. The third variable, the educational quality of the children, is, as Douglas (1968) points out, strongly influenced by the home background of the child; but this parental influence is much less amenable to control than the teacher training system and the educational administration system, and is the opportunity for the wider social structure to have a considerable impact on the school experience of the child.

Parents interested in their children's education introduce teachable children into the school and these children interact with the teachers to produce a learning environment. The parental interest is, in its turn, a product of the educational experience of the parent. The schoolchild is therefore caught in one of two circles of forces: the first producing well educated children of well educated parents and the second producing poorly educated children of poorly educated parents. By force of I.Q. and a favourable school environment, it is possible for the child to escape in some measure from that system to which by parental attitude he belongs.

The study by Jackson and Marsden (1962) suggests that two distinct factors are discouraging the parents belonging to the less prestigious social strata, i.e. the manual class in this country, from developing an interest in their children's educational life. The first is the relative ignorance of these parents of the educational system and of the actual process of academic learning which is a consequence of their own dearth of educational experience. As the educational system is the selection procedure for the occupational system, these educationally ignorant parents will cluster in these lower social strata. The second is the low status of these parents relative to the teachers and administrators in the schools which implies that contact with the schools has to span status and cultural differences, a task that is invariably painful for the person of lower status.

The manual families are in a disadvantageous position in an enduring social structure. As long as the educational system is a training and selection process for occupational status, the manual workers will be in general, relative failures; and as long as the family system endures, those parents who have failed will have children who fail relatively more frequently. Short of separating the educational and occupational systems or abolishing or severly weakening the influence of families, equality of opportunity in education, in terms of every child developing his special abilities, is unattainable.

7. Patterns of spending

Equality of incomes has not produced immediate similarity in spending. Traditionally, the manual household's expenditure has been relatively concentrated on personal consumption reflecting the institution of the ' husband's money ', i.e., a substantial proportion of the weekly pay reserved exclusively to the husband. Alcohol, tobacco and betting are predominant items in the expenditure of this money. In contrast the clerical expenditure is relatively concentrated on family consumption reflecting the institution of joint marital roles in allocating resources. Houses, household durable goods, services and holidays are predominant items in this spending.

The distribution of ownership of durable goods, Table VIII, follows the patterns of expenditure; the C1 households are more frequently owners than the C2 and D households. The differences are not large but the aggregate figures hide many variations in quality and price, for example second-hand or new. More of the washing machines in the C1 households are of the more expensive automatics than in the C2 and D households, and the detailed Survey of the Motoring Market (1964) found 79 per cent. of cars owned by C2, D and E households to be second hand in contrast to 50 per cent. of cars owned by C1 households, and in addition, 65 per cent. of the former households owned cars more than five years old compared to 50 per cent. of the latter. The proportions taking a holiday and owning a car, however, differ markedly between the two groups, the clerical figures being in each case twice the manual figures. The manual tradition of not

Table VIII

PURCHASING AND OWNERSHIP OF CONSUMER DURABLES BY SOCIAL CLASS

	Made a purchase during 1962-1967		Ownership in 1967	
	I.P.A. Social Group		I.P.A. Social Group	
	C1	C2, D	C1	C2, D
	%	%	%	%
Television[1]	45	47	92	92
Hair dryer[1]	16	15·6	43	35
Washing machine[1]	29	28·5	68	52
Spin/tumbler dryer[1]	8	9	15	14
Vacuum cleaner[1]	32	31	91	80
Refrigerator[1]	27	21	63	47
Food Mixer[1]	7	3	10	4
Holidays in 1968[2]				
in Britain	—	—	54·5	42*
abroad	—	—	17·5	7*
none	—	—	28	51*
Owning a car[3]				
1956			24	10·5*
1965			57	28·2*

Sources: 1. *Woman and the National Market*: Domestic Appliances 1967, Press.
2. *Patterns in British Holiday Making* 1951-68, B.T.A. 1969.
3. *The Motorist Today*, A.A. 1966.
* An average of C2's, D's, and E's.

going on a holiday or of having a holiday at home endures among the young as well as the old.

Affluence does not radically change the manual household spending patterns. Table IX compares the expenditure on a number of traditionally sensitive items of average manual and clerical households and those in the highest income category of more than £35 per week. The masculine expenditures on alcohol and tobacco appear, augmented, in the affluent manual budgets and so do the amounts spent on household durables and services in the affluent clerical budgets. The affluent manual householders have, however, channelled higher proportions of their larger incomes into two items: motor cars and holidays. The former is most certainly an extension of the husband's exclusive spending; for the evidence for this pattern of family organisation is present in the affluent budgets and the motor car is an almost exclusively male preserve.[14] The latter, in contrast, shows a tendency to follow the non-manual habit of going on a holiday.

Table IX

COMPARATIVE EXPENDITURES OF AVERAGE AND AFFLUENT HOUSEHOLDS: BY MANUAL AND CLERICAL GROUPS 1968

	All households average weekly expenditure				Household earnings more than £35 p.w average weekly expenditure			
			Percentage greater expenditure				Percentage greate expenditure	
	Manual	Clerical	Manual expenditure greater %	Clerical expenditure greater %	Manual	Clerical	Manual expenditure greater	Cleric: expend ture greate
	Shillings (a)	Shillings (b)	$\frac{(a-b)}{b}$	$\frac{(b-a)}{a}$	Shillings (c)	Shillings (d)	$\frac{(c-d)}{d}$	$\frac{(d-c}{c}$
Food	144	134	7·4	—	185	173	7	—
Alcohol	24·5	19	29	—	40·5	28·5	43	—
Tobacco	32	24·5	30	—	44	31·5	40	—
Purchase, maintenance motor vehicles	52	53	—	2	95	78	24	—
H/H durables	33	38	—	15	43·5	57	—	31
Services (inc. holidays)	37·5	55·5	—	48	58	72·5	—	11
Domestic help	1·5	2	—	25	2	4	—	200

Source: Family Expenditure Survey. 1968. H.M.S.O.

This, together with the growth in house ownership, suggests that some of the affluent manual workers are using the non-manual group as a normative reference for their spending, and the positive correlation between manual house-ownership and manual car ownership found in Atkins' (1964) study

[14] The New Housewife (1967, Table 7-7).

of people and their cars adds weight to this inference. The movement is, however, only a trickle, and there is evidence of considerable cultural inertia which will hinder this trickle from becoming a stream.

8. *Housing*

There is a slogan which was painted on a wall in Manchester's Moss Side only a few years ago proclaiming: 'Homes not mortgage traps'. To the middle class house buyers scrambling for the cheap building society ticket into the property boom this is an obscurantist viewpoint, but it does reflect a working class tradition of renting houses and an attitude inbred through this tradition of reluctance to take on the long-term burden of buying a house and of financing its intermittent and expensive maintenance. The habit of renting is the result of economic circumstances as much as it is the result of a learnt way of living; for should the manual worker wish to purchase his house a lack of wealth and an insecurity of income severely hinder the fulfilment of this aim. The increasing proportion of manual households buying their houses suggest that the traditional attitudes are waning as affluence rises and that the financiers, especially the Building Societies, are reassessing the creditworthy status of the manual workers.

Table X

PERCENTAGE OF INCOME GROUPS OWNING THEIR OWN HOUSES BY OCCUPATIONAL
GROUPS

	Ownership and expenditure on houses; manual and clerical households 1962 and 1968; by income groups					
	Household income in pounds per week					
1962 amounts 1968 „	Less than £10 £15	10 - 15 15 - 20	15 - 20 20 - 25	20 - 30 25 - 35	30 & more 35 & more	All H/H's
	Percentage owing houses					
Manual						
1962	14·6	24·6	30·0	32·4	33·4	29
1968	22·6	28·4	33·3	40·5	45·5	38
Clerical						
1962		39		56		47
1968	31		46	62	64	55

In 1968, compared with 1962, 9 per cent. more of manual households and 8 per cent. more of clerical households owned their houses (Table X). This has happened despite the increase in the costs of ownership from 32 shillings to 75 shillings per week (rates plus insurance plus mortgage payments), an increase from 7·8 per cent. to 12·3 per cent. of gross income before any deductions, and in spite of renting becoming cheaper than owner-ship during this period. Affluence is an important factor in this trend towards house-ownership; for the highest percentage increase belongs to the highest income group in the manual class, £35 or more per week. The trend, however, is spread throughout the whole class with a rate of growth roughly proportionate to income[15] (Table X).

Affluence in an inflationary economy is encouraging the manual workers to follow the middle class into house-ownership; however, the clerical workers are no less encouraged and are maintaining their considerable lead over the manual workers: in 1968 55 per cent. of clerical households owned their house compared with 38 per cent. of manual households. They are doing this with a very slight advantage in income and at a higher price: the average cost is approximately 100 shillings per week, 15 per cent. of the average clerical household gross income. This difference will partially be a reflection of the varying cultural traditions of manual and clerical workers but an equal if not stronger influence producing this contrast is the working of the credit market.

Apart from personal qualities which can multifariously influence the size and availability of a loan, the most important characteristic of a mortgage applicant is his income and on this point, the average manual worker is at a twofold disadvantage relative to the average clerical worker[16]: his income contains a higher proportion of non-regular amounts, and he is not on an income scale which more or less guarantees a future increase in income.

According to the D.E.P. survey of earnings in 1968 an average manual worker earning £30 per week obtained £4·8 from overtime and £3·5 from bonuses, whereas a clerical worker earning the same amount has only £1·75 overtime and £0·5 from bonuses. Overtime and bonuses are not necessarily fluctuating in amount in the contemporary economy, but they are less secure than the basic wage in principle and often in practice: a financial company would want to inquire about the permanency of the manual wage level which they would assume to be characteristic of the clerical salary. There is an important emphasis here which encourages the prudent financier to assess the borrowing capacity of the manual income lower than the clerical. In addition to this, the clerical worker is frequently on a salary scale, and the mortgager can take this into account. A record of regularly negotiated wage increases for the manual worker is not extrapolated into the future as a similar basis for credit. Consequently, the average manual worker with a weekly income of £30 can expect to be able to borrow probably £3,000 and possibly £3,500, while the average clerical workers with the same aggregate income can expect to be able to borrow probably £3,750 and possibly £4,500.

---

[15] The out-of-step 8 per cent. increase during the period 1962 to 1968 in the lowest income group appears to be due to a high proportion of workers over the official age of retirement, who cluster in the below £15 per week income group and who, in richer days, will have paid for their house: 87 per cent. of this group have no mortgage on the house they own.

[16] We are grateful to the managers of two large Building Society Branches who generously explained at length the various factors they have to weigh in considering an application for a mortgage.

There are, of course, houses available throughout the money range £3,000 to £4,500, but this does not mean that the manual worker will buy more frequently because he is channelled towards the cheaper houses. The cheaper houses are mainly the older houses and the less attractive to purchase; and their age will be grounds for requiring a higher initial percentage deposit making the absolute amount of the deposit as large as that for a newer, more expensive house. The market structure not only hinders the manual house-purchaser, but also, by directing the manual and clerical households towards different types of property, reinforces the contemporary pattern of neighbour-hood separation of the two occupational groups. The cultural barriers to mixing socially persist into the present[17] and the structural factors of the housing market contribute towards their continuation rather than their erosion.

9. The family

The differing class experiences in housing extends beyond the buying and renting of houses to the sharing of houses with their relatives. A national study of young housewives aged 16-34 in 1964 explored some of the ideas thrown up by the community studies of the 1950s using a national representa-tive sample (*The New Housewife*, 1967). It records almost universal agree-ment with the proposition that a newly married couple should live at first on their own, but the actual experience of the respondents did not fulfil their wishes. The newly wed middle class were able to set up their own homes more quickly than the working class: —

	A.B.C.1.	C.2.D.E.
Couples who set up their own home immediately	65%	44%
Couples who lived with parents and other relatives	28%	48%
Couples who lived with other people	7%	8%

And of the couples who lived at first with others the middle class set up their homes more quickly: —

Couples who set up their own home within one year	27%	21%
Couples who set up their own home between one and two years after marriage	33%	15%

When the couples eventually do set up their own homes, the manual families settle nearer to their parents than the non-manual in spite of the agreement of these occupational groups on the topic of living near to the wife's parents: —

	A.B.C.1.	C.2.D.E.
Now living with wife's parents	2·5%	7%
Now living within walking distance of wife's parents	25%	34·5%
	27·5%	41·5%
Think that they should live near to wife's parents	39%	40%

[17] Cf. Goldthorpe (1968).

The middle class families, in spite of living further away from their parents, are not hindered from contact with them: 32 per cent. of the wives see their mother at least once or twice a week, a proportion similar to the 30 per cent. of working class wives who see their mother this frequently. The two groups seem to have a different meaning of the word ' near ' which will depend upon the type of transport they normally use and the sort of contact that is desired. The manual households use the bus services much more than the clerical who frequently have a private motor car available and who use the railway more than the buses. (Family Expenditure Survey, 1968.) Bus journeys are generally shorter than rail journeys and fit the working class pattern of living in local communities, typified by a semi-communal living which the middle classes would regard as destroying their privacy. The family visiting in Bethnal Green,[18] though similar in frequency to the visiting in Cardiff,[19] was different in content: the former is a perpetuation of pre-marital family life while the latter is an attempt to preserve relationships which marriage has attacked.

The community studies also emphasised a tendency for manual families to have more contact with relatives than with friends, the converse of the middle class, and for the manual husbands and wives to have separate groups of friends. These family living patterns are reflected in the national sample, but hardly as dramatically as in the commnnity studies.: 84 per cent. of middle class couples see friends together in contrast to 75 per cent. of working class couples and the percentage who visited and were visited by friends and relatives during the past week are : —

	A.B.C.1.	C.2.D.E.
Visited relatives	47%	58%
Visited by relatives	44%	58%
Visited friends	60%	49%
Visited by friends	60%	49%

(*The New Housewife,* 1967, Table 3.16.)

There are indications in the community studies that the young members of the traditional communities were adopting different styles of living, a development which was accelerated by moving to newer housing areas, and were becoming privatised. The New Housewife Study of a national sample suggests that any such movement to a non-traditional life has been peripheral to the working class; the patterns emerging in the study testifying to the persistence of the sub-cultures in Britain which are resisting any homogenising influence of mass media and the disruptive influence of mass production.

[18] Wilmott and Young (1957).
[19] Rosser and Harris (1965).

IV

Status and Behaviour

We have been able to show, using official statistics and survey materials, the extent to which the status of the manual worker has changed; at least in our definition of these terms. We have also been able to point out, in passing, how the situation of the manual worker has improved, in absolute terms. All this tells us little about the processes by which improvement in relative or absolute position affects the behaviour of manual workers in their relationships with managers at the place of work, or in relation to members of family and neighbourhood or in judgments of their social prestige relative to other occupations. We conclude with a brief reference to these matters.

1. *The place of work*

With the progressive shortening of the hours of work of the manual worker, the differences in hours worked between manual and clerical workers has diminished, at least as far as the basic week is concerned. The manual worker has kept up his working hours by overtime (Gowler, 1969). But even ' regular ' overtime has its uncertainties; it is, in the last analysis, in the gift of the management. Bonus earnings might also be uncertain if management's plans for deploying men and machines (in response to pressures in product markets and interruptions in work flow) adversely affect the capacity to earn regular bonus. These things by themselves might be perceived by the worker to cancel out some of the apparent status gain that absolute and relative improvements in take-home pay may appear to have conferred. This is not to mention the obvious point that the job of the manual worker is at greater short-term risk than most professional, managerial and clerical jobs. When his job *is* at risk, it is the difference between his usual earnings and his State redundancy and unemployment benefit that measure the extent of job insecurity.

The manual worker is arguably the greatest risk-taker in modern industry. Managers faced with severe price competition or seasonal fluctuations in demand, or shortage of credit, or the pressure to reduce costs, might well decide to cut down overtime, tighten performance standards, or reduce the working force. In doing so, they virtually transfer the problem to the worker to deal with if unions will allow it or are unable to prevent it. The worker is now confronted with the short run difficulty of allocating a smaller or fluctuating income over the same set of regular commitments. Is it any wonder that workers adopt measures such as fiddling bonus schemes to even out earnings, and putting pressure on foremen to share out jobs equitably and to hand out ' manufactured ' overtime regularly and fairly.

Much modern industrial relations in the work place would make more sense than it does if it were seen as a disagreement about who was to be left to cope with the consequences of uncertainties in labour markets and product markets. For all the apparent power of the unions, they have neither the information nor the resources with which to gain control of these uncertainties. On the whole, the advantage still lies with manager and owner. To the extent that this is so, the worker's perception of his position in society is affected. The world may be seen as peopled with 'theys' with their hands on the levers of power. The manual worker probably still sees himself as a cog in the machine, the more so since advances in technology and administrative technique are tending to reduce the discretion in his job, anyway. This process has gone far enough to produce a literature on 'alienation' and a fashion for 'job enlargement' and 'job enrichment' to counteract the tendency, and to diminish its supposed effects on worker motivation, and hence production efficiency.

Some of the risks and uncertainties of manual work have of course been recently compensated for by the growth of state and company schemes of redundancy payment, the growth of pension funds, manpower planning to take care of redundancy by natural wastage, improved sick benefit schemes, and so on. There have also been moves to consolidate bonus earnings into high regular rates, to reduce or abolish overtime working, by many large companies; and in some cases to give some guarantee of security of employment to manual workers. Insofar as status, or one man's view of it, is related to the security of his income, it could then be said that the industrial manual worker's status has increased slightly and may increase more. If his income continues to become more secure, as it might well do in the increasing number of large firms whose industrial size and power enables them to reduce some of the uncertainty, then we might see a long term continuing impovement in the security of job and pay packet.

2. Family community and style of life

If this were to happen, then the manual worker might find it easier to save, or to buy his own house on mortgage and, as our figures show, there is already a trend of increasing private ownership of homes by manual workers. To what extent then, might his patterns of expenditure, and his patterns of social relationships within and without the family, change to correspond more nearly to those typical of professional and managerial occupations? The limited evidence on this point shows little movement in this direction. The fact that some manual workers buy washing machines, cars, and refrigerators, and take holidays abroad, is not an indication that they have changed their style of life in the sense of changing the nature and meaning of their relationships with others. The evidence of community studies over the past couple of decades suggests that substantial increases in real wages have increased material possessions but have had little impact on style of life. The circle of friends and acquaintances does not, it seems, widen with increased income. Indeed, as a result of movements into new housing estates and flats the circle might close around a family bereft of kin and friends close by. But in a generation the old extended kin relationships typical of older workers can re-establish themselves (Wilmott, 1963).

If it could be shown that there were the openings for manual workers, most of whom still leave school at fifteen or sixteen, to move to jobs in managements or the professions, or that sufficient sons and daughters of manual workers were moving into management and into professions, then a change in relationships and style of life might be expected. But it seems probable that the increasing numbers of graduate sons of non-manual workers who enter industry move in as managers or professionals, thus closing up avenues for manual workers' promotion beyond supervisory level. It also seems to be the case that those sons and daughters of manual workers who complete higher education move into management and the professions and take on middle class modes of living and patterns of relationship in the process and become cut off both socially and geographically from their places of origin and relationships there. The frequency of social inter-course at work and in the community outside of the workplace, between manual workers and professional and managerial workers has apparently not increased. The Luton study found little commerce between manual and clerical workers. But even the most superficial observations will serve to show that at work the sharp functional and authority divisions between shop floor and management have not eroded at all, and certainly it would be a matter for comment if the relationships between manual workers and those professions whom they meet outside the work place, i.e. doctors, dentists, solicitors, local government officials, etc., were to be continued outside the professional-client relationships. One might be prepared to say that manual workers and their families are less awestricken in the presence of professionals than they used to be, but this is probably as much due to the change in the professionals' attitude as that of the manual worker.

3. Perception of status

The concept of status we have used in this study has two integral components: a role and an evaluation. We have suggested that the system of allocating economic rewards in British society is constrained or legitimised by a status system which is defined by a series of occupational roles and a measure for making a comparative evaluation of them. Both the type of role that is considered and the evaluative measure are in large part culturally defined in the sense that they are ways of perceiving the ' real ' world which are learnt in the intergenerational socialisation process. In Britain, and in most industrial countries[20] the roles used in the allocative system are those of professional, non-manual and manual workers in broad outlines, and each of these is sub-divided into major and minor professions, e.g., doctors and teachers, responsible and routine non-manual workers, e.g., personal secretaries and filing clerks, and skilled and unskilled manual workers. The evaluative measure is descriptive, not analytical; it states that professional

[20] Inkeles and Rossi (1959).

roles are more worthy than non-manual roles which are more worthy than manual roles, and in doing this it expresses the prevailing pattern of reward distribution. As are all socially learnt ways of looking at the ' real ' world this status system has a strong conservative bias.

Although we argue that the broadly outlined occupational status system pervades the whole of British Society we do not imply by this that it is the only evaluative framework which is used. The crude categories of roles that it uses may not be relevant to a specific situation, for example, a distinction of skilled and unskilled manual work is not refined enough to compare plumbers and electricians, and the distinction of major and minor professions is not refined enough to compare doctors and lawyers. Additionally occupational roles may not be the most significant in the evaluative situation, for example on the roads where the make and size of car is the most salient variable which discriminates individuals, or amongst the neighbourhood network of housewives where for example success in child rearing is a salient variable. In an attempt to understand behaviour based on status perception it is, therefore, important to define the context in which the behaviour takes place, and to seek in this context the reasons why a particular set of roles and a particular evaluative measure was used. It is part of our argument for the persistence of the system of rewards allocation as it now is in Britain that there are in the contemporary society techniques for thrusting the allocative mechanisms, i.e. the negotiations on income levels, into the public forum in which context the salient perceptual framework is the broadly defined status system as we have described it.

The individual, on his own, can choose to use any one of a myriad of sole and evaluative references[21], a relative, for example, or a special friend or someone he has just read about in a magazine. For a group to make a status evaluation, however, there must be some agreement on the salience of both roles and evaluative measures. In the recent industrial relations activity in the Ford Motor Company[22] the definition of the situation by the shop stewards, as one of relative deprivation because some other car workers were being paid more than the Ford workers, was not accepted by the majority of workers. In contrast, in a demarcation dispute there is a deeply felt consensus amongst the disputants which is baffling to an outsider. This need for agreement limits the number of roles and evaluative criteria which can be relevant to a specific situation. The roles must be salient to all the individuals and both the roles and the criteria must be part of a historically developed localised culture. For example, the behaviour of a man's children is irrelevant to his role in the work situation, and the physical height of the individual workers though relevant in a brawl, would rarely be the subject for status evaluation in the workplace. This need for agreement also limits the adaptability of the status frame of reference, because of the inertia of learnt behaviour, which will be an obstacle to any new evaluation system. For example, in the recent Pressed Steel dispute (D.E.P.

[21] Cf. Hyman (1942) and Runciman (1966).
[22] *The Times,* Feb. 1970.

1968) about job grading the pattern makers insisted that their differential over the toolroom should be maintained despite the evidence of job evaluation and justified this by using the traditional concept of differences in skills.

Each specific situation, workplace, home, neighbourhood, voluntary society, has a status system peculiar to itself in some ways and also reflecting a wider embracing situation, e.g. the total society, in some ways. Feelings of status deprivation or satisfaction can be aroused in the perceptual framework of any status system though we suggest that the more immediate is the situational context of status the more potent it will be to arouse these feelings. Consequently, although the national status system powerfully influences the allocation of rewards in the whole society any attempt to explain the detailed behaviour within a particular negotiating mechanism must be in terms of the details of the highly localised situation.

Manchester Business School

REFERENCES

ATKIN, C. K. (1964). People and their Motor Car, Birmingham Univ. Dept. of Transportation and Environmental Planning, Vol. 1.
BOWLEY, A. L. and STAMP, Sir J. (1924). *The National Income,* Oxford Univ. Press.
DAVIES, K. (1961). *Human Society.* Macmillan.
D.E.P. (1968). Report of the Court of Inquiry into a Dispute concerning wage structure proposals for time workers employed at Pressed Steel, Fisher Ltd., Cowley, Cmnd. 3688. London, H.M.S.O.
D.E.P. (1969). New Survey of Earnings, *Employment and productivity Gazette,* May to September 1969.
DOUGLAS, J. W. B. *et al.* (1968). *All our Future,* Peter Davies.
GOLDTHORPE, J. H. *et al.* (1968). *The Affluent Worker: Industrial Attitudes and Behaviour,* Cambridge Univ. Press.
GOWLER, D. (1969). Determinants of the Supply of Labor to the Firm, *Journal of Management Studies,* Vol. 6. No. 1. Feb. 1969.
HYMAN, H. (1942). The Psychology of Status, *Archives of Psychology,* No. 269, N.Y.
INDUSTRIAL SOCIETY (1966a) Survey of Comparative Terms of Employment, Report No. 133.
INDUSTRIAL SOCIETY (1966b). Holidays—Current Practices and Trends, Report No. 134.
INDUSTRIAL SOCIETY (1969). Holidays—Current Practices and Trends, Report No. 153.
INKELES, A. and ROSSI, P. (1959). National Comparisons of Occupational Prestige, *American Journal of Sociology,* Vol. 55-56 pp. 329-39.
INSTITUTE OF OFFICE MANAGEMENT (1946). Clerical Salaries Analysis.
KRIESBURG, L. (1962). The Basis of Occupational Prestige, *American Sociological Review* (27) pp. 238-44.
JACKSON, B. and MARSDEN, D. (1962). *Education and the Working Class,* R. K. Paul.
LASLETT, P. (1965). *The World We Have Lost,* Methuen.
LENSKI, G. (1966). *Power and Prestige,* McGraw-Hill.
LITTLE, A. and WESTGAARD, S. (1964). The Trend of Class Differentials in Educational Opportunity in England and Wales, *British Journal of Sociology,* Vol. XV. No. 4.

MARSH, J. (1963). Shop Floor and Office, *Marriage Guidance*.

M.P.N.I. (1964). Enquiry into the Incidence of Incapacity to Work, Ministry of Pensions and National Insurance, London, H.M.S.O.

N.B.P.I. (1968). Standing Reference on the Pay of University Teachers, Report 98. Cmnd. 3866. London, H.M.S.O.

N.B.P.I. (1969). Top Salaries in the Private Sector and Nationalised Industries, Report 107. Cmnd. 3970. London, H.M.S.O.

The New Housewife (1967). J. Walter Thompson & Co. Ltd.

New Survey of London: Life and Labour (1934). Vol. 8, p. 284, P. S. King.

P.E.P. (1961). Family Needs and the Social Services, Political and Economic Planning, London, 1961.

PLOWDEN REPORT (1967). Children and their Primary Schools, Central Advisory Council for Education (England), London, H.M.S.O.

ROSSER, C. and HARRIS, C. (1965). *The Family and Social Change*, R. K. Paul.

RUNCIMAN, G. (1966). *Relative Deprivation and Social Justice*, R. K. Paul.

SOCIAL SURVEY (1968). Workplace Industrial Relations, London, H.M.S.O.

Survey of the Motoring Market (1964). Odhams Press.

WILMOTT, P. and YOUNG, N. (1957). *Family and Kinship—East London*, R. K. Paul.

WILMOTT, P. (1963). *The Evolution of a Community*, R. K. Paul.

ZWEIG, F. (1961). *The Worker in an Affluent Society*. Heinemann.

THE MANAGEMENT
OF HUMAN RESOURCES

D. J. FLUNDER

I

THE ENVIRONMENT

So many factors affect management's attitudes and ability to change that it seems necessary to begin this contribution with some broad assumptions about the social and economic climate that the U.K. can expect in the 1970s.

It is likely that the balance of payments problem will continue, although the figures will be better than we have been used to in the 1960s. Some fluctuation is to be expected.

The rate of growth (Gross National Product) will probably be insufficient, particularly in the early years, to allow easy repayment of international debts. This will, if anything, increase the pressure for higher productivity as a major requirement for manufacturing industry. International financial institutions, not least the International Monetary Fund, will look to Britain to improve its general economic health and much international attention will be focussed on the productivity of British manufacturing industry— and, of course, the behaviour of organised labour. Similar problems will arise from conditions for entry into the European Economic Community and if the U.K. does in fact enter the Community during the 1970s, other pressures will be created, mainly on cost per unit of production.

Another trend, already apparent, will surely increase rapidly. Investors, both individual and institutional, but particularly the latter, will become much more skilful and sophisticated in their assessments of companies' performance. Companies, to remain successful, must obviously have access to the capital they need, when they need it. The onus will be more heavily on them to convince the better informed and better equipped money market that they should have what they are asking for.

A feature of the 1960s, particularly the later years, has been a welcome increase in the emphasis on marketing within British industry. The 1970s will see an intensification of this movement and as a natural corollary, a much better performance by companies in forecasting sales and consequently production schedules. This has very important implications in the management of labour.

The rise in productivity which will occur will, if the experience of other industrial countries is meaningful, be due more to increased mechanisation than other single factor. This, in turn, will tend, in traditional manufacturing areas, to create surplus labour although the tendency will be offset by political influences and government moves against any rise in unemployment. It should also be offset by a movement towards ' service ' industries where the U.K. still has considerable room for expansion. It should not be forgotten that by the end of the 1970s a very high proportion of British managers will have spent their entire working lives in a period of very high employment—when full employment was in fact an element of government policy. This will probably predispose them to accept the need to produce a climate that is generally favourable to labour. If we accept that, we must also accept that fresh legislation will almost certainly be introduced during the period; this will to some extent define and limit management/labour relationships.

There is only one other environmental factor which seems important at this stage. Industry is already beginning to feel a shortage of school leavers, educated to ' O ' and 'A' level standards. These have been the main source of management and administrative staff for industry in the past. We are approaching quite rapidly now a situation in which graduates, in some disciplines, will be plentiful—possibly in oversupply. Until now graduates have been brought up by the system to expect higher status positions throughout society. Industry, certainly, has competed for them as for a scarce commodity. With a profound and surprisingly rapid change in the supply position we are beginning to move into a situation where they become the normal recruits of industry and fill junior and middle management grades, not always with contentment.

II

CHANGES IN THE UTILISATION OF MANPOWER

The previous section has dealt with environmental change and should lead us to one conclusion which is fundamental to much of the rest—that manufacturing industry will become more capital intensive and that increasing mechanisation will itself produce an imperative demand for greater plant utilisation. It is perhaps in this area that some of the biggest changes of thought are required on both sides of industry.

An obvious prime requirement is for expensive plant to be used more continuously. This implies reversing the present trend away from shift working and moving towards more shift working and more sophisticated shift working systems, e.g. those which permit round-the-clock operation for seven days a week.

The next obvious requirement with a high plant cost element of unit cost is to reduce the labour cost in a period when mechanisation makes less physical but more mental demands on a labour force. It is idle to talk of lower wages and the savings must be made in manning levels. Obvious tensions develop here. An important one from management's point of view is to understand much more about time off the job—absence for all reasons and holidays. Some need may well arise for standby elements, possibly provided by older people on a part-time basis.

Capital intensity will increase the proportion of indirect to direct labour. This has important implications for the education system, for the systems of recruitment and training and particularly for systems of payment. Much of the indirect element must be provided by a different type of man. He will need to be educated to a higher standard (it seems doubtful if the one year addition to the school leaving age will wholly meet this requirement) and the proportion to be catered for by the educational system on the one hand and training within industry on the other is a matter for argument and early resolution.

The present trend to rationalise payment structures will be accelerated in the period under review. Mechanisation everywhere reduces the direct contribution of the individual in terms of physical effort and dexterity. As this reduces, it becomes less possible to reward the individual for his own performance. The increasing numbers loosely grouped together as ' indirect ' cannot be rewarded on the basis of individual performance in most cases.

All of this must mean in the decade ahead of us a faster move away from individual incentive systems (piece-work) than we have seen before. This is not to say that individually or group based incentive systems will vanish. They are in the industrial blood of the nation and they remain quite a good basis for rewarding people for work, where there is direct individual contribution.

The general position of women in industry will undergo considerable change in the 1970s. A social change has been taking place already, which is pre-disposing women to enter fields which have been almost exclusively male and into which society now accepts them. Women will in any case become necessary in greater quantities in industry, for those jobs in which because of dexterity or responsibility factors they are preferable to men. Some of the country's fastest growing industries are those which employ by choice large numbers of women, for example, electronics.

Better medical facilities, improved family planning, an increased emphasis on a higher family standard of living, demanding expensive consumer durable goods, make it likely that more married women will be available to industry and that they will be available at an earlier age. Against this tendency will be a move towards equal pay in the period, which will make it less likely that women will be employed for purely cost reasons. Other legislation will accompany equal pay legislation which will reduce some of the present hindrances to the employment of women, e.g. night shift working. The conclusion must surely be that by the end of the 1970s industry must have revised its ideas about female employment and both employers and trade unions must come to terms with the profound change from the present restricted situation.

One other factor affecting the utilisation of manpower is worth mention. The continuing development and application of techniques to measure work and performance will take increasing effect from the shop floor to the boardroom. Techniques based on targets for the performance of managers, techniques like clerical work measurement, like job evaluation and ever more sophisticated work study systems will achieve much wider application during the decade and again will require changes of attitude by both management and trade unions. If the country is to remain internationally competitive, management will have to set the pace.

And, of course, if we are to remain internationally competitive, and if we enter the European Common Market during this period, we shall need to come to terms with the international mobility of labour under E.E.C. rules. Labour from the less developed areas of Europe may well, in the early years, become available in increasing quantity. An early task for management, together with the trade union movement, will be to learn how to be ready to meet this situation and how to digest the numbers involved.

III

REMUNERATION

In a continuing inflationary situation during the 1970s the strains arising from comparability of earnings levels will continue. The problem will be eased by the widespread and thorough application of scientific systems of evaluation, such as skills analysis and job evaluation, which will permit just wage settlements. Excessive wage awards, granted by ill-informed managements after pressure from labour, will only generate similar claims in other companies and industries that will stimulate inflation and further discontent.

Comparability problems arise within geographical areas but seldom too seriously. They arise more seriously within large corporations or industries doing similar work in different parts of the country. Again the policy for the next decade must be directed towards evaluation and a more systematic approach.

Differentials within large plants provide some of the classic problems of industry. In the imperfect but improved state of relationships, one answer lies in the thorough application, jointly by management and employee representatives, of job evaluation techniques.

Broader groupings of jobs, with the comparability fairly established by teams of both management and shop floor representatives, can do more for stability than any amount of weak management and easy concession.

IV

BARGAINING SYSTEMS

This conclusion leads naturally to a consideration of bargaining systems. It is often said that in this country we should spend less time arguing about what the job is, and what its performance standards are, and concentrate more on establishing how large a slice of the cake should accrue to the labour force. It is logical to develop that argument and say that conditions are more easily established and stabilised than wages. The bargaining in a locality or in a plant can properly centre on wages whereas conditions, hours of work, holidays etc. need to be more broadly established so that they can be excluded from local negotiations. Thus, industry wide bargaining systems which provide for national bargaining over conditions and the setting of a minimum wage, leaving detailed wages for plant bargaining, seem in present circumstances to be preferable to most others. They fit better with the mood and the climate than over-centralised systems, on the one hand, and wide, general, almost anarchic systems on the other.

It would be idle to pretend that all industries are quite ready for this approach and there will surely be some for which other systems are preferable—yet the approach remains valid for a larger part of manufacturing industry than is, at present, admitted.

One particularly important feature of bargaining systems which always requires special attention is the disputes procedure. Disputes procedures always have been important but become very much more so in an era of plant bargaining. One feature of an industry's national agreement which deserves very great care is that part of the procedure which is applied when the in-plant procedure is exhausted. It is better still if the general pattern for in-plant procedure can also be laid out at national level. Both sides of industry have a great deal to do in the 1970s to bring these procedures up to scratch. The better procedures in this country have been very good indeed and have stood the test of many years. It is surprising how often we come across inadequate procedures and how often indeed we find none at all.

V

STATUS AND TRADE UNIONISM

There is little doubt that we are entering a period during which employer acceptance of trade unions will be required by law. Even if this were not so, acceptance is growing rapidly among the smaller companies who have provided the resistance for so long.

One particular problem of the 1970s will centre round staff trade unions. Many companies, even the largest, have not yet come to terms with staff trade unionism during this period. Once obliged by law to recognise the unions, they will still have the problem of whom to recognise, for what categories of staff and how to keep a tidy bargaining situation.

For many years staff workers have felt insecure as the real differentials, both in conditions and pay between them and manual workers have been steadily eroded. In much of industry this has produced a more equitable situation but, of course, anomalies remain. Staff have felt in many sectors that they need the protection of union membership. Many cases are evident of such staff being uncertain what type of union they want to join. We are approaching a situation which will mean, if we are not careful, staff unions concentrating on restoring inequitable differentials, and this may well be one of management's most pressing problems of the next decade. A related issue which has become apparent only recently is the struggle between manual workers' unions to attract staff workers into special sections, in competition with purely staff trade unions. The employer, unfortunately, gets all of the kicks and none of the ha'pence in this struggle. In an age of mergers, corporations become larger and have greater difficulty with the increased proliferation of trade unions.

The emergence of powerful staff trade unions underlines the need to reduce the number of trade unions with whom individual employers currently need to have bargaining arrangements. It is fair to say that the trend is in the right direction, but the British employer is still in a particularly difficult position compared with his international competitors. The present trend of trade union amalgamations will continue into the 1970s and should be accelerated.

These paragraphs on trade unionism and status cannot be left without some discussion of the feeling of insecurity displayed by wide areas of middle management in British industry, as we enter this difficult decade. A great deal has been done and rightly done, to raise the status and standing in the community of the shop floor worker. During that period the middle manager has, by comparison, stood still. He has had to cope with a great deal of legislation designed, again rightly, to protect the employee, and to secure his position and his livelihood in almost any event. Top management has the opportunity and the need to organise the broader picture and understand the reasons for much of the social change which has come about. Middle management can be forgiven for wondering just who is on their side in the demanding and difficult job they are required to do. They require some very special attention in the years ahead—and the matter cannot just be resolved by adjusting earnings.

These remarks on the problems of the next decade are naturally speculative, but management priorities in the 1970s can be forecast with more confidence because they stem at least in part from the policies and programmes of the 1960s.

VI

PRIORITIES FOR MANAGEMENT ACTION

In Britain's competitive situation, management has the lion's share of the task of rapid change during the 1970s. It has much to do in all the different aspects of the industrial world but not least are the priority tasks in the management of people for whom it is responsible.

In the essential move towards higher efficiency we have both to reduce manpower and to make those who remain more productive. The priorities can be summarised into four headings:

Bargaining Systems

Management has a commercial responsibility to achieve its goals for profitability, production and sales, and also a social responsibility to ensure that its employees share in the prosperity generated by the organisation. The precise nature of that share and all that it involves, hours of work, basic and other rates of pay, welfare, fringe benefits, conditions at the work place, is bound to create problems of understanding and communication and occasionally dissension and dispute. It is essential that management and labour agree in advance the methods and communications that are applied during negotiations and disputes, so that both sides know and understand how grievances and claims are being resolved and accept that their interests are being protected.

Bargaining systems and disputes procedures can and must vary according to circumstances. There is no one answer or system, merely some principles that must be applied.

In the first place, common systems can only apply to common situations. Basic wages and standard hours of work can be agreed for an industry on a national scale. Other matters, such as protection against health hazards in a manufacturing process or incentives for particular operative tasks cannot be decided at national level. National officials of unions and companies—and other employing institutions such as nationalised industries, would be overwhelmed with detail; and they would usually have too little knowledge of conditions in individual areas and factories. If trade union structures are to remain meaningful, it seems necessary for national officials to have a proper place in the bargaining system and certainly in procedures.

At the same time a policy of leaving such local matters to be decided at local levels makes it possible for local grievances affecting comparatively few people to be settled quickly before they can spread and affect a great many. Thus, management's task for the 1970s is to ensure that it can cope quickly and flexibly with the requirement—to bargain about the right thing in the right place. This means having not only the right systems, but also the right people suitably trained and qualified at all levels of the organisation so that these systems can be put to proper use.

Effectiveness of work

Techniques and systems to establish and improve the effectiveness of work are management's bread and butter in a period of change. Many proven techniques, such as job evaluation, skills analysis, work study, value analysis and other aspects of industrial engineering are available. Management's tasks in the 1970s will be to make proper use of them and to ensure that their employees understand what these techniques are designed to achieve.

Management must not only recruit and train people in these techniques but be prepared to face hard negotiation in support of their work. Much change of this sort requires specific and detailed long term planning—critical path techniques are quite appropriate.

Change for the better must not only be continuous, it must be as rapid as the people concerned can assimilate it. This does not merely apply to the benefits of these specialist techniques, but also to changes of a more general nature, such as changes in plant layout, increased or continuous shift working and reduction in plant down-time—during annual holidays as well as between production runs.

Finally, it should not be forgotten that great improvements can be effected by adding to management knowledge of the production situation, particularly in multi-product plants where knowledge of what is being processed, and where, is often inadequate. Improvements in information flows can often be as beneficial as improvements in technique.

Communications and Consultation

Management is of course responsible for making the decisions and giving the instructions necessary for the running of the business, but it will do so much more effectively in the 1970s if it seeks to secure the co-operation of its workforce in the goals it is attempting to achieve, and if decisions which affect its employees are broadly understood and accepted by them. To achieve this aim, management must keep its employees informed of policies and progress, keep in touch with the attitudes of its employees, take account of these attitudes in the formulation of policy and ensure that plans which affect employment and working conditions are understood.

To achieve good communication, management has to devise and implement a systematic and comprehensive chain of communication groups from top management to the shop floor—the larger the company, the more complicated that task is. Much communication is of course related to the passage of work instructions and explanations of management decisions and policies and involves what is primarily a one-way flow of information both written and verbal. However, there is also the need for managers deliberately and systematically, to obtain, understand and react appropriately to the views and attitudes of employees.

At the junior levels of management, foremen (or department managers) usually have a clear picture of the attitudes and views of the people they supervise. Sound organisation and good training methods will ensure that such attitudes reach top management; moreover, deliberate use of the formal organisation will help to support the foreman's status and reinforce his standing with his team. Employees' attitudes to their employer and to their tasks are influenced firstly by the behaviour and attitudes of foremen (or however first line management are designated). All formal procedures must support and enhance this relationship, although we must accept that the foreman will himself act as a filter. In any case, reliance on this medium as the only two-way channel is not without risk. Employees may become sceptical about the views which reach top management through this medium and often demand a more direct means of communication. Obviously this is most likely to happen where employee dissatisfaction is widespread, but the urge to ' talk to the boss ' directly is strong.

As a very necessary supplement to normal line management communications, joint consultative systems (Works Councils) are helpful in permitting the free discussion of events within a company, and in permitting grievances to be ventilated and settled. Where these exist in British industry they are often based on arrangements made earlier this century—designed at the time to combat trade unionism. Whilst these now are usually unionised, they are seldom fully representative of all employees on a site—process workers, maintenance engineers, foremen, staff etc. By any standards, it seems a high priority task for management in the 1970s to create fully representative joint consultative systems within their companies. 'Participation' and 'involvement' are fashionable words. It is surely important to realise that either of them can only patiently be built from a firm point of contact in the place of work.

Some comments have been made earlier in this contribution about a special vulnerability of middle management in special circumstances. Managements would be well advised in the years immediately ahead of us to make special arrangements for periodic but regular consultation between those who direct the affairs of a business and their middle management.

Planning and Research

Manpower planning is a subject which attracts a great deal of attention both written and oral. Most of us would be honest if we admitted we did not yet quite understand what the words mean. The obvious requirement is to plan ahead to have the right skills available in the right quantities at the right time and place—an enormously difficult task. In essence, this means identifying as early as possible the areas of management, staff and labour, where there is likely to be over or under manning by suitably qualified people. Forecasts of this kind will never be entirely accurate, but they will inevitably reduce the losses, both human and financial, suffered when either of these two variances is experienced. Therefore, manpower planning will inevitably lead to much detailed work: nevertheless, it requires complete and continuing support from top management to ensure that forecasts receive proper attention from other areas of management, and to ensure that manpower planning is adequately co-ordinated with sales forecasting and production scheduling, from which it must stem.

The second need under this general heading is to find out a great deal more about even the more commonplace problems. Managements tend to have little information available about absence and the real reasons for it. They are normally unable to differentiate between absenteeism and genuine absence due to sickness or some other respectable cause. Our knowledge of motivation remains rudimentary even today and industry's extraordinarily tentative approach to the behavioural sciences is astonishing in a nation which has earned a living from the products of manufacturing industry for so many years.

The Dunlop Company Limited
London

THE ROLE OF GOVERNMENT AGENCIES

H. A. CLEGG

I

TRADITIONAL FUNCTIONS

For three-quarters of a century from the establishment of the Labour Department of the Board of Trade in 1886, the central function of government in the British labour market was the maintenance of industrial peace by smoothing the way for collective agreements, and government agencies were designed to assist in this. The department, subsequently the Ministry of Labour and now the Department of Employment and Productivity, keeps in touch with negotiations and provides a conciliation service where disputes threaten. Where their own efforts fail, officials may suggest arbitration by a special arbitrator or board, or by the permanent Industrial Court, and several public services have their own permanent arbitration tribunals. In an unusually complex and difficult industrial relations problem a Court of Inquiry or committee may be set up to investigate.

In recent years these arrangements have faced mounting criticism. They assume that the right outcome of an industrial dispute is whatever the two sides can agree, and that where they fail to agree by themselves they should be assisted towards the settlement most likely to be acceptable. By now, however, we are all familiar with the argument that a settlement which increases costs and prices may damage the economy and therefore be the wrong outcome of an industrial dispute. If so it follows that the government's job is not to secure peace at any price, but peace at the right price, and there may be need of a special agency to determine the right price in any particular set of circumstances.

The argument can be taken further. An increase in pay which raises costs when taken in isolation may not do so when it is part of a ' productivity agreement' which alters methods of production and working arrangements so as to use manpower more economically. Consequently the determination of the right price is not simply a matter of studying the economic indicators to see whether the economy can stand a 2 per cent. increase in pay, or one of 3 per cent. It may involve a review of productive methods to discover whether a productivity bargain is possible, and the parties may need guidance in reaching and applying the agreement if the expected savings are to be achieved.

The existing arrangements can also be criticised on the grounds that they do not achieve even the limited traditional objectives. Conciliation, arbitration and inquiry are designed to come to the assistance of employers and unions who have already used their own joint procedures for dealing with disputes and failed to reach agreement. But today 95 per cent. of recorded strikes are unofficial, lacking the sanction of the appropriate trade union authority, and almost all of these are also ' unconstitutional ' which means that work has been stopped before the joint procedures have been fully utilised. With the solitary exception of coalmining, which once provided the bulk of British strikes, the number of recorded strikes is rising in every major British industry, and there are many small unrecorded strikes, overtime bans and ' go-slows ' which are also unconstitutional.

The conciliation service is gravely handicapped in an unofficial and unconstitutional strike because it can deal only with the union officials. Discussions with unofficial leaders would undermine union authority. Arbitration of an unofficial dispute is unthinkable. It is possible to institute an inquiry into the causes of unrest in an industrial trouble-spot, and this has been done on several occasions. But, at least until the last few years, the main outcome of such inquiries has been a series of homilies on the wickedness of breaking agreements.

Moreover, if voluntary bargaining is not working satisfactorily the fault may lie in the defects of employers' associations and trade unions. The government has no means of compelling or inducing these bodies to ' put their house in order '.

Finally, despite long-established official support for voluntary collective bargaining, the government lacks any means of compelling private employers to recognise trade unions. Consequently voluntary bargaining has generally developed only in areas where unions are strong enough to secure recognition for themselves.

II

RECENT DEVELOPMENTS

Successive governments have shown growing awareness of the force of some of these criticisms, and new agencies have been established to serve new objectives, most of them since 1964. The three most important are the National Board for Prices and Incomes, the Manpower and Productivity Service and the Commission for Industrial Relations.

The National Board for Prices and Incomes

The Board is the senior of the three, and has the longest antecedents. The post-war Labour Government instituted a period of wage-restraint in 1948, but created no special agency to apply it. In 1958 a Council on Productivity, Prices and Incomes began to issue a series of warnings on the dangers of wage inflation. Partly as a consequence of its final report the National Economic Development Council was set up in 1962 as a tripartite organisation of government, union and employer representatives with a general remit to work towards an economic plan, which it was hoped would include the planning of incomes. About the same time the Conservative Government began to give guidance on the rate of increase in incomes which could be tolerated, and a National Incomes Commission was appointed to review particular increases in pay. But it had virtually no powers, and the unions chose to ignore it.

Over the winter of 1964-5 the new Labour Government persuaded the Trades Union Congress and the employers' organisations to accept a prices and incomes policy which had a good deal in common with the Conservative White Paper of 1962, except that criteria for price increases were included along with guidance on pay rises, and the Commission was replaced by a National Board for Prices and Incomes, more representative and with wider powers and a larger staff.

The bases of the policy were price stability and an increase in incomes of 3·5 per cent. a year to be covered by rising productivity. The White Paper particularised circumstances in which prices might be allowed to rise, and circumstances in which they should fall, and set out four grounds which might justify exceptional pay increases. These were: contributions to increasing productivity, shortage of labour, low pay and comparability (although comparisons, along with the cost of living, were to play a smaller part in pay settlements than they had in the past). Ostensibly, therefore, it was the job of the Board, on a reference from the government, to consider proposals for raising prices, or for increasing pay above 3·5 per cent., and to report whether they fell within the criteria for special treatment.

There was a difficulty about this right from the start. Prices were not stable. They were rising. The index of wage rates was increasing by a good deal more than 3·5 per cent. a year and actual earnings faster still. This state of affairs continued until July 1966 when the government announced a complete standstill on pay increases for six months and pushed through a bill giving statutory backing to this standstill. Until the end of the year there were virtually no pay increases. The rule for 1967 was that all increases had to be justified against the criteria, even those of less than 3·5 per cent.; and once more it became clear that most workers had exceptional claims, for most of them had a pay increase. From 1968 onwards a 'ceiling' of 3·5 per cent. replaced the 3·5 per cent. 'norm', but in practice prices and pay behaved much as they had in 1965.

This happened despite a considerable tightening up of the machinery of control. In 1965 the government's only recourse was to refer a proposed increase to the Board, hoping that it would not be applied before the Board's report, and that the Board's report would be accepted. By 1967 there was a vetting procedure, backed by an Act of Parliament, which imposed an obligation to report proposals to increase pay or prices. Implementation could be delayed until the Board reported and for a further period if the Board's report was adverse. In the summer of 1968 the period of delay was extended to a total of twelve months.

The powers were used. The Board found against an increase in busmen's pay in December 1967 and it was held up for a year. During the following autumn the threat of withholding the whole of a pay increase which the Board found to be excessive persuaded the building unions to renegotiate the increase at a lower figure. However, such instances are the exceptions. The general experience has been a succession of pay increases over and above the level thought to be compatible with price stability. Consequently, a good deal of the business of administering the policy has amounted to stretching its clauses to cover increases which the administrators deem it politic to allow through. The cabinet have taken the lead, showing special generosity to doctors and dockers, and their lead has been followed by the Manpower and Productivity Service within the Department of Employment and Productivity which has the duty of vetting pay increases in the first instance.

From time to time the Board have been forced to play the same game. They almost caused a strike at the beginning of 1966 when they backed the British Railways Board in refusing to improve upon an offer to the railway unions. The Prime Minister saved the day at the cost of relatively minor additional concessions. The occasion was still in the minds of the Board in May when they had to judge a 6·6 per cent. increase for London busmen already negotiated but not yet paid. An adverse judgement would almost certainly have led to a strike. The Board found the increase justified on productivity grounds. It is not easy to see how their reasoning would pass the tests for a productivity agreement which they later set out in the report on *Productivity Agreements* (National Board for Prices and Incomes, 1967). Among other groups for whose pay increases the Board have devised imaginative justifications are higher civil servants, the fire brigades, and employees in electricity supply. At the beginning of 1969 they found that an increase for farmworkers could not be justified within the terms of the current policy but suggested that the government should allow it nevertheless.

However, it would be grossly unfair to the Board to suggest that they have played fast and loose with the successive statements of policy. They have given ground where they thought they must, but generally they have been restrictive in their use of the criteria for exceptional treatment. They have condemned special ' comparability ' formulae for transmitting pay increases from one industry to another wherever they have found them. They have pointed out that in a period of full employment almost everyone can claim an increase on grounds of labour shortage, which, they suggest, can be more effectively remedied by making better use of the manpower which is available. In several instances they have diagnosed low productivity as the cause of low pay, so that in these instances a productivity increase could provide the remedy for low pay without an increase in costs. Finally, although they have been very ready to discover opportunities for productivity agreements, they have also set up strict tests for determining whether proposed productivity agreements are acceptable.

The need to find excuses for increases above the norm, and their own reluctance to use the other criteria, would inevitably have driven the Board into the consultancy business as advisers on the preparation, negotiation and application of productivity agreements. But there was no need for driving. Aubrey Jones, the chairman, has always emphasised that the 1964 Declaration of Intent inaugurated a policy on *productivity,* prices and incomes. Nor was consultancy confined to pay references. The Board was quick to point out that proposed price increases could be avoided or reduced if resources were used more effectively, and many of their reports on prices have suggested improvements in manpower utilisation which might form the basis of a productivity agreement.

Although it is as an advocate of productivity improvements that Aubrey Jones has captured public attention, his Board's consultancy work has not been universally successful, nor invariably convincing. Among the productivity proposals which have not yet been applied on any scale are those for local authority and hospital employees, and for industrial civil servants. A series of reports on buses and road haulage have failed to get to grips with the problem of excessive overtime on road services. The Board have laboured under the double burden of having to produce quick reports on complex issues and having in many instances to devise recommendations to cover the whole of an industry containing a wide range of size of unit and of circumstances. The thoroughness of their work has suffered from their chairman's readiness to take on any assignment and consider its feasibility and relevance afterwards. Consequently, the Board's reputation has not been established by the acceptance of their recommendations. It rests on their willingness to tackle jobs, their manifest determination to seek improvements in efficiency in season and out, their exposure of problems and their determination to throw light on the dark places of industrial relations.

If the policy is to be judged by the extent to which its precepts have been applied, then it unquestionably failed, except for the second half of 1966. On the other hand econometricians inform us that, taking into account such relevant factors as the level of employment and changes in import prices, wages have been rising since 1965 by almost one per cent. less than might have been expected in the circumstances, so that it may be argued that the policy had some restraining effect up to 1969. Either way, however, the credit or blame belongs primarily to the government, not the Board. On the one hand, it is the government which has given the lead in stretching their own policy, and the decisions of the Manpower and Productivity Service are the responsibility of the government. On the other hand if the policy has succeeded in imposing a degree of restraint, the cabinet and officials of the Department of Employment and Productivity deserve the credit. It is they who have decided when they could afford to take a firm stand, when employers or unions could be cajoled or frightened into lowering their sights, and when pay increases could be postponed if not prevented.

Another test of the policy is its effects on productivity. In 1969 the Board noted that output per head had been rising over the previous two years at a rate which normally occurs only when unemployment is falling rapidly, whereas unemployment had been relatively high and stable. (National Board for Prices and Incomes, 1969a.) The Board are properly cautious in explaining these figures, but if they are due to more effective utilisation of labour by British management, and if this is due to the spread of productivity bargaining, then the Board deserve the lion's share of the praise. They gave a clear lead on productivity bargaining. The government and the Department of Employment and Productivity followed, with the Treasury dragging its feet.

In the long run, however, the Board's greatest success may turn out to be their contribution to the informed discussion of industrial relations problems. Contrary to the tradition of arbitrators and Courts of Inquiry they insist on discovering what workers are paid before making recommendations about what they should be paid. They are not content with figures of rates of pay. They want to know what employees actually earn. They will not be put off with average figures for an industry. They want to know the range of earnings in each grade and each group. They want to know how much is due to overtime, how much to payment by results and how much to other additions and supplements. Even when a narrow time-limit has been imposed upon them, the Board have often found time to conduct their own earnings surveys, and their inquiries into the levels and distribution of pay in engineering, building, road haulage and drapery, for example, were highly informative and laid down standards for public pay investigations far ahead of anything the old Ministry of Labour had dreamed.

In addition the Board has made extensive use of case studies, and has from time to time employed a considerable part of the qualified staff of British universities to assist them. The main virtue of the Board's two reports on *Productivity Agreements* and their report on *Job Evaluation* is that they are based on careful investigation of a considerable number of instances, and this basis is even more evident in their report on *Payment by Results,* which is incomparably the most important contribution ever made to the discussion of this crucial aspect of industrial relations.[1]

The Manpower and Productivity Service

The Manpower and Productivity Service was inaugurated soon after the transformation of the Ministry of Labour into the Department of Employment and Productivity and the appointment of Barbara Castle as First Secretary, as part of the change of the department's image from a ministry for administering regulations and conciliating disputes to an agency in which these functions are subordinated to the promotion of the efficient use of manpower. Whereas the structure and functions of the Board were evolved from a number of previous experiments and those of the Commission on Industrial Relations were the result of the deliberations of a Royal Commission, the Service was the department's own creation, announced to the world with little prior warning.

[1] National Board for Prices and Incomes (1967); (1969b); (1968b); (1968a).

In the regions the Service came into being by altering the title of industrial relations officers to 'manpower advisers', and adding to their existing duties of conciliation and administering incomes policy the task of advising managers. At headquarters there is a central consultancy service of full-time specialists available to the regions on request. The director is George Cattell, a senior manager with experience of productivity bargaining and overhauling pay structures.

The 'main task' of the Service is 'to diagnose what is standing in the way of a better performance and then prescribe a programme for reform and reconstruction' (Department of Employment and Productivity, 1969). The diagnosis is offered free of charge to companies, industries and trade unions, and is usually expected to be the outcome of two or three weeks' investigation. If the implementation of the programme of reform requires the assistance of specialists the client is normally expected to find these elsewhere, although the service will give guidance on where to look.

There are, however, a number of exceptional assignments in which headquarters consultants are more heavily engaged. For example, George Cattell is chairman of the Docks Modernisation Committee, and the Service provides continuing assistance to this committee and to the local modernisation committees in the ports. Most of these continuing commitments are in the public services, including the ministries of Defence and Public Works, universities, local authorities and hospitals.

In the early months there were whispers that the Service would fail because managers in private industry would be unwilling to use it, although a few government departments might be dragged reluctantly along. This prophecy has proved false. Within a year the Service was overloaded, the bulk of its clients being private firms. This may have been partly the consequence of making no charge, but the main reason was probably that a new facility was being offered to existing clients. Being in contact with firms in the course of their existing duties the manpower advisers in the regions naturally pointed out to them instances in which they could assist in their new capacity.

The Service's early successes suggest that it is best fitted to cope with a situation in which a company is in the middle of productivity negotiations or a manpower reorganisation and has run into difficulties with the unions or shop stewards. The manpower advisers and headquarters consultants are well qualified to investigate what has gone wrong in such a situation and to suggest ways of making progress. Where the Service has to deal with a firm which has not yet begun to plan for change, or even to see the direction in which it wishes to change, a longer time must elapse before changes can be implemented and the risk of failure is greater. So far the Service may have been creaming off the easy successes, and it is far too early for any rounded assessment of its work.

Two problems have emerged. The first is the multiple activities of the regional advisers and their triple or quadruple responsibility to separate headquarters officials. As well as George Cattell and his subordinates, these

include the officials in charge of conciliation and those who administer
incomes policy. Consequently a firm could follow the productivity proposals
of one of the Service's consultants without any assurance that they would
be found to be in accordance with incomes policy when embodied in an
agreement. Alternatively a consultant could find himself under some pressure
to resolve a dispute by producing proposals for a new pay system without
giving meticulous attention to their contribution to efficiency.

The second concerns the wide range of the Service. It claims that its
' broad aim ' is to ' raise industrial, commercial and administrative efficiency
in order to contain and wherever possible reduce costs. It is concerned with
efficiency in the widest sense and not solely with the efficient use of manpower.' (Department of Employment and Productivity, 1969.) These are
bold words, but the expertise of most of the members of the service is in
industrial relations. It would not be easy to find a body of men and women
better qualified to advise on industrial relations problems. It would be easy
for most of them to make mistakes, even of diagnosis, in advising on the
resolution of problems involving the use of work study, job evaluation techniques, costing, control systems and so on. Perhaps the Service could with
advantage show a little more modesty in describing what it sets out to
accomplish.

The Commission on Industrial Relations

The Royal Commission on Trade Unions and Employers' Associations
which reported in 1968 found that the ' central defect ' of our system of
industrial relations is ' the disorder in factory and workshop relations and
pay structures ', which is responsible for, among other things, the high and
rising rate of unofficial strikes. In the Commission's view most industry-
wide agreements were not and could not be effective means of regulating
relations in the factory, and they suggested that in most industries the instru-
ment of reform should be comprehensive factory agreements. The main
responsibility for introducing the agreements must rest on companies themselves, but they might be assisted by a permanent Commission on Industrial
Relations with the task of promoting a general reconstruction of industrial
relations. Besides advising on the development of factory agreements and
investigating particular cases and problems, the Commission were to be
empowered to deal with disputes concerning trade union recognition (including disputes between unions concerning recognition). They were to be
authorised to recommend that unions should be given the right to unilateral
arbitration against an employer who refused recognition where the Commission thought it justified or where formal recognition had been granted
but the employer was exploiting union weakness ' to reduce bargaining to a
mockery '.

In a White Paper issued seven months later the government accepted
these recommendations and added to them (*In Place of Strife*, 1969.) The
Secretary of State was, as a last resort, to be empowered to enforce the

Commission's recommendations concerning recognition on both employers and trade unions by means of an order supported by financial penalties. The government also decided that the Royal Commission did ' not go far enough in its recommendations for modernising the trade union movement ', and proposed to empower the Commission on Industrial Relations to make grants or loans to assist union mergers, training schemes, research facilities, and the employment of management consultants by trade unions.

However, these proposals were overshadowed in the eyes of the public and of the unions by plans for enforceable strike ballots and a compulsory conciliation pause in prolonged and serious unconstitutional strikes. As a result of trade union pressure the government withdrew these plans in return for an extension of the authority of the Trades Union Congress to intervene in inter-union and industrial disputes, and promised to drop all proposals for penalties on individuals and unions. It is now far from certain that there will be any Industrial Relations Act at all before the next election.

Meanwhile the Commission on Industrial Relations were established by royal warrant, with George Woodcock as chairman. They began work in March 1969, bringing together an impressive staff. In May they received their first three references, two recognition cases and an investigation of the procedures of Birmid Qualcast, a Midlands engineering firm. No further references reached them until the autumn. When they came most of them were recognition cases, but there was also a general reference on shop steward facilities. The first reports began to appear early in 1970. They are slim and modest documents, reporting successful conciliation in one or two recognition disputes, and offering proposals for the reform of Birmid's procedures.

One of the Donovan Commission's proposals, to which they attached great importance, was a statutory obligation upon companies, in the first instance those with more than five thousand employees, to register their collective agreements with the Department of Employment and Productivity. Their purpose was to impress upon companies the need for effective joint regulation of industrial relations and to provide an indication of where and to what issues the Commission on Industrial Relations should direct its attention. The government accepted the principle, but, under pressure from the Trades Union Congress and the Confederation of British Industry, decided to limit registration to procedure agreements, whereas the Royal Commission had argued that ' in practice procedural and substantive agreements are closely intermeshed in the working of industrial relations '. Pending legislation the government decided to introduce voluntary registration of procedural agreements by major companies, and registration must remain voluntary until there is an Industrial Relations Act. The job was given to the Manpower and Productivity Service, where it was decided to use the opportunity for a purpose different from that of the Royal Commission—the collection of detailed information, not only on company procedural agreements, but also on practices, understandings and customs. Consequently lengthy questionnaires were prepared and circulated. Companies found themselves faced with the prospect of a great deal of detailed work if they took registration seriously, and the danger that by writing down and registering customs and arrangements they would accord authority and permanence to a large number of practices which the Donovan Commission were seeking to change. However, at least some large companies are using the occasion as a means of informing themselves on the procedures which exist in their factories with a view to reform where they feel this is needed.

III

LESSONS FOR THE FUTURE

If these agencies were able to fulfil all that was promised when they were established, then Britain would have a set of government agencies competent to remedy the major defects in the traditional pattern of state intervention in industrial relations. Negotiators would know the level at which they could settle pay claims without harm to the national interest, and would be under pressure to settle at this level. They would be shown how to plan agreements leading to more effective use of manpower and reduced costs, and they would be helped to negotiate and apply the agreements. They would be assisted to reconstruct defective procedures and pay systems, leading to a diminution in unofficial and unconstitutional strikes. Trade unions would have a tribunal of appeal in recognition disputes, and the state would have the means to spur the unions into remedying defects in their organisation.

However, the original promises have not been wholly fulfilled. There is ample evidence to show that the new objectives of government labour policy have failed to dislodge industrial peace from its pre-eminent position as the over-riding goal of state intervention. Over the last five years there have been many instances when avoiding or settling a strike has seemed to entail relaxing incomes policy, or slurring over the provisions concerning performance in a productivity agreement, and in most of them the concessions have been made, on some occasions after the intervention of the Secretary of State or the Prime Minister himself.

Concessions of this kind played their part in the decline of incomes policy from 1967 onwards. By the end of 1969 it was clear that the burial of the policy could not be long delayed. Still one more variation on the original version had been promulgated to cover 1970, but the statutory period for which settlements might be delayed had been reduced to four months, it was evident that the government intended to abandon statutory control over pay before long, and they had announced their intention to merge the Board with the Monopolies Commission.

The burial of the present policy need not be the end of incomes policy for all time. Sooner or later every post-war government have been driven to intervene in the process of pay settlement—the Attlee administration in 1948, the Conservatives with their 1961 pay pause, and the present administration on taking office. The problems which faced these governments have not yet been solved, and it is therefore reasonable to expect that a government of one party or the other will be driven by the same pressures to adopt a similar expedient during the next few years. If so, they might be expected to draw lessons from the Board's experience.

The current policy was not originally intended merely as a temporary check to rising incomes. It was also to bring a more rational and equitable distribution of incomes. The main responsibility for working out how this was to be done was placed upon the Board, but the business of taking the day-to-day decisions stayed with the government and its departments, with a few cases selected for reference to the Board. The course of events was influenced much more by the government's decisions than by the reports of the Board, and because of the pressures on the government the direction their decisions took was neither rational nor equitable.

Since all governments have a variety of objectives and work under pressures from many directions this might be regarded as the inevitable consequence of the machinery set up to apply the policy. The alternative would have been for the Board to administer the policy, and to publish reasons for all their decisions so that practice and principles would be forced together. Final responsibility would still have been the government's, together with the power to issue directions to the Board. Had this been done there would have been need of an even more powerful Board, perhaps with direct representation from the Trades Union Congress and the Confederation of British Industry. Overseas experience provides precedents. Among the most rigorous and widely accepted incomes policies have been those of the United States during the second world war, and of Holland for a dozen years after the war. The interpretation of policy and the vetting of claims were in the hands of semi-independent agencies, the National War Labour Board in the United States and the Board of Mediators in Holland. The first was a tripartite body of government, trade union and employer representatives, and on major decisions the Mediators in Holland were required to consult the Foundation of Labour, a joint organisation of unions and employers' associations.

In the end, however, even these policies were abandoned, and many people take the view that a continuing rational and equitable incomes policy is a chimera. If so, all that can be achieved is a temporary restraint when a crisis threatens in the balance of payments or foreign creditors require reassurance, and there is no need for a body like the Board. The Department can do the vetting, the cabinet can take the major decisions, and if there is need for statutory powers to delay increases, these powers do not have to hang on an investigation by the Board.

Whatever happens to incomes policy, there will still be a need for improved use of manpower, for reform of collective bargaining and for reconstruction in the unions. In these tasks the Manpower and Productivity Service can continue to play a modest but useful part. It is all to the good that, in addition to conciliating and offering arbitration, its officials can furnish a diagnostic service on industrial relations and manpower problems.

There is, however, no strong reason why there should be a team of specialists at headquarters. The regional team could call in the specialists when required even if they were attached to some other body, such as the Commission on Industrial Relations; and given the overriding concerns of the Department such an attachment might provide the specialists with a more congenial environment.

At the moment, however, the Commission's future seems uncertain. In its first nine months the National Board for Prices and Incomes had gone far towards establishing its reputation. Over a similar period of time the Commission have achieved very little. To date they have settled one or two of the trade union recognition disputes referred to them, but they are not likely to make much headway in this field without some sanction against recalcitrant employers. So far neither the Donovan Commission's recommendations nor the government's have been embodied in legislation, and the Commission must make do with conciliation. If effective legislation is passed the Commission might expect a heavy load of work, and the outcome could be a rapid extension of trade union membership and of collective bargaining, especially among white collar employees.

The original intention both of the Donovan Commission and of the government was that inter-union disputes also should be handled by the Commission on Industrial Relations, but the arrangement with the Trades Union Congress has left such disputes to them. It remains to be seen whether Congress can be more successful in this field in the future than it has been in the past. If not there will be increasing pressure for intervention by a government agency. Congress has given a chilly reception to the government's proposal for a ' trade union development fund ' administered by the Commission on Industrial Relations.

The central task of the Commission, however, is the reform of collective bargaining, and so far the Department of Employment and Productivity has been slow in making weighty references. Whether the Commission will succeed when, and if, they are given a serious job to do depends (amongst other things) upon how they conduct and report their investigations, upon their relationship with other bodies, and upon whether Parliament decides to back their reports by sanctions.

George Woodcock is reputed to have laid down that the aim of the Commission on Industrial Relations is ' results, not reports '. If he has, the results will be thin. The Commission's job is to change industrial relations, and providing another conciliation and arbitration service specialising in recognition disputes and procedural problems will not change very much. We have had skilled and experienced conciliators and arbitrators at work for many years now. The National Board for Prices and Incomes have not made an incomes policy work but they have accomplished a change in opinions and attitudes due to the skill as educators and publicists which they have shown in their reports. The Commission must also be educators and publicists, and they would do well to learn from the Board.

Indeed it is because they must achieve their objectives by means of their reports that the Commission's job, like the Board's, cannot be done by a government department. Civil servants are not publicists, and even when they are writing for the public to read they cannot be allowed the freedom to criticise which is essential where the job in hand is the reform of industrial relations. Moreover, the business of exposing the facts of industrial relations and analysing its problems cannot be adequately carried out by a government department because of the remarkable, and often unconscious, ignorance of industrial relations shown by all but a tiny minority of senior civil servants, due both to their training and to their experience.

At the moment the Commission are excluded from pay agreements and from manpower questions. These fall within the scope of the Manpower and Productivity Service and the Board, soon to be absorbed in the Commission on Industry and Manpower. But the indication is that this new Commission will give most of their attention to monopolistic practices, price policies, mergers and the like. There is no good reason why they should be the sole public body, outside the Department of Employment and Productivity, with general responsibility for pay problems, pay structures and the effective use of manpower. The Commission on Industrial Relations, on the other hand, have every reason for extending their interest into these areas. Procedure agreements, after all, cannot be examined and judged without regard for the issues they are supposed to handle, and in many industrial situations there is need for the reconstruction of procedures and the reform of pay structures to proceed hand in hand. There is room here for a redistribution of responsibilities.

Argument cannot settle the issue between those who believe that industrial relations can be reformed only by persuasion and those who think there must be sanctions against recalcitrant unions and unconstitutional strikers. Perhaps the Commission can prove that sanctions are not needed by showing results before the clamour for sanctions grows to such a pitch that legislation to provide them becomes unavoidable. If not, Parliament might impose penalties (civil or criminal) against strikes in breach of agreement. If these worked, then the case for sanctions would be proved. If they failed (as I would expect) then the Commission would still have a chance to succeed with persuasion. An alternative proposal to the enforcement of agreements is to enforce only the recommendations made by the Commission. But if Parliament enacted powers to allow this, and they failed, there would be a grave risk that the Commission's reputation would crumble along with the sanctions. In making proposals on these lines, *In Place of Strife* tried to protect the Commission by entrusting the imposition of penalties to a separate Industrial Board. There is no convincing reason for supposing that would save the Commission.

Meanwhile all the traditional agencies bequeathed to the sixties will still be with us in the seventies. It is true that arbitrators have been doing relatively little business. In his evidence to the Donovan Commission, Sir Roy Wilson argued that this was the consequence of incomes policy. Whether the awards are dictated by the policy or not, clients fear that they will be, and stay away. But the proposal that arbitration tribunals should be absorbed into the Prices and Incomes Board, canvassed in 1966, has now been forgotten, and the tribunals still do a modest business which might pick up again. Courts of inquiry, on the other hand, are doing a brisk trade with the rising trend in strikes promising even more to come.

Given the hopes and fears of five years ago it is remarkable that so many of the traditional objectives and agencies of government labour policy are still with us at the beginning of a new decade, looking set for years to come. But in the National Board for Prices and Incomes those five years have also seen the greatest experiment in government labour policy since the first world war. Is it wholly unreasonable to hope that the Commission on Industrial Relations might make an even greater contribution to reform over the next ten years?

University of Warwick

REFERENCES

DEPARTMENT OF EMPLOYMENT AND PRODUCTIVITY (1969). *The Manpower and Productivity Service.*
In Place of Strife. Cmnd. 3888. London, H.M.S.O.
NATIONAL BOARD FOR PRICES AND INCOMES (1967). *Productivity Agreements.* Report No. 36. Cmnd. 3311. London, H.M.S.O.
NATIONAL BOARD FOR PRICES AND INCOMES (1968a). *Payment by Results Systems.* Report No. 65. Cmnd. 3627. London, H.M.S.O.
NATIONAL BOARD FOR PRICES AND INCOMES (1968b). *Job Evaluation.* Report No. 83. Cmnd. 3772. London, H.M.S.O.
NATIONAL BOARD FOR PRICES AND INCOMES (1969a). *Fourth General Report.* Report No. 122. Cmnd. 4130. London, H.M.S.O.
NATIONAL BOARD FOR PRICES AND INCOMES (1969b). *Productivity Agreements.* Report No. 123. Cmnd. 4136. London, H.M.S.O.

BRITISH AND AMERICAN LABOR MARKET TRENDS: A CASE OF CONVERGENCE?*

JOSEPH W. GARBARINO

I

For at least the past decade, discussions of the future of British industrial relations institutions and procedures have included the possibility that one direction of change might be toward the adoption of some of the features of the industrial relations system of the United States. With the appointment of the Royal Commission on Trade Unions and Employers' Associations in 1965 and the flow of Research Reports that followed, the publication of the Conservative Party's statement, *Fair Deal At Work,* in April 1968, the *Report* of the Royal Commission in June of the same year (Donovan 1968), and the publication of the Labour Government's White Paper, *In Place of Strife,* in January 1969, the range of potential reforms broadened significantly.[1]

From an American point of view, the debate on the direction and extent of reform has almost seemed at times to be over whether the U.K. would enact a version of the U.S. Wagner Act of 1935, providing for the protection of the employee's right to organize, compulsory recognition and bargaining in good faith, or whether Britain would proceed immediately to an enactment of the equivalent of the U.S. Taft-Hartley Act of 1947. The Donovan Report leaned towards the first approach in some of its recommendations, while *Fair Deal's* proposals resembled the latter possibility with its call for the legal enforceability of contracts, 'cooling off' periods in strikes, and strike ballots. The White Paper seemed to combine something of both approaches. In addition, the Donovan Report's major thrust was toward the replacement of the 'two systems' of industrial relations it identified as prevalent in Britain with one formal, comprehensive system at the level of the factory or establishment. It appeared to be generally believed that this would also be a move toward the bargaining structure and practices prevailing in the United States. An observer of the British scene might reasonably have concluded that, by the end of the 1970's, the British industrial relations system would have moved much closer to the American model.

* The author expresses appreciation for the assistance provided by the Division of Research and Planning of the Department of Employment and Productivity, and the Comparative Studies Program of the Institute of International Studies, University of California.
[1] For full references, see the list at the end of this paper.

Sincere as this form of flattery might be if it were to materialize, this paper is based on three propositions that reflect a somewhat different view of the prospects. They are: (1) that although it is probably true that certain features of the U.S. sysem might be both useful and workable in the British context, American experience suggests some skepticism about the necessity for some types of drastic change and doubt about the benefits of others of the reform proposals; (2) that the differences in the way the two systems work are sometimes exaggerated, sometimes to the advantage of one and sometimes to the advantage of the other system; and (3) that the convergence of the two systems, if it occurs, will be from both directions rather than just one. This last proposition is based on the assumption that the American arrangements are coming under some of the same pressures that have already been experienced in the U.K., and that they may respond in similar ways.

II

TRANSFERRING INDUSTRIAL RELATIONS PRACTICES

Most of the changes in British industrial relations that have appeared in the three major documents that make up the trilogy can be grouped under two headings. One series of proposals is concerned with changes in the rights and obligations of the parties and in the procedures under which the system operates. The other is concerned with major changes in the structure of collective bargaining. The prime example of the latter is, of course, the Donovan Report's stress on making the company or the establishment the basic bargaining unit in the system to replace the employers' association (in American terms, a shift from multi-employer to single employer bargaining). Other proposals for structural change are aimed at reducing multi-unionism within plants, at rationalizing trade union structure generally and at inducing 'amalgamations and changes in organization' among employer organizations as well.

Illustrations of the proposed changes in rights, duties and procedures have already been cited in the earlier references to items such as compulsory recognition, good faith bargaining and the improvement of dispute settlement procedures. Considerable discussion of the utility of a possible transfer of procedures such as those from the United States to the United Kingdom has already taken place. Less consideration has been given to what might be learned from American experience with its more decentralized bargaining structure that would be relevant to the new structure proposed for Britain.

Turning first to a discussion of procedures, the writer's evaluation of the possibilities of transfer of some mechanisms has been presented at length elsewhere, and it will only be summarized here (Garbarino, 1969). On the assumption that the decision is made to move to a more formal, comprehensive system of collective agreements, the most useful device in the American tool kit is third party arbitration of grievance disputes. This mechanism helps to reduce the impact of one type of conflict and to order other types of conflict by making long term agreements and the exercise of managerial initiative possible. Unless the parties can count on agreements, once reached, being accepted as binding for a moderately long period of time (say one year), it is hard to see any large scale change in wage payments, dispute procedures and manpower utilization coming about. Perhaps, more important, it provides a form of ' industrial jurisprudence ' that can be used to secure the individual worker a range of recognized rights in his day-to-day working life without the necessity of resorting to industrial guerrilla warfare through direct action. The usual arguments that the lack of written agreements and the reliance on custom makes arbitration unworkable in Britain are not convincing. Adoption of a binding grievance system does not require that all types of disputes be included in its coverage nor does it depend on establishing the over-emphasized distinction between conflicts over rights and conflicts over interests. What is required is that the parties be willing to distinguish between types of disputes and to decide on principles to be applied by mutually agreed on third parties in the settlement of one or more types. The simplest example would be disputes over discipline and discharge, the most common type of case in the United States, and a type handled under industrial ' common law ' with virtually no guidance from contract language other than a stipulation that action must be based on ' just cause '. More serious obstacles to transfer may be a lack of experienced personnel and the money costs of the system.

Some form of recognition procedure that included a provision for worker choice of an exclusive representative with a well designed system of bargaining unit determination might help to ease the difficulties in extending organization to unorganized sectors. In the process some slight change in union structure might be induced while a reduction of multi-unionism would almost certainly result. United States experience with enforcing the obligation to bargain in good faith suggests more caution than the British seem disposed to display in proposing that this question be handled through unilateral arbitration.

Giving collective bargaining agreements legal status would hardly be a cure-all, but it would have some of the same symbolic force in expressing community concepts of appropriate behaviour that legal proscription of racial discrimination provides.

In the light of the British talent for making informal procedures work far better than any reasonable man would expect them to work, little formal administrative machinery would be required for the adaptations that might be thought to be desirable. A reluctance to adopt the American practice in representation elections, for example, is understandable in the light of the approximately 8,000 elections a year currently being conducted by the United States National Labour Relations Board in the fourth decade after the passage of the Wagner Act. (In addition, about one third of all representation cases brought to the board are settled without recourse to an election.)

An effective alternative might well be the special tribunal proposed by Allan Flanders (Donovan, 1968 pp 64-65).

The Americans themselves have discovered the potential workability of less formal procedures in at least some areas of the economy in that many governmental jurisdictions, including the Federal Government, are relying on a variety of relatively informal methods to settle questions that are handled by the N.L.R.B. in the private sector. In adopting a new industrial relations policy for Federal employees, the government itself rejected the private sector system for settling recognition disputes in favour of a different approach. Some of the considerations underlying this action may be relevant to the question of handling the extension of organization to white collar workers in Britain, and the approach shows one way multiple union claims to recognition might be handled.

Like white collar workers in the private sector of the United Kingdom, the great majority of the white collar workers in the Federal Government are unorganized, although substantial numbers are members of employee associations and a smaller number are enrolled in traditional unions. To deal with the representation problem, the government devised different types of recognition.

The two types provided for are : (1) national consultation rights, available to organizations with a ' substantial ' number of members in an agency and providing for the right to be notified of and to comment on proposed changes in policy; (2) exclusive recognition, available to an organization winning the votes of a majority of all the employees in a unit. Management in effect is required to bargain in good faith with exclusive representatives.

The effect of this approach is to provide some status for new organizations while employees make decisions about the pattern of representation they desire without committing the agencies to permanent relationships with numerous smaller unions and to bargaining structures that might not be appropriate at full scale organizational levels.

In Place of Strife reflects some of the same concern for the problem of introducing new organizations into an unorganized system when it remarks of minority unionism that ' increased support and membership, follow, not precede, recognition ' (p. 19).

In the Federal system the agencies are limited in their obligations to bargain with unions that remain in a minority status. Should one union gain majority status, the agency's obligations increase, but in compensation, other organizations are eliminated from the situation completely. Experience with this system has not been extensive enough for an evaluation of its operation. In theory at least, it retains the concept of exclusive representation as the normal state toward which an evolution through temporary states of multi-unionism occurs.

As of 1969 Britain seems to be moving toward a greater intervention by governmental bodies into industrial relations in the future, but without establishing large scale, permanent agencies with direct administrative responsibilities. The device of the *ad hoc* court of inquiry and the new

Commission on Industrial Relations, backed by the unusual variety of judicial and quasijudicial bodies seems to be an appropriate pattern for future development. It follows the United States pattern in the sense that the *substance* of intervention may be similar, but the *methods* are more in the British tradition and quite probably more appropriate to the character of the problems in their current form.

The current ferment in public sector industrial relations in the United States clearly indicates that the American substance can be implemented by methods much like those the British seem to prefer. Many techniques other than the reliance on the all encompassing administrative agency exemplified by the N.L.R.B. have been tried with considerable success in recent years. The reliance on detailed surveillance of a newly developing industrial relations system by a quasi-judicial agency operating in a context of explicit, comprehensive statutory law probably reflects the situation of the 1930s as much as it does the much remarked propensity for legal structures in the United States.

In the burgeoning area of public employee bargaining, the Americans have tended to retain the substance of the private sector system such as formal bargaining unit determination, representation elections, exclusive representation (at least as a goal), comprehensive written agreements, and grievance procedures with third party intervention. Though retaining the substance, however, they have displayed much more flexibility and informality in administrative procedures. Bargaining units are established initially by administrative decision in the Federal government with the unions then having the right of challenge and submission of the dispute to a new Federal Labour Relations Council for determination. Some use has been made of part-time administrative boards largely made up of 'public' members to administer bargaining legislation, e.g., in huge Los Angeles County. Representation elections have had their ground rules established and the voting conducted by private agencies such as the American Arbitration Association, by individual arbitrators acting case-by-case by agreement of the parties, or by officials of state or the Federal mediation and conciliations services acting on the same basis. In some states, e.g. Wisconsin, 'fact finding' panels of private citizens are provided by the administrative agencies and informal third party intervention in a variety of forms has been used by all levels of government to deal with both procedural questions of organizing the collective bargaining system as well as in matters of substance. In some jurisdictions, of course, formal administrative agencies matching their private sector counterparts have been established in the public sector (e.g., New York State), but the variety of approaches to implementation testifies to the workability in informal procedures that accomplish many of the purposes served by the N.L.R.B. mechanisms.

These developments lend weight to the possibility that some of the American industrial relations practices proposed for Britain might be introduced while at the same time the British propensity for reliance on informal procedures in implementation was spreading in the United States.

III

ON THE QUESTION OF BARGAINING STRUCTURES

Perhaps something like the feeling of intellectual euphoria often engendered by incomplete knowledge is necessary to an attempt to assess the objectives and the likelihood of realization of these objectives of a proposal to effect massive change in one nation's industrial relations system. The case for the defence rests on the circumstance that the documentation of the strategy of reform has been unusually complete and the direction of change is expected to be toward the arrangements found in the observer's own country.

On the evidence of the pamphlet *Fair Deal at Work,* the Conservative Party places much less emphasis on reforming the basic structure of bargaining than does the Labour Party in the White Paper or the members of the Royal Commission. The stress in the statements of the latter two groups is on the existence of ' two systems of industrial relations '. The first is the formal system embodied in industry-wide agreements between unions and associations of employers covering most but not all of the private sector. The second is the informal system created by the actual behaviour of the parties, their leadership, and their members, largely within the separate establishments that make up the industries.

The formal and the informal systems are seen to be in conflict. Examples of difficulties are . . . ' The gap between industry-wide agreed rates and actual earnings continues to grow. . . . Procedure agreements fail to cope adequately with disputes arising within factories. . . . Nevertheless, the assumptions of the formal system . . . prevent the informal system from developing into an effective and orderly method of regulation. . . . Factory bargaining remains informal and fragmented. . . . The unreality of industry-wide pay agreements leads us to the use of incentive schemes and overtime payments for purposes quite different from those they were designed to serve.' (Donovan, 1968, p. 36.) The Report calls for the drastic curtailment if not the abandonment of the industry-wide agreements in ' most industries ' and the conversion of the present informal system into a new formal system of factory or establishment level agreements. These new factory agreements '. . . can regulate actual pay, constitute a factory negotiating committee and grievance procedures which suit the circumstances, deal with such subjects as redundancy and discipline and cover the rights and obligations of shop stewards.' (Donovan, 1968, p. 262.)

In a broader context, the conflict between the two systems is charged with making the implementation of incomes policy more difficult, with hindering technological change in general and the negotiation of productivity bargains in particular, and with contributing to ' disorder ' in factory and workshop relations, particularly through a large number of unofficial strikes.

The Donovan Report's prescription for Britain's industrial relations ills has not escaped criticism.[2] The seriousness of the ill effects of the existence of the two systems has been challenged, the magnitude of the strike problem, particularly the unofficial strike problem emphasized in Donovan, has been doubted, the shortage of knowledgeable industrial relations personnel in both management and the unions needed to operate the comprehensive, decentralized system has been pointed out, and the feasibility of decentralizing bargaining to the establishment level in an economy of national unions has been questioned.

Rather than comment extensively on the whole range of problems, this section will suggest the possibility that the degree of change in the British bargaining structure necessary to accomplish the goals of the reformers is overstated in the usual formulation of the Commission's recommendations. Although the Report's major conclusions are qualified in many places, the main stress is clearly on the irreconcilable conflict between the formal and the informal systems of industrial relations and the need, in effect, to move to a 'one system' model by abandoning the present formal system and acting to 'formalize' the existing informal system. American experience suggests that not only is it impossible to implement a once-for-all, exclusive choice between systems, but that, luckily, it is unnecessary to do so in any event.

The first step in the argument is to advance the proposition that the American bargaining structure is, functionally if not formally, more centralized than commonly assumed by foreign observers. Study of employer organization and behaviour in bargaining is as relatively neglected in the United States as it is reported to be in the United Kingdom, so it is difficult to assess the extent of the equivalent of the British version of 'national bargaining' in the United States. The usual estimate is that about one-third of organized employees are in 'multi-employer bargaining units'. But the last serious attempt to arrive at a national figure was based on 1953 data, and a multi-employer unit was defined as 'a bargaining unit which includes under one agreement employees of more than one employer'.[3] This is a conservative definition of a multi-employer situation because many employer associations include in their membership only a portion (though the major portion) of the employers in the industry. The non-members are 'free-riders' who avoid the costs of association but sign the same contract in what is only nominally a separate bargain. The effect of including this group of contracts as multi-employer contracts probably would not change the estimate of the degree of coverage drastically, but it points up the importance of the question of definition.

[2] See for example, the November 1968 issue of the *British Journal of Industrial Relations*, devoted to a series of papers analyzing the *Report*.

[3] Chamberlain (1956) reported 42 percent of organized employees in multi-employer units against the earlier figure of one-third reported by the Bureau of Labor Statistics (p. 12). What appears to be a later classification of industries by type of employer unit but with no numerical estimates, appears in Bloom and Northrup (1969, p. 207). This table suggests to the writer that the proportion in multi-employer units would be close to two-thirds, an estimate that seems more reasonable at this time.

Although the pattern of practice varies from industry to industry, in general American employer associations negotiate contracts with the unions representing their members' employees that are very similar to those negotiated in single company bargaining. They are as formal and comprehensive, covering much the same broad set of topics. Company ' local supplements ' are sometimes used, but they are typically brief, specific, and often temporary. The typical company member of an association probably departs from the master agreement in handling a ' local problem ' more often than a plant unit operating under a parent company agreement does. There are, however, certainly some associations that maintain more uniformity among the practices of their member companies than some companies do over their own plant units.

To cite two of many examples of association participation: A member company telephoned its association to check on what policy had been adopted with regard to Monday attendance and working schedules in a year when Christmas fell on Tuesday; at a regular meeting of members' industrial relations personnel, one association staff used role playing techniques to lead into a policy discussion on how to deal with the very contemporary problem of bearded, long-haired male workers at a food processor. (They agreed to enforce the existing regulations applied to female workers including hair nets over the beards.) They are spurred to this detailed intervention by aggressive pressure to ' level up ' any concession won in contract administration, and by the availability of arbitration to ensure that ' custom and practice ' has weight in contract interpretation. (A suspicion arises that some British employers may feel that the effort involved in this approach is more than the elimination of the kind of ' disorder ' that disturbed the Donovan commission is worth.) Informal ' deals ' in the shop can never be eliminated, but a great many multi-employer units make something similar to the British system of industry bargaining work much like the new system the Royal Commission seems to have had in mind.

IV

COMPANY BARGAINING PATTERNS IN THE UNITED STATES

A brief sketch of the evolution of the bargaining system in the basic steel and automobile industries in the United States will illustrate the difficulties of evaluating the American version of company bargaining.[4] At least until 1955, bargaining in the steel industry during the postwar period would have been described as company bargaining. The situation was a classic example of ' pattern bargaining ', in which separate negotiations occurred between each company and the union, with a ' key bargain ' with one major company (usually, but not always, United States Steel) setting the pattern for the settlements in the other negotiations. The unions had long desired industry-wide negotiations, but the companies refused to accept the practice.

---

[4] For one excellent review, see U.S. Department of Labor (1961), particularly Part III.

In 1955 David McDonald, president of the union, sat as Chairman of all the separate union committees at the individual company negotiations. By the next year, twelve of the major producers had agreed to form a joint four-man bargaining committee to meet with the union to bargain on major issues. Although the meetings occurred in the same room, the companies claimed that the process was still individual company bargaining. In 1959, when the three-year contract negotiated in 1956 was up for renewal, the same company bargaining arrangements were set up, this time with all contract provisions covered by the negotiations. Since that time the same general pattern of joint bargaining has prevailed, except that Kaiser Steel, one of the original twelve, left the committee during the 1959 strike to sign separately with the union. (Kaiser has continued to negotiate separately in the context of its Long Range Sharing Plan, an early example of a plant-wide productivity agreement, but has guaranteed that its employees will do at least as well as those in the rest of the industry.)

During the past quarter century the companies in the basic steel industry and the Steelworkers' union have agreed to a uniform job evaluation plan for the entire industry (more than a half-million workers). As the result of a recent arbitration award, they have agreed on the minimum percentages of workers (85 percent as a company average) that are to be paid by wage incentives along with guidelines for the size of the incentive premiums by broad classes of jobs. Uniform wage changes by job classifications are negotiated industry-wide, a uniform escalator clause is negotiated, and other major issues are handled at the industry level as well. The steel industry is clearly an example of multi-employer bargaining although it might not be called a multi-employer ' unit ' since there is no industry-wide ' contract ' as such, although there are memoranda of agreement for the group as a whole. It seems fair to say that the American steel industry has adopted national bargaining much in the British pattern, covering a broad range of basic issues. But this is coupled with a great deal of ' formal, comprehensive ' company bargaining as well. The separate companies each continue to produce the pocket size printed company-union contract booklets of 75 to 200 pages that are characteristic of the United States collective bargaining system. Although the range of issues dealt with at the industry level has been expanding, company bargaining is alive and well and living in Pittsburgh and Chicago.

In short, the American steel industry seems to have two systems of industrial relations and, while it may be due to a failure of perception, the parties concerned do not seem to regard their simultaneous existence as a major problem. The Kaiser Steel situation does validate the Donovan position that unorthodox experiments require breaking away from the formal national system.

The American automobile industry is probably regarded in the United Kingdom as the model of company bargaining. The ' big three ', General Motors, Ford, and Chrysler, are huge, prosperous, highly viable companies with large operations in the British automobile industry. Walter Reuther, the president of the Auto Workers' union, is a colorful, able, and articulate union leader who has made the U.A.W. one of the world's most effective unions. General Motors has not only been the leader in the automobile industry in size and profitability, but in industrial relations practices as well.

The bargaining structure in the automobile industry is the leading example of pattern bargaining as described earlier in connection with the pre-1959 system in the steel industry. Since 1955 the key bargain has been made with the Ford Motor Company, with the other two major companies following the pattern in separate negotiations. There has never been anything resembling joint negotiations on the company side, although Reuther may participate in all the separate negotiations. The union usually charges that consultation and collaboration occurs behind the scenes at each negotiation, and it has been fairly well accepted that something like consultation has taken place in the last several negotiations at least. On occasion (one example occurring after the 1955 negotiations with Ford produced the first of the ' guaranteed wage ' contracts) the chief executives of both Ford and Chrysler have expressed the opinion that joint action of the three major companies would be desirable, but General Motors has remained aloof.

Unlike the steel industry, the auto industry as a whole produces no joint memoranda or agreements so that, on its face, there is nothing like a two-tiered system of bargaining. It is clear, however, that in the British sense, the automobile industry works under something close to *de facto* national bargaining. The biggest departure from the usual United Kingdom national agreement practice is the failure to specify the level of wage rates, minimum or otherwise, in the company contracts in the United States. What comes out of the key bargain is not an agreed-on *level* of wages, but a set of agreed-on *changes* in wages in the form of annual increases during the term of the contract and a formula for adjusting wages to offset changes in consumer prices. Major fringe benefits such as the supplemental unemployment benefit, pensions, and new paid holidays have been introduced in the various companies simultaneously and changed uniformly over successive bargaining years. Details of contract language covering this type of contract provision differ from one company's contract to another, but the substance of the provisions is the same.

The best way to relate the automobile situation to the two system model described by the Royal Commission is to depict the key bargain as providing the equivalent of a national agreement on the size and the composition of the ' package ' of economic items for that year's set of separate company contracts. Items such as the size of the wage increases, the details of the escalator formula, the financing system, eligibility requirements and benefit structure of the unemployment benefits, and the number of paid holidays are handled uniformly as they are included in the various company agreements. Many other elements, including some important cost elements, are handled differently in the several contracts. The automobile industry bargaining pattern is much less of a two-tier system than is that of the United States steel industry, but it is an open question whether an individual automobile company is more or less constrained by the industry key bargain pattern in the United States than a British company is by its associations' formal national agreement in the United Kingdom.

Company bargaining of the foregoing type within the confines of a key bargain has been the predominant pattern for many years in most industries in the United States that do not have a tradition of overt multi-employer bargaining. The official pattern in an industry often appears to be one of single company bargaining, or perhaps one of a number of small multi-employer units in local or regional areas, but closer inspection of the bargaining process in action will usually turn up unmistakable evidence of pattern following in important sections of the nominally separate contracts. Any count of separate contracts and separate negotiations will provide a misleading impression of the degree of 'decentralization' that exists in the United States' system of industrial relations. The extent to which major contracts in the same industry differ from one another varies from industry to industry and over time as well, but the degree of uniformity on major cost items is usually high and has probably been rising.

The sporadic attempts of United States policy makers to implement a national wage policy offers evidence of the extent of this interrelationship. These efforts are explicitly based on the premise that there are a small number of key settlements on which pressure can be exerted with consequent dampening effects over the entire system.

Some Implications

In the preceding section three patterns of bargaining in the United States have been identified and related to the British two system model. The types are (1) one-tier formal multi-employer unit bargaining which corresponds to national or industry bargaining in British terminology, but which is detailed and comprehensive in scope and is effectively implemented at the company or workshop level; (2) functional multi-employer bargaining as in the steel industry with elaborate formal joint agreements on certain major subjects at the industry level, but with a full set of company agreements added to provide a dual system in which each level is explicit and detailed in form and content; and (3) company bargaining in the automobile industry style marked by nominally independent company bargaining producing detailed comprehensive contracts, with no formal industry agreements, but with informal practices that produce uniform actions over a wide range of detailed subject matter. The three types thus include one in which there is a formal industry system and only a rudimentary, if any, company system; one in which there are fairly complete formal systems at both levels; and one with an informal but very real industry system and a full scale formal company system. The great majority of collective bargaining relationships in the United States fit into one of these patterns. In all three types workshop relations appear to be fairly uniformly and thoroughly regulated by the appropriate formal agreements.

If there is any useful conclusion to be drawn from this account, it would seem to be that the relatively close correspondence between the behaviour called for by the formal agreements and the actual behaviour in the plant in the United States is not the result of a particular form of bargaining structure. It is the result of a more complex combination of social, legal and economic factors, the attitudes and ideology of the parties, and other general environmental causes. It does not seem unreasonable, however, to attribute some of the results to the development and the imaginative application of the kinds of industrial relations apparatus described in the first section of this paper. The Royal Commission recommended the development of similar practices and procedures, but it assumed that a major structural change will necessarily precede the implementation of these changes. United States experience suggests that reform may be more a matter of elaborating and developing more fully the existing structures and less a question of fundamental redesign. However the question of bargaining is handled, all three reform programs agree that the development of more detailed formal bargaining practices and procedures is desirable. It is essentially optimistic to argue that these developments may be accommodated within various structures and that it may not be necessary, in addition, to make wholesale changes in bargaining structures and institutions at the same time. It is only partly facetious to suggest that Britain's problem may not be that there is a surplus of systems, but rather that there may be a shortage.

V

IS THE AMERICAN SYSTEM WORKING?

It is difficult to answer a question like the one posed above without an agreement as to what 'working' means and how performance is to be measured. An industrial relations system might be graded as to how well it keeps the (industrial) peace; how well it promotes, or at least permits, technological change and progress; how well it helps the community realize other economic goals such as the wage and price behaviour that are deemed to be appropriate; or how well it works in providing a vehicle for the desired level of industrial democracy.

In this section the record of the United States system will be examined with respect to the keeping of industrial peace and the behaviour of wages. As in the previous section, the background for the assessment will be the major criticism of the British systems by the Donovan Report, *In Place of Strife*, and, to some extent, *Fair Deal*. The questions to be investigated are: Is the American system working better than the British in the areas of (1) unofficial strikes, and (2) the distortion of payment systems? What are the prospects for the future?

Discussion of relative strike frequency begins by stipulating that the United States is one of the more strike-prone of the world's nations. H. A. Turner has argued that Britain's strike problem is greatly exaggerated particularly if the comparison is with the United States. I have argued elsewhere that the evaluation of strike effects requires the consideration not only of the number of strikes, but their size, causes, frequency and predictability (Garbarino, 1969). It is a question not only of the quantity of conflict but also of its character. The British authors of the triology stress the 'character' of conflict by emphasizing that about 95 per cent. of British strikes, accounting for just under 75 per cent. of working days lost in recent years have been 'unofficial', i.e., not called by the official union leadership. (*In Place of Strife*, p. 39.) Many of these unofficial strikes are also 'unconstitutional' in that they occur before an agreed-on procedure for settling disputes has been exhausted.

In the United States unofficial and unconstitutional strikes occur, but there is no official statistical record of them. Because American contracts have legal status, and because more than 90 per cent. of them call for binding arbitration during the contract term and include an explicit or implicit no-strike agreement, it has sometimes been assumed that few American strikes occur during contract periods. This assumption was explicitly challenged by James Kuhn (1961). Kuhn argued that if strikes of 1-3 days duration in the United States could be assumed to be 'illegitimate strikes', then the number occurring was large and showed no signs of declining.[5]

Since Kuhn's study was prepared, the United States Bureau of Labor Statistics has begun publication of data on strikes that occur during the term of agreements. Because some agreements do not provide for arbitration and because some that do permit strikes over certain types of issues, all such strikes are not 'illegitimate', or, in British terms, unofficial and/or unconstitutional. It is virtually certain, however, that a large majority of these strikes are illegitimate and these stoppages may be a better estimate of such strikes than are the data on short stoppages used by Kuhn.

Table I shows the data for the years since 1961 for the number of strikes of 1-3 days duration, the number during the term of agreements, and the number that combine these two characteristics. All series show a rise in the absolute number of strikes occurring, beginning in 1964 for the 1-3 days series and in 1963 for both of the other estimates. Neither the rise in strikes of short duration nor the rise in strikes combining the two criteria seems to have outstripped the rise in the total of all strikes. The percentages these two types of stoppages are of the total has not changed significantly. In the case of the total of strikes during the terms of agreements, the absolute rise in the number of strikes seems to have exceeded the rise in all types of strikes for the years 1964-1967 inclusive. The period as a whole was one of economic expansion and rising wages, prices and profits. It seems plausible that the same factors that led to an increase in strikes overall, led to an increase in the special classes of strikes considered here. The relative increase in strikes during the term of agreements could indicate that employee

---

[5] Kuhn (1961), pp. 54-5. Stieber (1968, p. 26), updated Kuhn's data and concluded that about 25 percent of all United States strikes accounting for only about 5 percent of lost time were in violation of contracts.

Table I

ESTIMATES OF THE INCIDENCE OF WORK STOPPAGES IN VIOLATION OF AGREEMENTS

Year	Strikes of 1-3 Days Duration	Percentage of All Strikes	Strikes During Term of Contracts	Percentage of all Strikes	Strikes Combining 1 and 3	Percent of all Strikes
1961	946	28·5	1084	32·2	547	16·5
1962	912	25·1	1078	29·8	492	13·6
1963	939	28·2	1204	35·8	593	17·8
1964	978	26·7	1317	36·0	611	16·7
1965	1012	25·5	1374	34·7	631	15·9
1966	1218	27·7	1608	36·5	758	17·2
1967	1238	27·0	1557	33·9	789	17·2
1968	1225	24·3	1585	31·4	N.A.	N.A.

Source: United States Bureau of Labor Statistics, *Analysis of Work Stoppages* (Annual series) Bulletins 1339, 1381, 1420, 1460, 1525, 1573, and 1611. Data for 1968 from the Preliminary Summary Report. The first two classes of stoppage accounted for 1·4 and 9·9 percent of all mandays lost in 1968.

discipline and contract observance has weakened as prosperity waxed, but the evidence is hardly overwhelming. As Kuhn and Stieber observed earlier, the proportion of all United States strikes that are probably in violation of contract is surprisingly high, but it seems to be fairly stable. Stieber's estimate that illegitimate strikes amount to something like 20-25 per cent. of all strikes, accounting for about 5 per cent. of lost time, seems to be on the mark.

In the United States collective bargaining agreements negotiated by the union leadership are submitted to the membership for ratification. In recent years the number of rejections of tentative agreements has been rising, and this is sometimes seen as a tendency towards ' disorder ' in the United States bargaining system. The Federal Mediation and Conciliation Service has reported the rejection rate in the ' joint-meeting case ' in which it has actively participated as rising from 8·7 in fiscal year 1964, to 10·0, 11·7, and 14·2 in the next three years. The absolute level of the true rate of rejection considering all contracts, is considerably lower, but the trend is worrisome.[6] The 1968 figure is unofficially reported to have fallen to about 12 per cent., however, suggesting a possible turning point.

Another disturbing element in the United States is that the negotiation of a growing number of ' local agreements ' has been holding up the final settlement of overall company bargaining agreements and causing local strikes, particularly in the auto industry, with increasing frequency. This may foreshadow a tendency towards something like ' workshop ' bargaining in the British pattern. Although the role of local or plant agreements is clearly growing, there are no quantitative estimates of their importance.

[6] Simkin (1968). The absolute number of rejections in 1967 was 1019.

In short, after several years of relatively high level operations of the economy, American industrial relations are showing some signs of the loss of overall control thought to be characteristic of the British system. The United States arrangements still seem to be working well in this respect, but this is one area in which the 1970s may see some convergence from the American side.

VI

IS WAGE DRIFT AN AMERICAN PROBLEM?

In its simplest form, wage drift refers to a tendency for the actual earnings of employees to diverge over time from the basic rates of pay for those employees. The Donovan Report provides several examples (pp. 14-16) illustrating both the magnitude of the gap at one point in time and its increase over time for a variety of job classifications and industries. (The footwear industry, for example, shows a gap for 1967 of £8.1.10 between the nominal rate for a 40 hours week of £11.12.6 and actual average weekly earnings of £19.14.4.) The three major elements identified as causing the gap are incentive earnings, company or plant additions to basic time rates, and overtime earnings. Not only were the gaps large in 1967, but they have been growing rapidly in recent years. Between 1962 and 1967, average weekly earnings for all industries reporting to the Ministry of Labour increased more than 50 per cent. faster than did average weekly rates (36·4 to 23·1 per cent.).

The much lower level of interest in this problem in the United States is itself probably the best evidence that wage drift is not serious. One American study of the relative behaviour of hourly wage rates and earnings for 1945-1957 reported that rates for thirteen industries increased $1.24 on the average while earnings increases averaged only $1.31. These results were heavily influenced by the fact that in four of the thirteen industries earnings actually lagged behind rates. Considering only the nine industries in which the earnings-rates gaps were positive, the average gap was still only 15.5 cents over twelve years.[7]

Data for the steel and the automobile industries have been calculated for periods in the 1960s more comparable to those cited for Britain in Donovan. In the steel industry the hourly wage rate schedules for the thirty-odd job classifications in the industry rose 24 per cent. between June 1962 and June 1969. Average hourly earnings in steel increased 23 per cent. over that span. Average weekly earnings went up substantially faster, however, rising by 34 per cent.[8] It appears that most of the increase in weekly earnings relative to hourly rates was the result of working overtime, however, and it is not clear why differences in the prevalence of overtime in different

[7] Mahar (1961, p. 279). The calculations above are the author's.

[8] In steel the wage rate changes were calculated from the 'standard hourly wage rates' in the appropriate collective bargaining contracts between United States Steel and the Steelworkers Union. Average hourly earnings are from the *Monthly Labor Review* series for the Blast Furnaces and Basic Steel Products industry.

periods in a cyclical industry should be regarded as evidence of ' disorder ' in pay structures. The steel record is particularly impressive since about two-thirds of its production workers are paid by one form or another of incentives and the administration of incentives is perhaps the most frequent problem area in controlling wage drift.

In the automobile industry negotiated hourly wage rate changes between July 1961 and October 1966 produced increases of 60.6 cents while average hourly earnings rose 70 cents. Although average hourly earnings rose only 25 per cent., once again average weekly earnings rose faster: 34 per cent.[9] Some part, but only a minor part, of this difference can be explained by an increase in overtime working.

The relatively close correspondence of changes in hourly earnings and rates implies that wage drift is not a problem in either steel or autos. There is a considerably larger divergence between rates of pay and average weekly earnings that may mean that some forms of drift are appearing. The measurement of drift is in such a statistically primitive state that only gross differences can be regarded as significant (measurement should be at the department level, but currently most comparisons are between company overall rates and industry earnings). In addition, wage drift may be reduced, not by tightening wage administration to bring earnings into line with rates, but by adjusting rates to validate the earnings results. It seems fair to conclude that United States pay structures may be reacting to higher demand pressures in the labour market to some extent, but that the reaction to date must be of limited magnitude.

In summary, judged by the tests of industrial unrest and the behaviour of pay structures, the United States industrial relations system can be said to be working fairly well. Illegitimate strikes are estimated to be considerably more common than usually assumed, and a slight upward trend may exist. Contract rejections have been rising, but may have reached a plateau. Only a limited amount of wage drift appears in the rudimentary measures available. Continued high level employment through the 1970s might well aggravate these symptoms leading to a repetition of some of the British experience.

VII

POTENTIAL DEVELOPMENTS IN PUBLIC POLICY

The most likely area in which American developments are likely to follow a British model concerns questions of public policy, including employee relations in the public sector. A number of possibilities will be briefly sketched.

(1) For more than thirty years the United States tradition has been one of government regulation of collective bargaining institutions and processes

[9] In automobiles, wage rate changes were taken from the *Wage Chronology, General Motors Corporation 1939-1966,* Bulletin No. 1532, Bureau of Labor Statistics. Hourly and weekly earnings data are from the *Monthly Labor Review* series for Motor Vehicles and Equipment.

while pursuing an American version of 'voluntarism' in employee relations in general. Britain's tradition has been almost the exact reverse.

Just as there has been no British counterpart of the Taft-Hartley Act governing union-management relations, there are no United States counterparts of the British Contracts of Employment Bill of 1963 or the Redundancy Payments Act of 1965. Some of the problems with which these laws have been concerned are handled under collective bargaining agreements or sometimes by unilateral employer policies in the United States. The White Paper proposed that the law protect all employees against unfair dismissal as well as provide protection for union members from unfair treatment by union officials. In the United States the unions through the grievance procedure furnish the employees they represent with a high degree of protection from unfair dismissal or any other discipline, but unorganized employees are protected only by the threat of organization or the force of example. It seems very likely that the next decade will see the introduction of 'due process' into employee relations in a formal way, particularly in view of the preoccupation with the issue among youth. In protecting union members' rights, Britain would, of course, be following policies already written into United States law. In this area of public policy, convergence should be substantially advanced by the end of the 1970s.

(2) Britain has a great deal more experience with organized public employees than the United States and some of the United Kingdom practices may be adapted to American problems. Bargaining by the teachers in American lower schools, for example, may well follow British patterns of centralization of salary setting and of financial support. The American states are well on the way toward centralization in the area of financial support, but are a long way from moving salary determination from local school districts to central bodies. In general, another weakness of American public sector bargaining is the identification of the 'employer' representative for bargaining purposes. The role of the Treasury on the Official Side of the Whitley Councils is an example of what appears to an American to be a desirable clarification of responsibility. Something like the Whitley Council approach to joint negotiation to avoid fragmented bargaining in American jurisdictions may be adopted in the United States system.

(3) Although its record of success could hardly be called inspiring, it appears highly probable that the United States will repeat most of the British pattern of incomes policy. Having abandoned what might be called the 'unemployment wage policy' in the early 1960s, the United States has been struggling to find a substitute, starting with the ill-fated guideposts for wages and prices in 1962. As of the beginning of the 1970s the Americans seem to be launched on their version of the stop-go policies of the postwar era in Britain. A melancholy progression through the stages of standstill, severe restraint, statutory control, productivity bargaining loopholes and all the rest may well be in prospect. Should either country by any chance hit upon an effective method of stabilization, it is certain that adoption would be instantaneous.

In summary, the decade of the 1970s may well see a significant convergence of the industrial relations policies of the United States and the United Kingdom. Britain may adopt some of the American private sector practices, and may become more interventionist in union-management relations. The United States will probably begin to show some of the disorder in her own industrial relations that is claimed to exist in Britain under the pressure of fuller employment, rising prices, and a general weakening of institutional authority. The United States may well intervene more actively in employee relations, and may borrow some practices from Britain's public sector. Finally, a more positive incomes policy will almost certainly have to be adopted by the United States. It seems safe to wager that at the end of the 1970s, the American and the British labour market and industrial relations system will resemble one another more closely than they do at the beginning of the decade.

University of California, Berkeley.

REFERENCES

BLOOM, G. and NORTHRUP, H. (1969). *Economics of Labor Relations,* Sixth Edition, Irwin.

CHAMBERLAIN, Neil W. (1956). ' The Structure of Bargaining Units in the United States.' *Industrial and Labor Relations Review,* 10:1, October 1956, pp. 3-25.

DONOVAN (1968). *Report* of the Royal Commission on Trade Unions and Employers' Associations. Cmnd. 3623. London, H.M.S.O.

Fair deal at Work (1968). Conservative Political Centre, No. 400. London.

GARBARINO, J. W. (1969). ' Managing Conflict in Industrial Relations: United States Experience and Current Issues in Britain.' *British Journal of Industrial Relations,* November 1969.

In Place of Strife (1969). Cmnd. 3888. London, H.M.S.O.

KUHN, James (1961). *Bargaining in Grievance Settlement.* Columbia.

MAHAR, John (1961). 'An Index of Wage Rates for Selected Industries.' *Review of Economics and Statistics,* August 1961.

SIMKIN, William E. (1968). ' Refusals to Ratify Contracts.' *Industrial and Labor Relations Review,* July 1968, pp. 518-540.

STIEBER, Jack (1968). ' Grievance Arbitration in the United States: an Analysis of its Functions and Effects,' *in* Royal Commission on Trade Unions and Employers' Associations *Three Studies in Collective Bargaining.* Research Paper 8. London, H.M.S.O.

U.S. DEPARTMENT OF LABOR (1961). *Collective Bargaining in the Basic Steel Industry.* U.S. Government Printing Office. Washington.

SUBJECT INDEX